Seven Databases
in Seven Weeks

A Guide to Modern Databases
and the NoSQL Movement

Eric Redmond

Jim R. Wilson

The Pragmatic Bookshelf

Dallas, Texas • Raleigh, North Carolina

Many of the designations used by manufacturers and sellers to distinguish their products are claimed as trademarks. Where those designations appear in this book, and The Pragmatic Programmers, LLC was aware of a trademark claim, the designations have been printed in initial capital letters or in all capitals. The Pragmatic Starter Kit, The Pragmatic Programmer, Pragmatic Programming, Pragmatic Bookshelf, PragProg and the linking *g* device are trademarks of The Pragmatic Programmers, LLC.

Every precaution was taken in the preparation of this book. However, the publisher assumes no responsibility for errors or omissions, or for damages that may result from the use of information (including program listings) contained herein.

Our Pragmatic courses, workshops, and other products can help you and your team create better software and have more fun. For more information, as well as the latest Pragmatic titles, please visit us at *http://pragprog.com*.

Apache, Apache HBase, Apache CouchDB, HBase, CouchDB, and the HBase and CouchDB logos are trademarks of The Apache Software Foundation. Used with permission. No endorsement by The Apache Software Foundation is implied by the use of these marks.

The team that produced this book includes:

Jackie Carter (editor)
Potomac Indexing, LLC (indexer)
Kim Wimpsett (copyeditor)
David J Kelly (typesetter)
Janet Furlow (producer)
Juliet Benda (rights)
Ellie Callahan (support)

Printed in the United States of America.
ISBN-13: 978-1-93435-692-0
Printed on acid-free paper.
Book version: P1..0—May 2012

Contents

Foreword   vii

Acknowledgments   ix

Preface   xi

1. Introduction   1
   1.1   It Starts with a Question   1
   1.2   The Genres   3
   1.3   Onward and Upward   7

2. PostgreSQL   9
   2.1   That's Post-greS-Q-L   9
   2.2   Day 1: Relations, CRUD, and Joins   10
   2.3   Day 2: Advanced Queries, Code, and Rules   21
   2.4   Day 3: Full-Text and Multidimensions   35
   2.5   Wrap-Up   48

3. Riak   51
   3.1   Riak Loves the Web   51
   3.2   Day 1: CRUD, Links, and MIMEs   52
   3.3   Day 2: Mapreduce and Server Clusters   62
   3.4   Day 3: Resolving Conflicts and Extending Riak   80
   3.5   Wrap-Up   91

4. HBase   93
   4.1   Introducing HBase   94
   4.2   Day 1: CRUD and Table Administration   94
   4.3   Day 2: Working with Big Data   106
   4.4   Day 3: Taking It to the Cloud   122
   4.5   Wrap-Up   131

5.   MongoDB   135
     5.1   Hu(mongo)us   135
     5.2   Day 1: CRUD and Nesting   136
     5.3   Day 2: Indexing, Grouping, Mapreduce   151
     5.4   Day 3: Replica Sets, Sharding, GeoSpatial, and GridFS   165
     5.5   Wrap-Up   174

6.   CouchDB   177
     6.1   Relaxing on the Couch   177
     6.2   Day 1: CRUD, Futon, and cURL Redux   178
     6.3   Day 2: Creating and Querying Views   186
     6.4   Day 3: Advanced Views, Changes API, and Replicating
           Data   200
     6.5   Wrap-Up   217

7.   Neo4J   219
     7.1   Neo4J Is Whiteboard Friendly   219
     7.2   Day 1: Graphs, Groovy, and CRUD   220
     7.3   Day 2: REST, Indexes, and Algorithms   238
     7.4   Day 3: Distributed High Availability   250
     7.5   Wrap-Up   258

8.   Redis   261
     8.1   Data Structure Server Store   261
     8.2   Day 1: CRUD and Datatypes   262
     8.3   Day 2: Advanced Usage, Distribution   275
     8.4   Day 3: Playing with Other Databases   291
     8.5   Wrap-Up   304

9.   Wrapping Up   307
     9.1   Genres Redux   307
     9.2   Making a Choice   311
     9.3   Where Do We Go from Here?   312

A1. Database Overview Tables   313

A2. The CAP Theorem   317
     A2.1 Eventual Consistency   317
     A2.2 CAP in the Wild   318
     A2.3 The Latency Trade-Off   319

     Bibliography   321

     Index   323

Foreword

Riding up the Beaver Run SuperChair in Breckenridge, Colorado, we wondered where the fresh powder was. Breckenridge made snow, and the slopes were immaculately groomed, but there was an inevitable sameness to the conditions on the mountain. Without fresh snow, the total experience was lacking.

In 1994, as an employee of IBM's database development lab in Austin, I had very much the same feeling. I had studied object-oriented databases at the University of Texas at Austin because after a decade of relational dominance, I thought that object-oriented databases had a real chance to take root. Still, the next decade brought more of the same relational models as before. I watched dejectedly as Oracle, IBM, and later the open source solutions led by MySQL spread their branches wide, completely blocking out the sun for any sprouting solutions on the fertile floor below.

Over time, the user interfaces changed from green screens to client-server to Internet-based applications, but the coding of the relational layer stretched out to a relentless barrage of sameness, spanning decades of perfectly competent tedium. So, we waited for the fresh blanket of snow.

And then the fresh powder finally came. At first, the dusting wasn't even enough to cover this morning's earliest tracks, but the power of the storm took over, replenishing the landscape and delivering the perfect skiing experience with the diversity and quality that we craved. Just this past year, I woke up to the realization that the database world, too, is covered with a fresh blanket of snow. Sure, the relational databases are there, and you can get a surprisingly rich experience with open source RDBMS software. You can do clustering, full-text search, and even fuzzy searching. But you're no longer limited to that approach. I have not built a fully relational solution in a year. Over that time, I've used a document-based database and a couple of key-value datastores.

The truth is that relational databases no longer have a monopoly on flexibility or even scalability. For the kinds of applications that we build, there are more appropriate models that are simpler, faster, and more reliable. As a person who spent ten years at IBM Austin working on databases with our labs and customers, this development is simply stunning to me. In *Seven Databases in Seven Weeks*, you'll work through examples that cover a beautiful cross section of the most critical advances in the databases that back Internet development. Within key-value stores, you'll learn about the radically scalable and reliable Riak and the beautiful query mechanisms in Redis. From the columnar database community, you'll sample the power of HBase, a close cousin of the relational database models. And from the document-oriented database stores, you'll see the elegant solutions for deeply nested documents in the wildly scalable MongoDB. You'll also see Neo4J's spin on graph databases, allowing rapid traversal of relationships.

You won't have to use all of these databases to be a better programmer or database admin. As Eric Redmond and Jim Wilson take you on this magical tour, every step will make you smarter and lend the kind of insight that is invaluable in a modern software professional. You will know where each platform shines and where it is the most limited. You will see where your industry is moving and learn the forces driving it there.

Enjoy the ride.

Bruce Tate
author of *Seven Languages in Seven Weeks*
Austin, Texas, May 2012

Acknowledgments

A book with the size and scope of this one cannot be done by two mere authors alone. It requires the effort of many very smart people with superhuman eyes spotting as many mistakes as possible and providing valuable insights into the details of these technologies.

We'd like to thank, in no particular order, all of the folks who provided their time and expertise:

Ian Dees   Mark Phillips   Jan Lenhardt

Robert Stam   Oleg Bartunov   Dave Purrington

Daniel Bretoi   Matt Adams   Sean Copenhaver

Loren Sands-Ramshaw   Emil Eifrem   Andreas Kollegger

Finally, thanks to Bruce Tate for his experience and guidance.

We'd also like to sincerely thank the entire team at the Pragmatic Bookshelf. Thanks for entertaining this audacious project and seeing us through it. We're especially grateful to our editor, Jackie Carter. Your patient feedback made this book what it is today. Thanks to the whole team who worked so hard to polish this book and find all of our mistakes.

Last but not least, thanks to Frederic Dumont, Matthew Flower, Rebecca Skinner, and all of our relentless readers. If it weren't for your passion to learn, we wouldn't have had this opportunity to serve you.

For anyone we missed, we hope you'll accept our apologies. Any omissions were certainly not intentional.

From Eric: Dear Noelle, you're not special; you're unique, and that's so much better. Thanks for living through another book. Thanks also to the database creators and commiters for providing us something to write about and make a living at.

From Jim: First, I have to thank my family; Ruthy, your boundless patience and encouragement have been heartwarming. Emma and Jimmy, you're two smart cookies, and your daddy loves you always. Also a special thanks to all the unsung heroes who monitor IRC, message boards, mailing lists, and bug systems ready to help anyone who needs you. Your dedication to open source keeps these projects kicking.

Preface

It has been said that data is the new oil. If this is so, then databases are the fields, the refineries, the drills, and the pumps. Data is stored in databases, and if you're interested in tapping into it, then coming to grips with the modern equipment is a great start.

Databases are tools; they are the means to an end. Each database has its own story and its own way of looking at the world. The more you understand them, the better you will be at harnessing the latent power in the ever-growing corpus of data at your disposal.

Why Seven Databases

As early as March 2010, we had wanted to write a NoSQL book. The term had been gathering buzz, and although lots of people were talking about it, there seemed to be a fair amount of confusion around it too. What exactly does the term *NoSQL* mean? Which types of systems are included? How is this going to impact the practice of making great software? These were questions we wanted to answer—as much for ourselves as for others.

After reading Bruce Tate's exemplary *Seven Languages in Seven Weeks: A Pragmatic Guide to Learning Programming Languages [Tat10]*, we knew he was onto something. The progressive style of introducing languages struck a chord with us. We felt teaching databases in the same manner would provide a smooth medium for tackling some of these tough NoSQL questions.

What's in This Book

This book is aimed at experienced developers who want a well-rounded understanding of the modern database landscape. Prior database experience is not strictly required, but it helps.

After a brief introduction, this book tackles a series of seven databases chapter by chapter. The databases were chosen to span five different database genres or styles, which are discussed in Chapter 1, *Introduction*, on page 1. In order, they are PostgreSQL, Riak, Apache HBase, MongoDB, Apache CouchDB, Neo4J, and Redis.

Each chapter is designed to be taken as a long weekend's worth of work, split up into three days. Each day ends with exercises that expand on the topics and concepts just introduced, and each chapter culminates in a wrap-up discussion that summarizes the good and bad points about the database. You may choose to move a little faster or slower, but it's important to grasp each day's concepts before continuing. We've tried to craft examples that explore each database's distinguishing features. To really understand what these databases have to offer, you have to spend some time using them, and that means rolling up your sleeves and doing some work.

Although you may be tempted to skip chapters, we designed this book to be read linearly. Some concepts, such as mapreduce, are introduced in depth in earlier chapters and then skimmed over in later ones. The goal of this book is to attain a solid understanding of the modern database field, so we recommend you read them all.

What This Book Is Not

Before reading this book, you should know what it won't cover.

This Is Not an Installation Guide

Installing the databases in this book is sometimes easy, sometimes challenging, and sometimes downright ugly. For some databases, you'll be able to use stock packages, and for others, you'll need to compile from source. We'll point out some useful tips here and there, but by and large you're on your own. Cutting out installation steps allows us to pack in more useful examples and a discussion of concepts, which is what you really want anyway, right?

Administration Manual? We Think Not

Along the same lines of installation, this book will not cover everything you'd find in an administration manual. Each of these databases has myriad options, settings, switches, and configuration details, most of which are well documented on the Web. We're more interested in teaching you useful concepts and full immersion than focusing on the day-to-day operations. Though the characteristics of the databases can change based on operational settings—and we may discuss those characteristics—we won't be able to go into all the nitty-gritty details of all possible configurations. There simply isn't space!

A Note to Windows Users

This book is inherently about choices, predominantly open source software on *nix platforms. Microsoft environments tend to strive for an integrated environment, which limits many choices to a smaller predefined set. As such, the databases we cover are open source and are developed by (and largely *for*) users of *nix systems. This is not our own bias so much as a reflection of the current state of affairs. Consequently, our tutorial-esque examples are presumed to be run in a *nix shell. If you run Windows and want to give it a try anyway, we recommend setting up Cygwin[1] to give you the best shot at success. You may also want to consider running a Linux virtual machine.

Code Examples and Conventions

This book contains code in a variety of languages. In part, this is a consequence of the databases that we cover. We've attempted to limit our choice of languages to Ruby/JRuby and JavaScript. We prefer command-line tools to scripts, but we will introduce other languages to get the job done—like PL/pgSQL (Postgres) and Gremlin/Groovy (Neo4J). We'll also explore writing some server-side JavaScript applications with Node.js.

Except where noted, code listings are provided in full, usually ready to be executed at your leisure. Samples and snippets are syntax highlighted according to the rules of the language involved. Shell commands are prefixed by $.

Online Resources

The Pragmatic Bookshelf's page for this book[2] is a great resource. There you'll find downloads for all the source code presented in this book. You'll also find feedback tools such as a community forum and an errata submission form where you can recommend changes to future releases of the book.

Thanks for coming along with us on this journey through the modern database landscape.

Eric Redmond and Jim R. Wilson

---

1.   http://www.cygwin.com/
2.   http://pragprog.com/book/rwdata/seven-databases-in-seven-weeks

## CHAPTER 1

Introduction

This is a pivotal time in the database world. For years the relational model has been the *de facto* option for problems big and small. We don't expect relational databases will fade away anytime soon, but people are emerging from the RDBMS fog to discover alternative options, such as schemaless or alternative data structures, simple replication, high availability, horizontal scaling, and new query methods. These options are collectively known as *NoSQL* and make up the bulk of this book.

In this book, we explore seven databases across the spectrum of database styles. In the process of reading the book, you will learn the various functionality and trade-offs each database has—durability vs. speed, absolute vs. eventual consistency, and so on—and how to make the best decisions for your use cases.

1.1 It Starts with a Question

The central question of *Seven Databases in Seven Weeks* is this: what database or combination of databases best resolves your problem? If you walk away understanding how to make that choice, given your particular needs and resources at hand, we're happy.

But to answer that question, you'll need to understand your options. For that, we'll take you on a deep dive into each of seven databases, uncovering the good parts and pointing out the not so good. You'll get your hands dirty with CRUD, flex your schema muscles, and find answers to these questions:

- *What type of datastore is this?* Databases come in a variety of genres, such as relational, key-value, columnar, document-oriented, and graph. Popular databases—including those covered in this book—can generally be grouped into one of these broad categories. You'll learn about each type and the kinds of problems for which they're best suited. We've specifically chosen databases to span these categories including one relational database (Postgres), two key-value stores (Riak, Redis), a column-oriented database (HBase), two document-oriented databases (MongoDB, CouchDB), and a graph database (Neo4J).

- *What was the driving force?* Databases are not created in a vacuum. They are designed to solve problems presented by real use cases. RDBMS databases arose in a world where query flexibility was more important than flexible schemas. On the other hand, column-oriented datastores were built to be well suited for storing large amounts of data across several machines, while data relationships took a backseat. We'll cover cases in which to use each database and related examples.

- *How do you talk to it?* Databases often support a variety of connection options. Whenever a database has an interactive command-line interface, we'll start with that before moving on to other means. Where programming is needed, we've stuck mostly to Ruby and JavaScript, though a few other languages sneak in from time to time—like PL/pgSQL (Postgres) and Gremlin (Neo4J). At a lower level, we'll discuss protocols like REST (CouchDB, Riak) and Thrift (HBase). In the final chapter, we present a more complex database setup tied together by a Node.js JavaScript implementation.

- *What makes it unique?* Any datastore will support writing data and reading it back out again. What else it does varies greatly from one to the next. Some allow querying on arbitrary fields. Some provide indexing for rapid lookup. Some support ad hoc queries; for others, queries must be planned. Is schema a rigid framework enforced by the database or merely a set of guidelines to be renegotiated at will? Understanding capabilities and constraints will help you pick the right database for the job.

- *How does it perform?* How does this database function and at what cost? Does it support sharding? How about replication? Does it distribute data evenly using consistent hashing, or does it keep like data together? Is this database tuned for reading, writing, or some other operation? How much control do you have over its tuning, if any?

- *How does it scale?* Scalability is related to performance. Talking about scalability without the context of what you want to *scale to* is generally fruitless. This book will give you the background you need to ask the right questions to establish that context. While the discussion on *how* to scale each database will be intentionally light, in these pages you'll find out whether each datastore is geared more for horizontal scaling (MongoDB, HBase, Riak), traditional vertical scaling (Postgres, Neo4J, Redis), or something in between.

Our goal is not to guide a novice to mastery of any of these databases. A full treatment of any one of them could (and does) fill entire books. But by the end you should have a firm grasp of the strengths of each, as well as how they differ.

1.2 The Genres

Like music, databases can be broadly classified into one or more styles. An individual song may share all of the same notes with other songs, but some are more appropriate for certain uses. Not many people blast Bach's *Mass in B Minor* out an open convertible speeding down the 405. Similarly, some databases are better for some situations over others. The question you must always ask yourself is not "Can I use this database to store and refine this data?" but rather, "Should I?"

In this section, we're going to explore five main database genres. We'll also take a look at the databases we're going to focus on for each genre.

It's important to remember that most of the data problems you'll face could be solved by most or all of the databases in this book, not to mention other databases. The question is less about whether a given database style could be shoehorned to model your data and more about whether it's the best fit for your problem space, your usage patterns, and your available resources. You'll learn the art of divining whether a database is intrinsically useful to you.

Relational

The relational model is generally what comes to mind for most people with database experience. Relational database management systems (RDBMSs) are set-theory-based systems implemented as two-dimensional tables with rows and columns. The canonical means of interacting with an RDBMS is by writing queries in Structured Query Language (SQL). Data values are typed and may be numeric, strings, dates, uninterpreted blobs, or other types. The types are enforced by the system. Importantly, tables can join and morph into new, more complex tables, because of their mathematical basis in relational (set) theory.

There are lots of open source relational databases to choose from, including MySQL, H2, HSQLDB, SQLite, and many others. The one we cover is in Chapter 2, *PostgreSQL*, on page 9.

PostgreSQL

Battle-hardened PostgreSQL is by far the oldest and most robust database we cover. With its adherence to the SQL standard, it will feel familiar to anyone who has worked with relational databases before, and it provides a solid point of comparison to the other databases we'll work with. We'll also explore some of SQL's unsung features and Postgres's specific advantages. There's something for everyone here, from SQL novice to expert.

Key-Value

The key-value (KV) store is the simplest model we cover. As the name implies, a KV store pairs keys to values in much the same way that a map (or hashtable) would in any popular programming language. Some KV implementations permit complex value types such as hashes or lists, but this is not required. Some KV implementations provide a means of iterating through the keys, but this again is an added bonus. A filesystem could be considered a key-value store, if you think of the file path as the key and the file contents as the value. Because the KV moniker demands so little, databases of this type can be incredibly performant in a number of scenarios but generally won't be helpful when you have complex query and aggregation needs.

As with relational databases, many open source options are available. Some of the more popular offerings include memcached (and its cousins memcachedb and membase), Voldemort, and the two we cover in this book: Redis and Riak.

Riak

More than a key-value store, *Riak*—covered in Chapter 3, *Riak*, on page 51— embraces web constructs like HTTP and REST from the ground up. It's a faithful implementation of Amazon's Dynamo, with advanced features such as vector clocks for conflict resolution. Values in Riak can be anything, from plain text to XML to image data, and relationships between keys are handled by named structures called *links*. One of the lesser known databases in this book, Riak, is rising in popularity, and it's the first one we'll talk about that supports advanced querying via mapreduce.

Redis

Redis provides for complex datatypes like sorted sets and hashes, as well as basic message patterns like publish-subscribe and blocking queues. It also has one of the most robust query mechanisms for a KV store. And by caching writes in memory before committing to disk, Redis gains amazing performance in exchange for increased risk of data loss in the case of a hardware failure. This characteristic makes it a good fit for caching noncritical data and for acting as a message broker. We leave it until the end—see Chapter 8, *Redis*, on page 261—so we can build a multidatabase application with Redis and others working together in harmony.

Columnar

Columnar, or column-oriented, databases are so named because the important aspect of their design is that data from a given column (in the two-dimensional table sense) is stored together. By contrast, a row-oriented database (like an RDBMS) keeps information about a row together. The difference may seem inconsequential, but the impact of this design decision runs deep. In column-oriented databases, adding columns is quite inexpensive and is done on a row-by-row basis. Each row can have a different set of columns, or none at all, allowing tables to remain *sparse* without incurring a storage cost for null values. With respect to structure, columnar is about midway between relational and key-value.

In the columnar database market, there's somewhat less competition than in relational databases or key-value stores. The three most popular are HBase (which we cover in Chapter 4, *HBase*, on page 93), Cassandra, and Hypertable.

HBase

This column-oriented database shares the most similarities with the relational model of all the nonrelational databases we cover. Using Google's BigTable paper as a blueprint, HBase is built on Hadoop (a mapreduce engine) and designed for scaling horizontally on clusters of commodity hardware. HBase makes strong consistency guarantees and features tables with rows and columns—which should make SQL fans feel right at home. Out-of-the-box support for versioning and compression sets this database apart in the "Big Data" space.

Document

Document-oriented databases store, well, documents. In short, a document is like a hash, with a unique ID field and values that may be any of a variety of types, including more hashes. Documents can contain nested structures, and so they exhibit a high degree of flexibility, allowing for variable domains. The system imposes few restrictions on incoming data, as long as it meets the basic requirement of being expressible as a document. Different document databases take different approaches with respect to indexing, ad hoc querying, replication, consistency, and other design decisions. Choosing wisely between them requires understanding these differences and how they impact your particular use cases.

The two major open source players in the document database market are MongoDB, which we cover in Chapter 5, *MongoDB*, on page 135, and CouchDB, covered in Chapter 6, *CouchDB*, on page 177.

MongoDB

MongoDB is designed to be *huge* (the name *mongo* is extracted from the word hu*mongo*us). Mongo server configurations attempt to remain consistent—if you write something, subsequent reads will receive the same value (until the next update). This feature makes it attractive to those coming from an RDBMS background. It also offers atomic read-write operations such as incrementing a value and deep querying of nested document structures. Using JavaScript for its query language, MongoDB supports both simple queries and complex mapreduce jobs.

CouchDB

CouchDB targets a wide variety of deployment scenarios, from the datacenter to the desktop, on down to the smartphone. Written in Erlang, CouchDB has a distinct ruggedness largely lacking in other databases. With nearly incorruptible data files, CouchDB remains highly available even in the face of intermittent connectivity loss or hardware failure. Like Mongo, CouchDB's native query language is JavaScript. Views consist of mapreduce functions, which are stored as documents and replicated between nodes like any other data.

Graph

One of the less commonly used database styles, graph databases excel at dealing with highly interconnected data. A graph database consists of nodes and relationships between nodes. Both nodes and relationships can have properties—key-value pairs—that store data. The real strength of graph databases is traversing through the nodes by following relationships.

In Chapter 7, *Neo4J*, on page 219, we discuss the most popular graph database today, Neo4J.

Neo4J

One operation where other databases often fall flat is crawling through self-referential or otherwise intricately linked data. This is exactly where Neo4J shines. The benefit of using a graph database is the ability to quickly traverse nodes and relationships to find relevant data. Often found in social networking applications, graph databases are gaining traction for their flexibility, with Neo4j as a pinnacle implementation.

Polyglot

In the wild, databases are often used alongside other databases. It's still common to find a lone relational database, but over time it is becoming popular to use several databases together, leveraging their strengths to create an ecosystem that is more powerful, capable, and robust than the sum of its parts. This practice is known as *polyglot persistence* and is a topic we consider further in Chapter 9, *Wrapping Up*, on page 307.

1.3 Onward and Upward

We're in the midst of a Cambrian explosion of data storage options; it's hard to predict exactly what will evolve next. We can be fairly certain, though, that the pure domination of any particular strategy (relational or otherwise) is unlikely. Instead, we'll see increasingly specialized databases, each suited to a particular (but certainly overlapping) set of ideal problem spaces. And just as there are jobs today that call for expertise specifically in administrating relational databases (DBAs), we are going to see the rise of their nonrelational counterparts.

Databases, like programming languages and libraries, are another set of tools that every developer should know. Every good carpenter must understand what's in their toolbelt. And like any good builder, you can never hope to be a master without a familiarity of the many options at your disposal.

Consider this a crash course in the workshop. In this book, you'll swing some hammers, spin some power drills, play with some nail guns, and in the end be able to build so much more than a birdhouse. So, without further ado, let's wield our first database: PostgreSQL.

## CHAPTER 2

PostgreSQL

PostgreSQL is the hammer of the database world. It's commonly understood, is often readily available, is sturdy, and solves a surprising number of problems if you swing hard enough. No one can hope to be an expert builder without understanding this most common of tools.

PostgreSQL is a relational database management system, which means it's a set-theory-based system, implemented as two-dimensional tables with data rows and strictly enforced column types. Despite the growing interest in newer database trends, the relational style remains the most popular and probably will for quite some time.

The prevalence of relational databases comes not only from their vast toolkits (triggers, stored procedures, advanced indexes), their data safety (via ACID compliance), or their mind share (many programmers speak and think relationally) but also from their query pliancy. Unlike some other datastores, you needn't know how you plan to use the data. If a relational schema is normalized, queries are flexible. PostgreSQL is the finest open source example of the relational database management system (RDBMS) tradition.

2.1 That's Post-greS-Q-L

PostgreSQL is by far the oldest and most battle-tested database in this book. It has plug-ins for natural-language parsing, multidimensional indexing, geographic queries, custom datatypes, and much more. It has sophisticated transaction handling, has built-in stored procedures for a dozen languages, and runs on a variety of platforms. PostgreSQL has built-in Unicode support, sequences, table inheritance, and subselects, and it is one of the most ANSI SQL–compliant relational databases on the market. It's fast and reliable, can handle terabytes of data, and has been proven to run in high-profile production

So, What's with the Name?

PostgreSQL has existed in the current project incarnation since 1995, but its roots are considerably older. The original project was written at Berkeley in the early 1970s and called the Interactive Graphics and Retrieval System, or "Ingres" for short. In the 1980s, an improved version was launched post-Ingres—shortened to Postgres. The project ended at Berkeley proper in 1993 but was picked up again by the open source community as Postgres95. It was later renamed to PostgreSQL in 1996 to denote its rather new SQL support and has remained so ever since.

projects such as Skype, France's Caisse Nationale d'Allocations Familiales (CNAF), and the United States' Federal Aviation Administration (FAA).

You can install PostgreSQL in many ways, depending on your operating system.[1] Beyond the basic install, we'll need to extend Postgres with the following contributed packages: tablefunc, dict_xsyn, fuzzystrmatch, pg_trgm, and cube. You can refer to the website for installation instructions.[2]

Once you have Postgres installed, create a schema called book using the following command:

```
$ createdb book
```

We'll be using the book schema for the remainder of this chapter. Next, run the following command to ensure your contrib packages have been installed correctly:

```
$ psql book -c "SELECT '1'::cube;"
```

Seek out the online docs for more information if you receive an error message.

2.2 Day 1: Relations, CRUD, and Joins

While we won't assume you're a relational database expert, we do assume you have confronted a database or two in the past. Odds are good that the database was relational. We'll start with creating our own schemas and populating them. Then we'll take a look at querying for values and finally what makes relational databases so special: the table join.

Like most databases we'll read about, Postgres provides a back-end server that does all of the work and a command-line shell to connect to the running

---

1. http://www.postgresql.org/download/
2. http://www.postgresql.org/docs/9.0/static/contrib.html

server. The server communicates through port 5432 by default, which you can connect to with the psql shell.

```
$ psql book
```

PostgreSQL prompts with the name of the database followed by a hash mark if you run as an administrator and by dollar sign as a regular user. The shell also comes equipped with the best built-in documentation you will find in any console. Typing \h lists information about SQL commands, and \? helps with psql-specific commands, namely, those that begin with a backslash. You can find usage details about each SQL command in the following way:

```
book=# \h CREATE INDEX
Command:     CREATE INDEX
Description: define a new index
Syntax:
CREATE [ UNIQUE ] INDEX [ CONCURRENTLY ] [ name ] ON table [ USING method ]
    ( { column | ( expression ) } [ opclass ] [ ASC | DESC ] [ NULLS { FIRST | ...
    [ WITH ( storage_parameter = value [, ... ] ) ]
    [ TABLESPACE tablespace ]
    [ WHERE predicate ]
```

Before we dig too deeply into Postgres, it would be good to familiarize yourself with this useful tool. It's worth looking over (or brushing up on) a few common commands, like SELECT or CREATE TABLE.

Starting with SQL

PostgreSQL follows the SQL convention of calling relations TABLEs, attributes COLUMNs, and tuples ROWs. For consistency we will use this terminology, though you may encounter the mathematical terms *relations*, *attributes*, and *tuples*. For more on these concepts, see *Mathematical Relations*, on page 12.

Working with Tables

PostgreSQL, being of the relational style, is a design-first datastore. First you design the schema, and then you enter data that conforms to the definition of that schema.

Creating a table consists of giving it a name and a list of columns with types and (optional) constraint information. Each table should also nominate a unique identifier column to pinpoint specific rows. That identifier is called a PRIMARY KEY. The SQL to create a countries table looks like this:

```
CREATE TABLE countries (
  country_code char(2) PRIMARY KEY,
  country_name text UNIQUE
);
```

Mathematical Relations

Relational databases are so named because they contain *relations* (i.e., tables), which are sets of *tuples* (i.e., rows), which map *attributes* to atomic values (for example, {name: 'Genghis Khan', p.died_at_age: 65}). The available attributes are defined by a *header* tuple of attributes mapped to some *domain* or constraining type (i.e., columns; for example, {name: string, age: int}). That's the gist of the relational structure.

Implementations are much more practically minded than the names imply, despite sounding so mathematical. So, why bring them up? We're trying to make the point that relational databases are *relational* based on mathematics. They aren't relational because tables "relate" to each other via foreign keys. Whether any such constraints exist is beside the point.

Though much of the math is hidden from you, the power of the model is certainly in the math. This magic allows users to express powerful queries and then lets the system optimize based on predefined patterns. RDBMSs are built atop a set-theory branch called *relational algebra*—a combination of selections (WHERE ...), projections (SELECT ...), Cartesian products (JOIN ...), and more, as shown below:

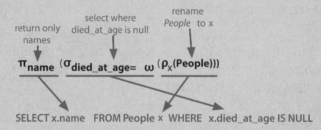

Imagining a relation as a physical table (an array of arrays, repeated in database introduction classes *ad infinitum*) can cause pain in practice, such as writing code that iterates over all rows. Relational queries are much more declarative than that, springing from a branch of mathematics known as *tuple relational calculus*, which can be converted to relational algebra. PostgreSQL and other RDBMSs optimize queries by performing this conversion and simplifying the algebra. You can see that the SQL in the diagram below is the same as the previous diagram.

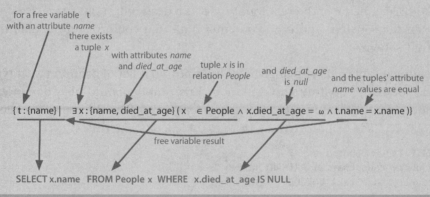

This new table will store a set of rows, where each is identified by a two-character code and the name is unique. These columns both have *constraints*. The PRIMARY KEY constrains the country_code column to disallow duplicate country codes. Only one us and one gb may exist. We explicitly gave country_name a similar unique constraint, although it is not a primary key. We can populate the countries table by inserting a few rows.

```
INSERT INTO countries (country_code, country_name)
VALUES ('us','United States'), ('mx','Mexico'), ('au','Australia'),
       ('gb','United Kingdom'), ('de','Germany'), ('ll','Loompaland');
```

Let's test our unique constraint. Attempting to add a duplicate country_name will cause our unique constraint to fail, thus disallowing insertion. Constraints are how relational databases like PostgreSQL ensure kosher data.

```
INSERT INTO countries
VALUES ('uk','United Kingdom');

ERROR:  duplicate key value violates unique constraint "countries_country_name_key"
DETAIL:  Key (country_name)=(United Kingdom) already exists.
```

We can validate that the proper rows were inserted by reading them using the SELECT...FROM table command.

```
SELECT *
FROM countries;

 country_code | country_name
--------------+---------------
 us           | United States
 mx           | Mexico
 au           | Australia
 gb           | United Kingdom
 de           | Germany
 ll           | Loompaland
(6 rows)
```

According to any respectable map, Loompaland isn't a real place—let's remove it from the table. We specify which row to remove by the WHERE clause. The row whose country_code equals ll will be removed.

```
DELETE FROM countries
WHERE country_code = 'll';
```

With only real countries left in the countries table, let's add a cities table. To ensure any inserted country_code also exists in our countries table, we add the REFERENCES keyword. Since the country_code column references another table's key, it's known as the *foreign key* constraint.

On CRUD

CRUD is a useful mnemonic for remembering the basic data management operations: *Create*, *Read*, *Update*, and *Delete*. These generally correspond to inserting new records (*creating*), modifying existing records (*updating*), and removing records you no longer need (*deleting*). All of the other operations you use a database for (any crazy query you can dream up) are *read operations*. If you can CRUD, you can do anything.

```
CREATE TABLE cities (
  name text NOT NULL,
  postal_code varchar(9) CHECK (postal_code <> ''),
  country_code char(2) REFERENCES countries,
  PRIMARY KEY (country_code, postal_code)
);
```

This time, we constrained the name in cities by disallowing NULL values. We constrained postal_code by checking that no values are empty strings (<> means *not equal*). Furthermore, since a PRIMARY KEY uniquely identifies a row, we created a compound key: country_code + postal_code. Together, they uniquely define a row.

Postgres also has a rich set of datatypes. You've just seen three different string representations: text (a string of any length), varchar(9) (a string of variable length up to nine characters), and char(2) (a string of exactly two characters). With our schema in place, let's insert *Toronto, CA*.

```
INSERT INTO cities
VALUES ('Toronto','M4C1B5','ca');
```

```
ERROR:  insert or update on table "cities" violates foreign key constraint
  "cities_country_code_fkey"
DETAIL:  Key (country_code)=(ca) is not present in table "countries".
```

This failure is good! Since country_code REFERENCES countries, the country_code must exist in the countries table. This is called *maintaining referential integrity*, as in Figure 1, *The REFERENCES keyword constrains fields to another table's primary key*, on page 15, and ensures our data is always correct. It's worth noting that NULL is valid for cities.country_code, since NULL represents the lack of a value. If you want to disallow a NULL country_code reference, you would define the table cities column like this: country_code char(2) REFERENCES countries NOT NULL.

Now let's try another insert, this time with a U.S. city.

```
INSERT INTO cities
VALUES ('Portland','87200','us');
```

```
INSERT 0 1
```

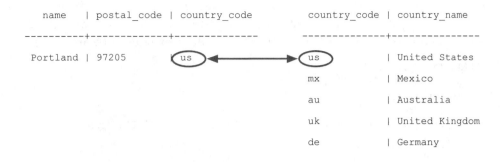

```
     name    | postal_code | country_code        country_code | country_name
  ----------+-------------+--------------       --------------+---------------
   Portland  |  97205      |   us  <------->  us             | United States
                                                mx             | Mexico
                                                au             | Australia
                                                uk             | United Kingdom
                                                de             | Germany
```

Figure 1—The REFERENCES keyword constrains fields to another table's primary key.

This is a successful insert, to be sure. But we mistakenly entered the wrong postal_code. The correct postal code for Portland is *97205*. Rather than delete and reinsert the value, we can update it inline.

```
UPDATE cities
SET postal_code = '97205'
WHERE name = 'Portland';
```

We have now Created, Read, Updated, and Deleted table rows.

Join Reads

All of the other databases we'll read about in this book perform CRUD operations as well. What sets relational databases like PostgreSQL apart is their ability to join tables together when reading them. Joining, in essence, is an operation taking two separate tables and combining them in some way to return a single table. It's somewhat like shuffling up Scrabble pieces from existing words to make new words.

The basic form of a join is the *inner join*. In the simplest form, you specify two columns (one from each table) to match by, using the ON keyword.

```
SELECT cities.*, country_name
FROM cities INNER JOIN countries
  ON cities.country_code = countries.country_code;
```

```
 country_code |    name    | postal_code | country_name
 -------------+----------+-------------+---------------
  us           | Portland  | 97205       | United States
```

The join returns a single table, sharing all columns' values of the cities table plus the matching country_name value from the countries table.

We can also join a table like cities that has a compound primary key. To test a compound join, let's create a new table that stores a list of venues.

A venue exists in both a *postal code* and a specific *country*. The *foreign key* must be two columns that reference both cities *primary key* columns. (MATCH FULL is a constraint that ensures either both values exist or both are NULL.)

```
CREATE TABLE venues (
  venue_id SERIAL PRIMARY KEY,
  name varchar(255),
  street_address text,
  type char(7) CHECK ( type in ('public','private') ) DEFAULT 'public',
  postal_code varchar(9),
  country_code char(2),
  FOREIGN KEY (country_code, postal_code)
    REFERENCES cities (country_code, postal_code) MATCH FULL
);
```

This venue_id column is a common primary key setup: automatically increment-ed integers (1, 2, 3, 4, and so on...). We make this identifier using the SERIAL keyword (MySQL has a similar construct called AUTO_INCREMENT).

```
INSERT INTO venues (name, postal_code, country_code)
VALUES ('Crystal Ballroom', '97205', 'us');
```

Although we did not set a venue_id value, creating the row populated it.

Back to our compound join. Joining the venues table with the cities table requires *both* foreign key columns. To save on typing, we can alias the table names by following the real table name directly with an alias, with an optional AS between (for example, venues v or venues AS v).

```
SELECT v.venue_id, v.name, c.name
FROM venues v INNER JOIN cities c
  ON v.postal_code=c.postal_code AND v.country_code=c.country_code;
```

```
 venue_id |       name       |  name
----------+------------------+----------
        1 | Crystal Ballroom | Portland
```

You can optionally request that PostgreSQL return columns after insertion by ending the query with a RETURNING statement.

```
INSERT INTO venues (name, postal_code, country_code)
VALUES ('Voodoo Donuts', '97205', 'us') RETURNING venue_id;
```

```
 id
- - - -
  2
```

This provides the new venue_id without issuing another query.

The Outer Limits

In addition to inner joins, PostgreSQL can also perform *outer joins*. Outer joins are a way of merging two tables when the results of one table must always be returned, whether or not any matching column values exist on the other table.

It's easiest to give an example, but to do that, we'll create a new table named events. This one is up to you. Your events table should have these columns: a SERIAL integer event_id, a title, starts and ends (of type *timestamp*), and a venue_id (foreign key that references venues). A schema definition diagram covering all the tables we've made so far is shown in Figure 2, *The crow's-feet entity relationship diagram (ERD)*, on page 18.

After creating the events table, INSERT the following values (timestamps are inserted as a string like *2012-02-15 17:30*), two holidays, and a club we *do not talk about*.

title	starts	ends	venue_id	event_id
LARP Club	2012-02-15 17:30:00	2012-02-15 19:30:00	2	1
April Fools Day	2012-04-01 00:00:00	2012-04-01 23:59:00		2
Christmas Day	2012-12-25 00:00:00	2012-12-25 23:59:00		3

Let's first craft a query that returns an event title and venue name as an inner join (the word INNER from INNER JOIN is not required, so leave it off here).

```
SELECT e.title, v.name
FROM events e JOIN venues v
  ON e.venue_id = v.venue_id;
```

title	name
LARP Club	Voodoo Donuts

INNER JOIN will return a row only *if the column values match*. Since we can't have NULL venues.venue_id, the two NULL events.venue_ids refer to nothing. Retrieving all of the events, whether or not they have a venue, requires a LEFT OUTER JOIN (shortened to LEFT JOIN).

```
SELECT e.title, v.name
FROM events e LEFT JOIN venues v
ON e.venue_id = v.venue_id;
```

title	name
LARP Club	Voodoo Donuts
April Fools Day	
Christmas Day	

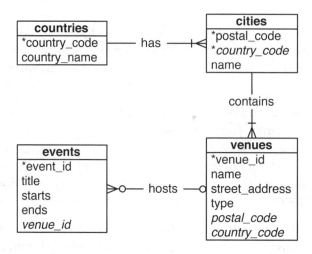

Figure 2—The crow's-feet entity relationship diagram (ERD)

If you require the inverse, all venues and only matching events, use a RIGHT JOIN. Finally, there's the FULL JOIN, which is the union of LEFT and RIGHT; you're guaranteed all values from each table, joined wherever columns match.

Fast Lookups with Indexing

The speed of PostgreSQL (and any other RDBMS) lies in its efficient management of blocks of data, reducing disk reads, query optimization, and other techniques. But those go only so far in fetching results fast. If we select the title of *Christmas Day* from the events table, the algorithm must scan every row for a match to return. Without an *index*, each row must be read from disk to know whether a query should return it. See the following.

```
matches "Christmas Day"? No.  ──────▶  LARP Club       |     2 |        1

matches "Christmas Day"? No.  ──────▶  April Fools Day |       |        2

matches "Christmas Day"? Yes! ──────▶  Christmas Day   |       |        3
```

An index is a special data structure built to avoid a full table scan when performing a query. When running CREATE TABLE commands, you may have noticed a message like this:

```
CREATE TABLE / PRIMARY KEY will create implicit index "events_pkey" \
for table "events"
```

PostgreSQL automatically creates an index on the primary key, where the key is the primary key value and where the value points to a row on disk, as shown in the graphic below. Using the UNIQUE keyword is another way to force an index on a table column.

You can explicitly add a hash index using the CREATE INDEX command, where each value must be unique (like a hashtable or a map).

```
CREATE INDEX events_title
  ON events USING hash (title);
```

For less-than/greater-than/equals-to matches, we want an index more flexible than a simple hash, like a B-tree (see Figure 3, *A B-tree index can match on ranged queries*, on page 20). Consider a query to find all events that are on or after April 1.

```
SELECT *
FROM events
WHERE starts >= '2012-04-01';
```

For this, a tree is the perfect data structure. To index the starts column with a B-tree, use this:

```
CREATE INDEX events_starts
  ON events USING btree (starts);
```

Now our query over a range of dates will avoid a full table scan. It makes a huge difference when scanning millions or billions of rows.

We can inspect our work with this command to list all indexes in the schema:

```
book=# \di
```

It's worth noting that when you set a FOREIGN KEY constraint, PostgreSQL will automatically create an index on the targeted column(s). Even if you don't like using database constraints (that's right, we're looking at you, Ruby on

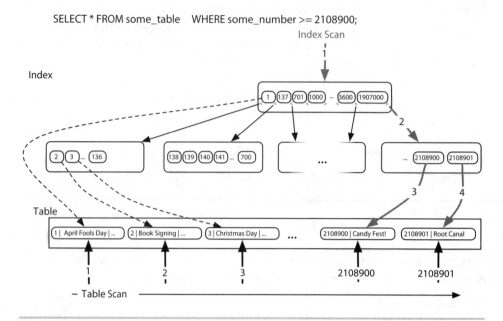

Figure 3—A B-tree index can match on ranged queries.

Rails developers), you will often find yourself creating indexes on columns you plan to join against in order to help speed up foreign key joins.

Day 1 Wrap-Up

We sped through a lot today and covered many terms. Here's a recap:

Term	Definition
Column	A domain of values of a certain type, sometimes called an *attribute*
Row	An object comprised as a set of column values, sometimes called a *tuple*
Table	A set of rows with the same columns, sometimes called a *relation*
Primary key	The unique value that pinpoints a specific row
CRUD	Create, Read, Update, Delete
SQL	Structured Query Language, the *lingua franca* of a relational database
Join	Combining two tables into one by some matching columns
Left join	Combining two tables into one by some matching columns or NULL if nothing matches the left table

Term	Definition
Index	A data structure to optimize selection of a specific set of columns
B-tree	A good standard index; values are stored as a balanced tree data structure; very flexible

Relational databases have been the *de facto* data management strategy for forty years—many of us began our careers in the midst of their evolution. So, we took a look at some of the core concepts of the relational model via basic SQL queries. We will expound on these root concepts tomorrow.

Day 1 Homework

Find

1. Bookmark the online PostgreSQL FAQ and documents.
2. Acquaint yourself with the command-line \? and \h output.
3. In the addresses FOREIGN KEY, find in the docs what MATCH FULL means.

Do

1. Select all the tables we created (and only those) from pg_class.
2. Write a query that finds the country name of the LARP Club event.
3. Alter the venues table to contain a boolean column called active, with the default value of TRUE.

2.3 Day 2: Advanced Queries, Code, and Rules

Yesterday we saw how to define schemas, populate them with data, update and delete rows, and perform basic reads. Today we'll dig even deeper into the myriad ways that PostgreSQL can query data. We'll see how to group similar values, execute code on the server, and create custom interfaces using *views* and *rules*. We'll finish the day by using one of PostgreSQL's contributed packages to flip tables on their heads.

Aggregate Functions

An aggregate query groups results from several rows by some common criteria. It can be as simple as counting the number of rows in a table or calculating the average of some numerical column. They're powerful SQL tools and also a lot of fun.

Let's try some aggregate functions, but first we'll need some more data in our database. Enter your own country into the countries table, your own city into the cities table, and your own address as a venue (which we just named *My Place*). Then add a few records to the events table.

Here's a quick SQL tip: rather than setting the venue_id explicitly, you can sub-SELECT it using a more human-readable title. If *Moby* is playing at the *Crystal Ballroom*, set the venue_id like this:

```
INSERT INTO events (title, starts, ends, venue_id)
  VALUES ('Moby', '2012-02-06 21:00', '2012-02-06 23:00', (
    SELECT venue_id
    FROM venues
    WHERE name = 'Crystal Ballroom'
  )
);
```

Populate your events table with the following data (to enter *Valentine's Day* in PostgreSQL, you can escape the apostrophe with two, such as *Heaven''s Gate*):

title	starts	ends	venue
Wedding	2012-02-26 21:00:00	2012-02-26 23:00:00	Voodoo Donuts
Dinner with Mom	2012-02-26 18:00:00	2012-02-26 20:30:00	My Place
Valentine's Day	2012-02-14 00:00:00	2012-02-14 23:59:00	

With our data set up, let's try some aggregate queries. The simplest aggregate function is count(), which is fairly self-explanatory. Counting all titles that contain the word *Day* (note: % is a wildcard on LIKE searches), you should receive a value of 3.

```
SELECT count(title)
FROM events
WHERE title LIKE '%Day%';
```

To get the first start time and last end time of all events at the Crystal Ballroom, use min() (return the smallest value) and max() (return the largest value).

```
SELECT min(starts), max(ends)
FROM events INNER JOIN venues
  ON events.venue_id = venues.venue_id
WHERE venues.name = 'Crystal Ballroom';
```

min	max
2012-02-06 21:00:00	2012-02-06 23:00:00

Aggregate functions are useful but limited on their own. If we wanted to count all events at each venue, we could write the following for each venue ID:

```
SELECT count(*) FROM events WHERE venue_id = 1;
SELECT count(*) FROM events WHERE venue_id = 2;
SELECT count(*) FROM events WHERE venue_id = 3;
SELECT count(*) FROM events WHERE venue_id IS NULL;
```

This would be tedious (intractable even) as the number of venues grows. Enter the GROUP BY command.

Grouping

GROUP BY is a shortcut for running the previous queries all at once. With GROUP BY, you tell Postgres to place the rows into groups and then perform some aggregate function (such as count()) on those groups.

```
SELECT venue_id, count(*)
FROM events
GROUP BY venue_id;

 venue_id | count
----------+-------
        1 |     1
        2 |     2
        3 |     1
          |     3
```

It's a nice list, but can we filter by the count() function? Absolutely. The GROUP BY condition has its own filter keyword: HAVING. HAVING is like the WHERE clause, except it can filter by aggregate functions (whereas WHERE cannot).

The following query SELECTs the most popular venues, those with two or more events:

```
SELECT venue_id
FROM events
GROUP BY venue_id
HAVING count(*) >= 2 AND venue_id IS NOT NULL;

 venue_id | count
----------+-------
        2 |     2
```

You can use GROUP BY without any aggregate functions. If you call SELECT... FROM...GROUP BY on one column, you get all unique values.

```
SELECT venue_id FROM events GROUP BY venue_id;
```

This kind of grouping is so common that SQL has a shortcut in the DISTINCT keyword.

```
SELECT DISTINCT venue_id FROM events;
```

The results of both queries will be identical.

GROUP BY in MySQL

If you tried to run a SELECT with columns not defined under a GROUP BY in MySQL, you may be shocked to see that it works. This originally made us question the necessity of window functions. But when we more closely inspected the data MySQL returns, we found it will return only a random row of data along with the count, not all relevant results. Generally, that's not useful (and quite potentially dangerous).

Window Functions

If you've done any sort of production work with a relational database in the past, you were likely familiar with aggregate queries. They are a common SQL staple. *Window functions*, on the other hand, are not quite so common (PostgreSQL is one of the few open source databases to implement them).

Window functions are similar to GROUP BY queries in that they allow you to run aggregate functions across multiple rows. The difference is that they allow you to use built-in aggregate functions without requiring every single field to be grouped to a single row.

If we attempt to select the title column without grouping by it, we can expect an error.

```
SELECT title, venue_id, count(*)
FROM events
GROUP BY venue_id;
```

```
ERROR:  column "events.title" must appear in the GROUP BY clause or \
        be used in an aggregate function
```

We are counting up the rows by venue_id, and in the case of *LARP Club* and *Wedding*, we have two titles for a single venue_id. Postgres doesn't know *which* title to display.

Whereas a GROUP BY clause will return one record per matching group value, a window function can return a separate record for each row. For a visual representation, see Figure 4, *Window function results do not collapse results per group*, on page 25. Let's see an example of the sweet spot that window functions attempt to hit.

Window functions return all matches and replicate the results of any aggregate function.

```
SELECT title, count(*) OVER (PARTITION BY venue_id) FROM events;
```

We like to think of PARTITION BY as akin to GROUP BY, but rather than grouping the results outside of the SELECT attribute list (and thus combining the results

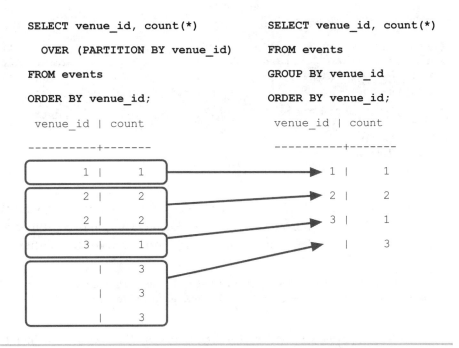

Figure 4—Window function results do not collapse results per group.

into fewer rows), it returns grouped values as any other field (calculating on the grouped variable but otherwise just another attribute). Or in SQL parlance, it returns the results of an aggregate function OVER a PARTITION of the result set.

Transactions

Transactions are the bulwark of relational database consistency. *All or nothing,* that's the transaction motto. Transactions ensure that every command of a set is executed. If anything fails along the way, all of the commands are rolled back like they never happened.

PostgreSQL transactions follow ACID compliance, which stands for Atomic (all ops succeed or none do), Consistent (the data will always be in a good state—no inconsistent states), Isolated (transactions don't interfere), and Durable (a committed transaction is safe, even after a server crash). We should note that *consistency* in ACID is different from *consistency* in CAP (covered in Appendix 2, *The CAP Theorem,* on page 317).

We can wrap any transaction within a BEGIN TRANSACTION block. To verify atomicity, we'll kill the transaction with the ROLLBACK command.

> ## Unavoidable Transactions
>
> Up until now, every command we've executed in psql has been implicitly wrapped in a transaction. If you executed a command, such as DELETE FROM account WHERE total < 20;, and the database crashed halfway through the delete, you wouldn't be stuck with half a table. When you restart the database server, that command will be rolled back.

```
BEGIN TRANSACTION;
  DELETE FROM events;
ROLLBACK;
SELECT * FROM events;
```

The events all remain. Transactions are useful when you're modifying two tables that you don't want out of sync. The classic example is a debit/credit system for a bank, where money is moved from one account to another:

```
BEGIN TRANSACTION;
  UPDATE account SET total=total+5000.0 WHERE account_id=1337;
  UPDATE account SET total=total-5000.0 WHERE account_id=45887;
END;
```

If something happened between the two updates, this bank just lost five grand. But when wrapped in a transaction block, the initial update is rolled back, even if the server explodes.

Stored Procedures

Every command we've seen until now has been declarative, but sometimes we need to run some code. At this point, you must make a decision: execute code on the client side or execute code on the database side.

Stored procedures can offer huge performance advantages for huge architectural costs. You may avoid streaming thousands of rows to a client application, but you have also bound your application code to this database. The decision to use stored procedures should not be arrived at lightly.

Warnings aside, let's create a procedure (or FUNCTION) that simplifies INSERTing a new event at a venue without needing the venue_id. If the venue doesn't exist, create it first and reference it in the new event. Also, we'll return a boolean indicating whether a new venue was added, as a nicety to our users.

postgres/add_event.sql
```
CREATE OR REPLACE FUNCTION add_event( title text, starts timestamp,
  ends timestamp, venue text, postal varchar(9), country char(2) )
RETURNS boolean AS $$
DECLARE
  did_insert boolean := false;
```

What About Vendor Lock?

When relational databases hit their heyday, they were the Swiss Army knife of technologies. You could store nearly anything—even programming entire projects in them (for example, Microsoft Access). The few companies that provided this software promoted use of proprietary differences and then took advantage of this corporate reliance by charging enormous license and consulting fees. This was the dreaded *vendor lock* that newer programming methodologies tried to mitigate in the 1990s and early 2000s.

However, in their zeal to neuter the vendors, maxims arose such as *no logic in the database*. This is a shame because relational databases are capable of so many varied data management options. Vendor lock has not disappeared. Many actions we investigate in this book are highly implementation specific. However, it's worth knowing how to use databases to their fullest extent before deciding to skip tools like stored procedures *a priori*.

```
    found_count integer;
    the_venue_id integer;
BEGIN
    SELECT venue_id INTO the_venue_id
    FROM venues v
    WHERE v.postal_code=postal AND v.country_code=country AND v.name ILIKE venue
    LIMIT 1;

    IF the_venue_id IS NULL THEN
        INSERT INTO venues (name, postal_code, country_code)
        VALUES (venue, postal, country)
        RETURNING venue_id INTO the_venue_id;

        did_insert := true;
    END IF;

    -- Note: not an "error", as in some programming languages
    RAISE NOTICE 'Venue found %', the_venue_id;

    INSERT INTO events (title, starts, ends, venue_id)
    VALUES (title, starts, ends, the_venue_id);

    RETURN did_insert;
END;
$$ LANGUAGE plpgsql;
```

You can import this external file into the current schema by the following command-line argument (if you don't feel like typing all that code).

```
book=# \i add_event.sql
```

Running it should return t (true), since this is the first use of the venue *Run's House*. This saves a client two round-trip SQL commands to the database (a select and then an insert) and instead does only one.

```
SELECT add_event('House Party', '2012-05-03 23:00',
  '2012-05-04 02:00', 'Run''s House', '97205', 'us');
```

The language we used in the procedure we wrote is PL/pgSQL (which stands for Procedural Language/PostgreSQL). Covering the details of an entire programming language is beyond our scope, but you can read much more about it in the online PostgreSQL documentation.[3]

In addition to PL/pgSQL, Postgres supports three more core languages for writing procedures: Tcl, Perl, and Python. People have written extensions for a dozen more including Ruby, Java, PHP, Scheme, and others listed in the public documentation. Try this shell command:

```
$ createlang book --list
```

It will list the languages installed in your database. The createlang command is also used to add new languages, which you can find online.[4]

Pull the Triggers

Triggers automatically fire stored procedures when some event happens, like an insert or update. They allow the database to enforce some required behavior in response to changing data.

Let's create a new PL/pgSQL function that logs whenever an event is updated (we want to be sure no one changes an event and tries to deny it later). First, create a logs table to store event changes. A primary key isn't necessary here, since it's just a log.

```
CREATE TABLE logs (
  event_id integer,
  old_title varchar(255),
  old_starts timestamp,
  old_ends timestamp,
  logged_at timestamp DEFAULT current_timestamp
);
```

Next, we build a function to insert old data into the log. The OLD variable represents the row about to be changed (NEW represents an incoming row, which we'll see in action soon enough). Output a notice to the console with the event_id before returning.

---

3. http://www.postgresql.org/docs/9.0/static/plpgsql.html
4. http://www.postgresql.org/docs/9.0/static/app-createlang.html

Choosing to Execute Database Code

This is the first of a number of places you'll see this theme in this book: does the code belong in your application or in the database? It is a difficult decision—one that you'll have to answer uniquely for every application.

The benefit is you'll often improve performance by as much as an order of magnitude. For example, you might have a complex application-specific calculation that requires custom code. If the calculation involves many rows, a stored procedure will save you from moving thousands of rows instead of a single result. The cost is splitting your application, your code, and your tests, across two different programming paradigms.

postgres/log_event.sql
```
CREATE OR REPLACE FUNCTION log_event() RETURNS trigger AS $$
DECLARE
BEGIN
  INSERT INTO logs (event_id, old_title, old_starts, old_ends)
  VALUES (OLD.event_id, OLD.title, OLD.starts, OLD.ends);
  RAISE NOTICE 'Someone just changed event #%', OLD.event_id;
  RETURN NEW;
END;
$$ LANGUAGE plpgsql;
```

Finally, we create our trigger to log changes after any row is updated.

```
CREATE TRIGGER log_events
  AFTER UPDATE ON events
  FOR EACH ROW EXECUTE PROCEDURE log_event();
```

So, it turns out our party at Run's House has to end earlier than we hoped. Let's change the event.

```
UPDATE events
SET ends='2012-05-04 01:00:00'
WHERE title='House Party';

NOTICE:  Someone just changed event #9
```

And the old end time was logged.

```
SELECT event_id, old_title, old_ends, logged_at
FROM logs;
```

event_id	old_title	old_ends	logged_at
9	House Party	2012-05-04 02:00:00	2011-02-26 15:50:31.939

Triggers can also be created before updates and before or after inserts.[5]

Viewing the World

Wouldn't it be great if you could use the results of a complex query just like any other table? Well, that's exactly what VIEWs are for. Unlike stored procedures, these aren't functions being executed but rather aliased queries.

In our database, all holidays contain the word *Day* and have no venue.

```
postgres/holiday_view_1.sql
CREATE VIEW holidays AS
  SELECT event_id AS holiday_id, title AS name, starts AS date
  FROM events
  WHERE title LIKE '%Day%' AND venue_id IS NULL;
```

So, creating a view is as simple as writing a query and prefixing it with CREATE VIEW some_view_name AS. Now you can query holidays like any other table. Under the covers it's the plain old events table. As proof, add *Valentine's Day* on *2012-02-14* to events and query the holidays view.

```
SELECT name, to_char(date, 'Month DD, YYYY') AS date
FROM holidays
WHERE date <= '2012-04-01';
```

```
     name        |        date
-----------------+--------------------
 April Fools Day | April      01, 2012
 Valentine's Day | February   14, 2012
```

Views are powerful tools for opening up complex queried data in a simple way. The query may be a roiling sea of complexity underneath, but all you see is a table.

If you want to add a new column to the view, it will have to come from the underlying table. Let's alter the events table to have an array of associated colors.

```
ALTER TABLE events
ADD colors text ARRAY;
```

Since holidays are to have colors associated with them, let's update the VIEW query to contain the colors array.

```
CREATE OR REPLACE VIEW holidays AS
  SELECT event_id AS holiday_id, title AS name, starts AS date, colors
  FROM events
  WHERE title LIKE '%Day%' AND venue_id IS NULL;
```

Now it's a matter of setting an array or color strings to the holiday of choice. Unfortunately, we cannot update a view directly.

```
UPDATE holidays SET colors = '{"red","green"}' where name = 'Christmas Day';
```

```
ERROR:  cannot update a view
HINT:  You need an unconditional ON UPDATE DO INSTEAD rule.
```

Looks like we need a RULE.

What RULEs the School?

A RULE is a description of how to alter the parsed *query tree*. Every time Postgres runs an SQL statement, it parses the statement into a query tree (generally called an *abstract syntax tree*).

Operators and values become branches and leaves in the tree, and the tree is walked, pruned, and in other ways edited before execution. This tree is optionally rewritten by Postgres rules, before being sent on to the query planner (which also rewrites the tree in a way to run optimally), and sends this final command to be executed. See Figure 5, *How SQL gets executed in PostgreSQL*, on page 32. What's more is that a VIEW such as holidays *is* a RULE.

We can prove this by taking a look at the execution plan of the holidays view using the EXPLAIN command (notice *Filter* is the WHERE clause, and *Output* is the column list).

```
EXPLAIN VERBOSE
  SELECT *
  FROM holidays;
```

```
                          QUERY PLAN
-----------------------------------------------------------------------------
 Seq Scan on public.events  (cost=0.00..1.04 rows=1 width=57)
   Output: events.event_id, events.title, events.starts, events.colors
   Filter: ((events.venue_id IS NULL) AND ((events.title)::text ~~ '%Day%'::text))
```

Compare that to running EXPLAIN VERBOSE on the query we built the holidays VIEW from. They're functionally identical.

```
EXPLAIN VERBOSE
  SELECT event_id AS holiday_id,
    title AS name, starts AS date, colors
  FROM events
  WHERE title LIKE '%Day%' AND venue_id IS NULL;
```

```
                          QUERY PLAN
-----------------------------------------------------------------------------
 Seq Scan on public.events  (cost=0.00..1.04 rows=1 width=57)
   Output: event_id, title, starts, colors
   Filter: ((events.venue_id IS NULL) AND ((events.title)::text ~~ '%Day%'::text))
```

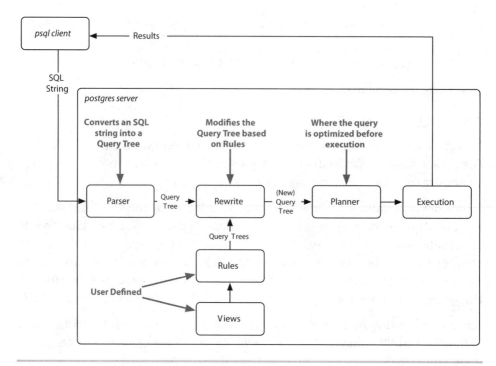

Figure 5—How SQL gets executed in PostgreSQL

So, to allow updates against our holidays view, we need to craft a RULE that tells Postgres what to do with an UPDATE. Our rule will capture updates to the holidays view and instead run the update on events, pulling values from the pseudorelations NEW and OLD. NEW functionally acts as the relation containing the values we're setting, while OLD contains the values we query by.

postgres/create_rule.sql
```
CREATE RULE update_holidays AS ON UPDATE TO holidays DO INSTEAD
  UPDATE events
  SET title = NEW.name,
      starts = NEW.date,
      colors = NEW.colors
  WHERE title = OLD.name;
```

With this rule in place, now we can update holidays directly.

```
UPDATE holidays SET colors = '{"red","green"}' where name = 'Christmas Day';
```

Next let's insert *New Years Day* on *2013-01-01* into holidays. As expected, we need a rule for that too. No problem.

```
CREATE RULE insert_holidays AS ON INSERT TO holidays DO INSTEAD
  INSERT INTO ...
```

We're going to move on from here, but if you'd like to play more with RULEs, try to add a DELETE RULE.

I'll Meet You at the Crosstab

For our last exercise of the day, we're going to build a monthly calendar of events, where each month in the calendar year counts the number of events in that month. This kind of operation is commonly done by a *pivot table*. These constructs "pivot" grouped data around some other output, in our case, a list of months. We'll build our pivot table using the crosstab() function.

Start by crafting a query to count the number of events per month, each year. PostgreSQL provides an extract() function that returns some subfield from a date or timestamp, which aids in our grouping.

```
SELECT extract(year from starts) as year,
  extract(month from starts) as month, count(*)
FROM events
GROUP BY year, month;
```

To use crosstab(), the query must return three columns: rowid, category, and value. We'll be using the year as an ID, which means the other fields are category (the month) and value (the count).

The crosstab() function needs another set of values to represent months. This is how the function knows how many columns we need. These are the values that become the columns (the table to *pivot* against). So, let's create a table to store a temporary list of numbers.

```
CREATE TEMPORARY TABLE month_count(month INT);
INSERT INTO month_count VALUES (1),(2),(3),(4),(5),(6),(7),(8),(9),(10),(11),(12);
```

Now we're ready to call crosstab() with our two queries.

```
SELECT * FROM crosstab(
  'SELECT extract(year from starts) as year,
    extract(month from starts) as month, count(*)
   FROM events
   GROUP BY year, month',
  'SELECT * FROM month_count'
);
```

```
ERROR:  a column definition list is required for functions returning "record"
```

Oops. An error occurred.

It may feel cryptic, but it's saying the function is returning a set of records (rows), but it doesn't know how to label them. In fact, it doesn't even know what datatypes they are.

Remember, the pivot table is using our months as categories, but those months are just integers. So, we define them like this:

```
SELECT * FROM crosstab(
  'SELECT extract(year from starts) as year,
    extract(month from starts) as month, count(*)
  FROM events
  GROUP BY year, month',
  'SELECT * FROM month_count'
) AS (
  year int,
  jan int, feb int, mar int, apr int, may int, jun int,
  jul int, aug int, sep int, oct int, nov int, dec int
) ORDER BY YEAR;
```

We have one column year (which is the row ID) and twelve more columns representing the months.

```
year | jan | feb | mar | apr | may | jun | jul | aug | sep | oct | nov | dec
-----+-----+-----+-----+-----+-----+-----+-----+-----+-----+-----+-----+-----
2012 |     |  5  |     |  1  |  1  |     |     |     |     |     |     |  1
```

Go ahead and add a couple more events on another year just to see next year's event counts. Run the crosstab function again, and enjoy the calendar.

Day 2 Wrap-Up

Today finalized the basics of PostgreSQL. What we're starting to see is that Postgres is more than just a server for storing vanilla datatypes and querying them; it is a data management engine that can reformat output data, store weird datatypes like arrays, execute logic, and provide enough power to rewrite incoming queries.

Day 2 Homework

Find

1. Find the list of aggregate functions in the PostgreSQL docs.
2. Find a GUI program to interact with PostgreSQL, such as Navicat.

Do

1. Create a rule that captures DELETEs on venues and instead sets the active flag (created in the Day 1 homework) to FALSE.

2. A temporary table was not the best way to implement our event calendar pivot table. The generate_series(a, b) function returns a set of records, from a to b. Replace the month_count table SELECT with this.

3. Build a pivot table that displays every day in a single month, where each week of the month is a row and each day name forms a column across the top (seven days, starting with Sunday and ending with Saturday) like a standard month calendar. Each day should contain a count of the number of events for that date or should remain blank if no event occurs.

2.4 Day 3: Full-Text and Multidimensions

We'll spend Day 3 investigating the many tools at our disposal to build a movie query system. We'll begin with the many ways that PostgreSQL can search actor/movie names using fuzzy string matching. Then we'll discover the cube package by creating a movie suggestion system based on similar genres of movies we already like. Since these are all contributed packages, the implementations are special to PostgreSQL and not part of the SQL standard.

Commonly, when designing a relational database schema, you'll start with an entity diagram. We'll be writing a personal movie suggestion system that keeps track of movies, their genres, and their actors, as modeled in Figure 6, *Our movie suggestion system*, on page 36.

As a reminder, on Day 1 we installed several contributed packages. Today we'll need them all. Again, the list we'll need installed is as follows: tablefunc, dict_xsyn, fuzzystrmatch, pg_trgm, and cube.

Let's first build the database. It's often good practice to create indexes on foreign keys to speed up reverse lookups (such as what movies this actor is involved in). You should also set a UNIQUE constraint on join tables like movies_actors to avoid duplicate join values.

```
postgres/create_movies.sql
CREATE TABLE genres (
        name text UNIQUE,
        position integer
);
CREATE TABLE movies (
        movie_id SERIAL PRIMARY KEY,
        title text,
        genre cube
);
CREATE TABLE actors (
        actor_id SERIAL PRIMARY KEY,
        name text
);
```

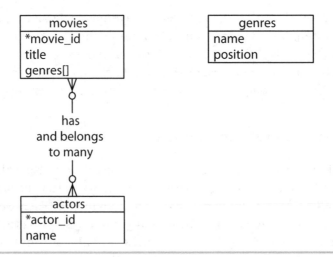

Figure 6—Our movie suggestion system

```
CREATE TABLE movies_actors (
        movie_id integer REFERENCES movies NOT NULL,
        actor_id integer REFERENCES actors NOT NULL,
        UNIQUE (movie_id, actor_id)
);
CREATE INDEX movies_actors_movie_id ON movies_actors (movie_id);
CREATE INDEX movies_actors_actor_id ON movies_actors (actor_id);
CREATE INDEX movies_genres_cube ON movies USING gist (genre);
```

You can download the movies_data.sql file as a file alongside the book and populate the tables by piping the file into the database. Any questions you may have about the genre cube will be covered later today.

Fuzzy Searching

Opening up a system to text searches means opening your system to inaccurate inputs. You have to expect typos like "Brid of Frankstein." Sometimes, users can't remember the full name of "J. Roberts." In other cases, we just plain don't know how to spell "Benn Aflek." We'll look into a few PostgreSQL packages that make text searching easy. It's worth noting that as we progress, this kind of string matching blurs the lines between relational queries and searching frameworks like Lucene.[6] Although some may feel features like full-text search belong with the application code, there can be performance and administrative benefits of pushing these packages to the database, where the data lives.

---

6.   http://lucene.apache.org/

SQL Standard String Matches

PostgreSQL has many ways of performing text matches, but the two big default methods are LIKE and regular expressions.

I Like LIKE and ILIKE

LIKE and ILIKE (case-insensitive LIKE) are the simplest forms of text search. They are fairly universal in relational databases. LIKE compares column values against a given pattern string. The % and _ characters are wildcards. % matches any number of any characters, and _ matches exactly one character.

```
SELECT title FROM movies WHERE title ILIKE 'stardust%';

        title
-------------------
 Stardust
 Stardust Memories
```

If we want to be sure the substring *stardust* is not at the end of the string, we can use the underscore (_) character as a little trick.

```
SELECT title FROM movies WHERE title ILIKE 'stardust_%';

        title
-------------------
 Stardust Memories
```

This is useful in basic cases, but LIKE is limited to simple wildcards.

Regex

A more powerful string-matching syntax is a *regular expression* (regex). Regexes appear often throughout this book, because many databases support them. There are entire books dedicated to writing powerful expressions—the topic is far too wide and complex to cover in depth. Postgres conforms (mostly) to the POSIX style.

In Postgres, a regular expression match is led by the ~ operator, with the optional ! (meaning, *not* matching) and * (meaning *case insensitive*). So, to count all movies that do *not* begin with *the*, the following case-insensitive query will work. The characters inside the string are the regular expression.

```
SELECT COUNT(*) FROM movies WHERE title !~* '^the.*';
```

You can index strings for pattern matching the previous queries by creating a text_pattern_ops operator class index, as long as the values are indexed in lowercase.

```
CREATE INDEX movies_title_pattern ON movies (lower(title) text_pattern_ops);
```

We used the text_pattern_ops because the title is of type text. If you need to index varchars, chars, or names, use the related ops: varchar_pattern_ops, bpchar_pattern_ops, and name_pattern_ops.

Bride of Levenshtein

Levenshtein is a string comparison algorithm that compares how similar two strings are by how many *steps* are required to change one string into another. Each replaced, missing, or added character counts as a step. The distance is the total number of steps away. In PostgreSQL, the levenshtein() function is provided by the fuzzystrmatch contrib package. Say we have the string *bat* and the string *fads*.

```
SELECT levenshtein('bat', 'fads');
```

The Levenshtein distance is 3 because—compared to the string *bat*—we replaced two letters (b=>f, t=>d), and we added a letter (+s). Each change increments the distance. We can watch the distance close as we step closer (so to speak). The total goes down until we get zero (the two strings are equal).

```
SELECT levenshtein('bat', 'fad') fad,
  levenshtein('bat', 'fat') fat,
  levenshtein('bat', 'bat') bat;
```

```
 fad | fat | bat
-----+-----+-----
   2 |   1 |   0
```

Changes in case cost a point too, so you may find it best to convert all strings to the same case when querying.

```
SELECT movie_id, title FROM movies
WHERE levenshtein(lower(title), lower('a hard day nght')) <= 3;
```

```
 movie_id |        title
----------+--------------------
      245 | A Hard Day's Night
```

This ensures minor differences won't over-inflate the distance.

Try a Trigram

A trigram is a group of three consecutive characters taken from a string. The pg_trgm contrib module breaks a string into as many trigrams as it can.

```
SELECT show_trgm('Avatar');
```

```
            show_trgm
-------------------------------------
 {"  a"," av","ar ",ata,ava,tar,vat}
```

Finding a matching string is as simple as counting the number of matching trigrams. The strings with the most matches are the most similar. It's useful for doing a search where you're OK with either slight misspellings or even minor words missing. The longer the string, the more trigrams and the more likely a match—they're great for something like movie titles, since they have relatively similar lengths.

We'll create a trigram index against movie names to start (we use Generalized Index Search Tree [GIST], a generic index API made available by the PostgreSQL engine).

```
CREATE INDEX movies_title_trigram ON movies
USING gist (title gist_trgm_ops);
```

Now you can query with a few misspellings and still get decent results.

```
SELECT *
FROM movies
WHERE title % 'Avatre';

  title
---------
 Avatar
```

Trigrams are an excellent choice for accepting user input, without weighing them down with wildcard complexity.

Full-Text Fun

Next, we want to allow users to perform full-text searches based on matching words, even if they're pluralized. If a user wants to search for certain words in a movie title but can remember only some of them, Postgres supports simple natural-language processing.

TSVector and TSQuery

Let's look for a movie that contains the words *night* and *day*. This is a perfect job for text search using the @@ full-text query operator.

```
SELECT title
FROM movies
WHERE title @@ 'night & day';

           title
-------------------------------
 A Hard Day's Night
 Six Days Seven Nights
 Long Day's Journey Into Night
```

The query returns titles like *A Hard Day's Night*, despite the word *Day* being in possessive form, and the two words are out of order in the query. The @@ operator converts the name field into a tsvector and converts the query into a tsquery.

A tsvector is a datatype that splits a string into an array (or a *vector*) of tokens, which are searched against the given query, while the tsquery represents a query in some language, like English or French. The language corresponds to a dictionary (which we'll see more of in a few paragraphs). The previous query is equivalent to the following (if your system language is set to English):

```
SELECT title
FROM movies
WHERE to_tsvector(title) @@ to_tsquery('english', 'night &amp; day');
```

You can take a look at how the vector and the query break apart the values by running the conversion functions on the strings outright.

```
SELECT to_tsvector('A Hard Day''s Night'), to_tsquery('english', 'night &amp; day');
```

```
      to_tsvector          |     to_tsquery
---------------------------+-----------------
 'day':3 'hard':2 'night':5 | 'night' & 'day'
```

The tokens on a tsvector are called *lexemes* and are coupled with their positions in the given phrase.

You may have noticed the tsvector for *A Hard Day's Night* did not contain the lexeme *a*. Moreover, simple English words like *a* are missing if you try to query by them.

```
SELECT *
FROM movies
WHERE title @@ to_tsquery('english', 'a');
```

```
NOTICE:  text-search query contains only stop words or doesn't \
     contain lexemes, ignored
```

Common words like *a* are called *stop words* and are generally not useful for performing queries. The English dictionary was used by the parser to normalize our string into useful English components. In your console, you can view the output of the stop words under the English tsearch_data directory.

```
cat `pg_config --sharedir`/tsearch_data/english.stop
```

We could remove *a* from the list, or we could use another dictionary like simple that just breaks up strings by nonword characters and makes them lowercase. Compare these two vectors:

```
SELECT to_tsvector('english', 'A Hard Day''s Night');

     to_tsvector
--------------------------
 'day':3 'hard':2 'night':5

SELECT to_tsvector('simple', 'A Hard Day''s Night');

             to_tsvector
-----------------------------------------
 'a':1 'day':3 'hard':2 'night':5 's':4
```

With simple, you can retrieve any movie containing the lexeme *a*.

Other Languages

Since Postgres is doing some natural-language processing here, it only makes sense that different configurations would be used for different languages. All of the installed configurations can be viewed with this command:

```
book=# \dF
```

Dictionaries are part of what Postgres uses to generate tsvector lexemes (along with stop words and other tokenizing rules we haven't covered called *parsers* and *templates*). You can view your system's list here:

```
book=# \dFd
```

You can test any dictionary outright by calling the ts_lexize() function. Here we find the English stem word of the string *Day's*.

```
SELECT ts_lexize('english_stem', 'Day''s');

 ts_lexize
-----------
 {day}
```

Finally, the previous full-text commands work for other languages too. If you have German installed, try this:

```
SELECT to_tsvector('german', 'was machst du gerade?');

   to_tsvector
--------------------
 'gerad':4 'mach':2
```

Since *was* (what) and *du* (you) are common, they are marked as stop words in the German dictionary, while *machst* (doing) and *gerade* (now) are stemmed.

Indexing Lexemes

Full-text search is powerful. But if we don't index our tables, it's also slow. The EXPLAIN command is a powerful tool for digging into how queries are internally planned.

```
EXPLAIN
SELECT *
FROM movies
WHERE title @@ 'night & day';
```

```
                           QUERY PLAN
-----------------------------------------------------------------------
 Seq Scan on movies  (cost=10000000000.00..10000000001.12 rows=1 width=68)
   Filter: (title @@ 'night & day'::text)
```

Note the line *Seq Scan on movies*. That's rarely a good sign in a query, because it means a whole table scan is taking place; each row will be read. So, we need the right index.

We'll use Generalized Inverted iNdex (GIN)—like GIST, it's an index API—to create an index of lexeme values we can query against. The term *inverted index* may sound familiar to you if you've ever used a search engine like Lucene or Sphinx. It's a common data structure to index full-text searches.

```
CREATE INDEX movies_title_searchable ON movies
USING gin(to_tsvector('english', title));
```

With our index in place, let's try to search again.

```
EXPLAIN
SELECT *
FROM movies
WHERE title @@ 'night & day';
```

```
                           QUERY PLAN
-----------------------------------------------------------------------
 Seq Scan on movies  (cost=10000000000.00..10000000001.12 rows=1 width=68)
   Filter: (title @@ 'night & day'::text)
```

What happened? Nothing. The index is there, but Postgres isn't using it. It's because our GIN index specifically uses the english configuration for building its tsvectors, but we aren't specifying that vector. We need to specify it in the WHERE clause of the query.

```
EXPLAIN
SELECT *
FROM movies
WHERE to_tsvector('english',title) @@ 'night & day';
```

```
                              QUERY PLAN
-------------------------------------------------------------------------
 Bitmap Heap Scan on movies  (cost=4.26..8.28 rows=1 width=68)
   Recheck Cond: (to_tsvector('english'::regconfig, title) @@ '''day'''::tsquery)
   -> Bitmap Index Scan on movies_title_searchable  (cost=0.00..4.26 rows=1 width=0)
        Index Cond: (to_tsvector('english'::regconfig, title) @@ '''day'''::tsquery)
```

EXPLAIN is important to ensure indexes are used as you expect them. Otherwise, the index is just wasted overhead.

Metaphones

We've inched toward matching less-specific inputs. LIKE and regular expressions require crafting patterns that can match strings precisely according to their format. Levenshtein distance allows finding matches that contain minor misspellings but must ultimately be very close to the same string. Trigrams are a good choice for finding reasonable misspelled matches. Finally, full-text searching allows natural-language flexibility, in that it can ignore minor words like *a* and *the* and can deal with pluralization. Sometimes we just don't know how to spell words correctly but we know how they sound.

We love Bruce Willis and would love to see what movies he's in. Unfortunately, we can't remember exactly how to spell his name, so we sound it out as best we can.

```
SELECT *
FROM actors
WHERE name = 'Broos Wlis';
```

Even a trigram is no good here (using % rather than =).

```
SELECT *
FROM actors
WHERE name % 'Broos Wlis';
```

Enter the metaphones, which are algorithms for creating a string representation of word sounds. You can define how many characters are in the output string. For example, the seven-character metaphone of the name Aaron Eckhart is *ARNKHRT*.

To find all films acted by someone sounding like Broos Wils, we can query against the metaphone output. Note that NATURAL JOIN is an INNER JOIN that automatically joins ON matching column names (for example, movies.actor_id= movies_actors.actor_id).

```
SELECT title
FROM movies NATURAL JOIN movies_actors NATURAL JOIN actors
WHERE metaphone(name, 6) = metaphone('Broos Wils', 6);
```

```
            title
----------------------------
 The Fifth Element
 Twelve Monkeys
 Armageddon
 Die Hard
 Pulp Fiction
 The Sixth Sense
 :
```

If you peek at the online documentation, you'd see the *fuzzystrmatch* module contains other functions: dmetaphone() (double metaphone), dmetaphone_alt() (for alternative name pronunciations), and soundex() (a really old algorithm from the 1880s made by the U.S. Census to compare common American surnames).

You can dissect the functions' representations by selecting their output.

```
SELECT name, dmetaphone(name), dmetaphone_alt(name),
  metaphone(name, 8), soundex(name)
FROM actors;
```

```
      name      | dmetaphone | dmetaphone_alt | metaphone | soundex
----------------+------------+----------------+-----------+--------
 50 Cent        | SNT        | SNT            | SNT       | C530
 Aaron Eckhart  | ARNK       | ARNK           | ARNKHRT   | A652
 Agatha Hurle   | AK0R       | AKTR           | AK0HRL    | A236
 :
```

There is no single best function to choose, and the optimal choice depends on your dataset.

Combining String Matches

With all of our string searching ducks in a row, we're ready to start combining them in interesting ways.

One of the most flexible aspects of metaphones is that their outputs are just strings. This allows you to mix and match with other string matchers.

For example, we could use the trigram operator against metaphone() outputs and then order the results by the lowest Levenshtein distance. This means "Get me names that sound the most like Robin Williams, in order."

```
SELECT * FROM actors
WHERE metaphone(name,8) % metaphone('Robin Williams',8)
ORDER BY levenshtein(lower('Robin Williams'), lower(name));
```

```
 actor_id |       name
----------+----------------
     2442 | John Williams
     4090 | Robin Shou
```

```
  4093 | Robin Williams
  4479 | Steven Williams
```

Note it isn't perfect. Robin Williams ranked at #3. Unbridled exploitation of this flexibility can yield other funny results, so be careful.

```
SELECT * FROM actors WHERE dmetaphone(name) % dmetaphone('Ron');
```

```
 actor_id |      name
----------+-------------
     3911 | Renji Ishibashi
     3913 | Renée Zellweger
:
```

The combinations are vast, limited only by your experimentations.

Genres as a Multidimensional Hypercube

The last contributed package we investigate is cube. We'll use the cube datatype to map a movie's genres as a multidimensional vector. We will then use methods to efficiently query for the closest points within the boundary of a hypercube to give us a list of similar movies.

As you may have noticed in the beginning of Day 3, we created a column named genres of type cube. Each value is a point in 18-dimensional space with each dimension representing a genre. Why represent movie genres as points in n-dimensional space? Movie categorization is not an exact science, and many movies are not 100 percent comedy or 100 percent tragedy—they are something in between.

In our system, each genre is scored from (the totally arbitrary numbers) 0 to 10 based on how strong the movie is within that genre—with 0 being nonexistent and 10 being the strongest.

Star Wars has a genre vector of (0,7,0,0,0,0,0,0,0,7,0,0,0,0,10,0,0,0). The genres table describes the position of each dimension in the vector. We can decrypt its genre values by extracting the cube_ur_coord(vector,dimension) using each genres.position. For clarity, we filter out genres with scores of 0.

```
SELECT name,
  cube_ur_coord('(0,7,0,0,0,0,0,0,0,7,0,0,0,0,10,0,0,0)', position) as score
FROM genres g
WHERE cube_ur_coord('(0,7,0,0,0,0,0,0,0,7,0,0,0,0,10,0,0,0)', position) > 0;
```

```
   name    | score
-----------+-------
 Adventure |     7
 Fantasy   |     7
 SciFi     |    10
```

We will find similar movies by finding the nearest points. To understand why this works, we can envision two movies on a two-dimensional genre graph, like the graph shown below.. If your favorite movie is *Animal House*, you'll probably want to see *The 40 Year Old Virgin* more than *Oedipus*—a story distinctly lacking in comedy. In our two-dimensional universe, it's a simple nearest-neighbor search to find likely matches.

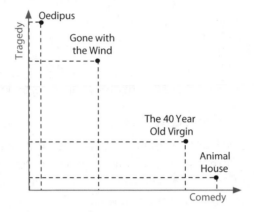

We can extrapolate this into more dimensions with more genres, be it 2, 3, or 18. The principle is the same: a nearest-neighbor match to the nearest points in genre space will yield the closest genre matches.

The nearest matches to the genre vector can be discovered by the cube_distance(point1, point2). Here we can find the distance of all movies to the *Star Wars* genre vector, nearest first.

```
SELECT *,
  cube_distance(genre, '(0,7,0,0,0,0,0,0,0,7,0,0,0,0,10,0,0,0)') dist
FROM movies
ORDER BY dist;
```

We created the movies_genres_cube cube index earlier when we created the tables. However, even with an index, this query is still relatively slow, since it requires a full-table scan. It computes the distance on every row and then sorts them.

Rather than compute the distance of every point, we can instead focus on likely points by way of a *bounding cube*. Just like finding the closest five towns on a map will be faster on a state map than a world map, bounding reduces the points we need to look at.

We use cube_enlarge(cube,radius,dimensions) to build an 18-dimensional cube that is some length (radius) wider than a point.

Let's view a simpler example. If we built a two-dimensional square one unit around a point (1,1), the lower-left point of the square would be at (0,0), and the upper-right point would be (2,2).

```
SELECT cube_enlarge('(1,1)',1,2);
```

```
 cube_enlarge
---------------
 (0, 0),(2, 2)
```

The same principle applies in any number of dimensions. With our bounding hypercube, we can use a special cube operator, @>, which means *contains*. This query finds the distance of all points contained within a five-unit cube of the *Star Wars* genre point.

```
SELECT title, cube_distance(genre, '(0,7,0,0,0,0,0,0,0,7,0,0,0,0,10,0,0,0)') dist
FROM movies
WHERE cube_enlarge('(0,7,0,0,0,0,0,0,0,7,0,0,0,0,10,0,0,0)'::cube, 5, 18) @> genre
ORDER BY dist;
```

title	dist
Star Wars	0
Star Wars: Episode V - The Empire Strikes Back	2
Avatar	5
Explorers	5.74456264653803
Krull	6.48074069840786
E.T. The Extra-Terrestrial	7.61577310586391

Using a subselect, we can get the genre by movie name and perform our calculations against that genre using a table alias.

```
SELECT m.movie_id, m.title
FROM movies m, (SELECT genre, title FROM movies WHERE title = 'Mad Max') s
WHERE cube_enlarge(s.genre, 5, 18) @> m.genre AND s.title <> m.title
ORDER BY cube_distance(m.genre, s.genre)
LIMIT 10;
```

movie_id	title
1405	Cyborg
1391	Escape from L.A.
1192	Mad Max Beyond Thunderdome
1189	Universal Soldier
1222	Soldier
1362	Johnny Mnemonic
946	Alive
418	Escape from New York
1877	The Last Starfighter
1445	The Rocketeer

This method of movie suggestion is not perfect, but it's an excellent start. We will see more dimensional queries in later chapters, such as two-dimensional geographic searches in MongoDB (see *GeoSpatial Queries*, on page 171).

Day 3 Wrap-Up

Today we jumped headlong into PostgreSQL's flexibility at string searches and used the cube package for multidimensional searching. Most importantly, we caught a glimpse of the nonstandard extensions that puts PostgreSQL at the top of the open source RDBMS field. There are dozens (if not hundreds) of more extensions at your disposal, from geographic storage to cryptographic functions, custom datatypes, and language extensions. Beyond the core power of SQL, contrib packages are what makes PostgreSQL shine.

Day 3 Homework

Find

1. Find online documentation of all contributed packages bundled into Postgres.

2. Find online POSIX regex documentation (it will also be handy for future chapters).

Do

1. Create a stored procedure where you can input a movie title or actor's name you like, and it will return the top five suggestions based on either movies the actor has starred in or films with similar genres.

2. Expand the movies database to track user comments and extract keywords (minus English stopwords). Cross-reference these keywords with actors' last names, and try to find the most talked about actors.

2.5 Wrap-Up

If you haven't spent much time with relational databases, we highly recommend digging deeper into PostgreSQL, or another relational database, before deciding to scrap it for a newer variety. Relational databases have been the focus of intense academic research and industrial improvements for more than forty years, and PostgreSQL is one of the top open source relational databases to benefit from these advancements.

PostgreSQL's Strengths

PostgreSQL's strengths are as numerous as any relational model: years of research and production use across nearly every field of computing, flexible queryability, and very consistent and durable data. Most programming languages have battle-tested driver support for Postgres, and many programming models, like object-relational mapping (ORM), assume an underlying relational database. The crux of the matter is the flexibility of the join. You needn't know how you plan to actually query your model, since you can always perform some joins, filters, views, and indexes—odds are good you will always have the ability to extract the data you want.

PostgreSQL is fantastic for what we call "Stepford data" (named for *The Stepford Wives*, a story about a neighborhood where nearly everyone was consistent in style and substance), which is data that is fairly homogeneous and conforms well to a structured schema.

Furthermore, PostgreSQL goes beyond the normal open source RDBMS offerings, such as powerful schema constraint mechanisms. You can write your own language extensions, customize indexes, create custom datatypes, and even overwrite the parsing of incoming queries. And where other open source databases may have complex licensing agreements, PostgreSQL is open source in its purest form. No one owns the code. Anyone can do pretty much anything they want with the project (other than hold authors liable). The development and distribution are completely community supported. If you are a fan of free(dom) software or have a long bushy beard, you have to respect their general resistance to cashing in on an amazing product.

PostgreSQL's Weaknesses

Although relational databases are undeniably the most successful style of database over the years, there are cases where it may not be a great fit.

Partitioning is not one of the strong suits of relational databases like Post-greSQL. If you need to scale out rather than up (multiple parallel datastores rather than a single beefy machine or cluster), you may be better served looking elsewhere. If your data requirements are too flexible to easily fit into the rigid schema requirements of a relational database or you don't need the overhead of a full database, require very high-volume reads and writes as key values, or need to store only large blobs of data, then one of the other data-stores might be a better fit.

Parting Thoughts

A relational database is an excellent choice for query flexibility. While Post-greSQL requires you to design your data up front, it makes no assumptions on how you use that data. As long as your schema is designed in a fairly normalized way, without duplication or storage of computable values, you should generally be all set for any queries you might need to create. And if you include the correct modules, tune your engine, and index well, it will perform amazingly well for multiple terabytes of data with very small resource consumption. Finally, to those for whom data safety is paramount, Post-greSQL's ACID-compliant transactions ensure your commits are completely atomic, consistent, isolated, and durable.

## CHAPTER 3

Riak

Anyone who has worked construction knows that rebar is a steel beam used to reinforce concrete. Just like Riak ("Ree-ahck"), you never use only one, but the multiple parts working together make the overall system durable. Each component is cheap and expendable, but when used right, it's hard to find a simpler or stronger structure upon which to build a foundation.

Riak is a distributed key-value database where values can be anything—from plain text, JSON, or XML to images or video clips—all accessible through a simple HTTP interface. Whatever data you have, Riak can store it.

Riak is also fault-tolerant. Servers can go up or down at any moment with no single point of failure. Your cluster continues humming along as servers are added, removed, or (ideally not) crash. Riak won't keep you up nights worrying about your cluster—a failed node is not an emergency, and you can wait to deal with it in the morning. As core developer Justin Sheehy once noted, "[The Riak team] focused so hard on things like write availability...to go back to sleep."

But this flexibility has some trade-offs. Riak lacks robust support for ad hoc queries, and key-value stores, by design, have trouble linking values together (in other words, they have no foreign keys). Riak attacks these problems on several fronts, which we'll discover in the next few days.

3.1 Riak Loves the Web

Riak speaks *web* better than any other database we'll see in this book (though CouchDB is a close second). You query via URLs, headers, and verbs, and Riak returns assets and standard HTTP response codes.

> ### Riak and cURL
>
> Since the goal of this book is to investigate seven databases and their concepts, and not teach new programming languages, we try to avoid introducing new languages where possible. Riak supplies an HTTP REST interface, so we're going to interact with it via the URL tool cURL. In production, you'll almost always use a driver in your language of choice. Using cURL allows us to peek at the underlying API without resorting to a particular driver or programming language.

Riak is a great choice for datacenters like Amazon that must serve many requests with low latency. If every millisecond spent waiting is a potential customer loss, Riak is hard to beat. It's easy to manage, easy to set up, and can grow with your needs. If you've ever used Amazon Web Services, like SimpleDB or S3, you may notice some similarities in form and function. This is no coincidence. Riak is inspired by Amazon's Dynamo paper.[1]

In this chapter, we'll investigate how Riak stores and retrieves values and how to tie data together using Links. Then we'll explore a data-retrieval concept used heavily throughout this book: mapreduce. We'll see how Riak clusters its servers and handles requests, even in the face of server failure. Finally, we'll look at how Riak resolves conflict that arises from writing to distributed servers, and we'll look at some extensions to the basic server.

3.2 Day 1: CRUD, Links, and MIMEs

You can download and install a build of Riak provided by Basho[2] (the company that funds its development), but we actually prefer to build this one since you get some preconfigured examples. If you really don't want to build it, just install a prebuilt version, and then grab the source code and extract the example dev servers. Erlang[3] is also required to run Riak (R14B03 or greater).

Building Riak from source requires three things: Erlang, the source code, and general Unix build tools like Make. Installing Erlang is easy enough (you'll also need Erlang for CouchDB in Chapter 6, *CouchDB*, on page 177), though it can take a while. We get the Riak source from its repository (link available via the Basho website—if you don't have Git or Mercurial installed, you can download a zipped package). All of the examples in this chapter were run on version 1.0.2.

---

1. http://allthingsdistributed.com/files/amazon-dynamo-sosp2007.pdf
2. http://www.basho.com/
3. http://www.erlang.org/

The Riak creators played Santa Claus for us new users, slipping a cool toy into our stockings. In the same directory you built Riak, run this command:

```
$ make devrel
```

When complete, we find three example servers. Just fire them up:

```
$ dev/dev1/bin/riak start
$ dev/dev2/bin/riak start
$ dev/dev3/bin/riak start
```

If you have a server fail to start because a port is in use, don't panic. You can change the dev1, dev2, or dev3 port by opening the offending server's etc/app.config file and altering the line that looks like this to use another port:

```
{http, [ {"127.0.0.1", 8091 } ]}
```

We should now have three Erlang processes running named beam.smp, representing individual Riak nodes (server instances), unaware of each other's presence. To create a cluster, we need to join the nodes using each server's riak-admin command named join and point them to any other cluster node.

```
$ dev/dev2/bin/riak-admin join dev1@127.0.0.1
```

It doesn't really matter which servers we point them at—in Riak, all nodes are equal. Now that dev1 and dev2 are in a cluster, we can point dev3 at either one.

```
$ dev/dev3/bin/riak-admin join dev2@127.0.0.1
```

Verify your servers are healthy by checking their stats in a web browser: http://localhost:8091/stats. It may prompt you to download the file, which contains lots of information about the cluster. It should look something like this (edited for readability):

```
{
  "vnode_gets":0,
  "vnode_puts":0,
  "vnode_index_reads":0,
  ...
  "connected_nodes":[
    "dev2@127.0.0.1",
    "dev3@127.0.0.1"
  ],
  ...
  "ring_members":[
    "dev1@127.0.0.1",
    "dev2@127.0.0.1",
    "dev3@127.0.0.1"
  ],
```

```
"ring_num_partitions":64,
"ring_ownership":
  "[{'dev3@127.0.0.1',21},{'dev2@127.0.0.1',21},{'dev1@127.0.0.1',22}]",
...
}
```

We can see that all servers are equal participants in the ring by pinging the other servers for stats on ports 8092 (dev2) and 8093 (dev3). For now, we'll stick with the stats from dev1.

Look for the *ring_members* property—it should contain all our node names and will be the same for each server. Next, find the value for *connected_nodes*. This should be a list of the other servers in the ring.

We can change the values reported by *connected_nodes* by stopping a node...

```
$ dev/dev2/bin/riak stop
```

...and reloading the /stats. Notice that dev2@127.0.0.1 is now gone from the *connected_nodes* list. Start dev2, and it will rejoin itself to the *Riak ring* (we'll discuss the ring on Day 2).

REST Is Best (or Doing cURLs)

REST stands for REpresentational State Transfer. It sounds like a mouthful of jargon, but it has become the *de facto* architecture of web applications, so it's worth knowing. REST is a guideline for mapping resources to URLs and interacting with them using CRUD verbs: POST (Create), GET (Read), PUT (Update), and DELETE (Delete).

If you don't already have it installed, install the HTTP client program cURL. We use it as our REST interface, because it's easy to specify verbs (like GET and PUT) and HTTP header information (like Content-Type). With the curl command, we speak directly to the Riak server's HTTP REST interface without the need for an interactive console or, say, a Ruby driver.

You can validate the curl command works with Riak by pinging a node.

```
$ curl http://localhost:8091/ping
OK
```

Let's issue a bad query. -I tells cURL that we want only the header response.

```
$ curl -I http://localhost:8091/riak/no_bucket/no_key
HTTP/1.1 404 Object Not Found
Server: MochiWeb/1.1 WebMachine/1.7.3 (participate in the frantic)
Date: Thu, 04 Aug 2011 01:25:49 GMT
Content-Type: text/plain
Content-Length: 10
```

Since Riak leverages HTTP URLs and actions, it uses HTTP headers and error codes. The 404 response means the same as a 404 when you encounter a missing web page: nothing to see here. So, let's PUT something in Riak.

The -X PUT parameter tells cURL that we want to perform an HTTP PUT action to store and retrieve on an explicit key. The -H attribute sets the following text as HTTP header information. In this case, we set the MIME content type to HTML. Everything passed to -d (also known as the body data) is what Riak will add as a new value.

```
$ curl -v -X PUT http://localhost:8091/riak/favs/db \
  -H "Content-Type: text/html" \
  -d "<html><body><h1>My new favorite DB is RIAK</h1></body></html>"
```

If you navigate to http://localhost:8091/riak/favs/db in a browser, you'll get a nice message from yourself.

PUT the Value in the Bucket

Riak is a key-value store, so it expects you to pass in a key to retrieve a value. Riak breaks up classes of keys into *buckets* to avoid key collisions—for example, a key for java the *language* will not collide with java the *drink*.

We're going to create a system to keep track of animals in a dog hotel. We'll start by creating a bucket of animals that contain each furry guest's details. The URL follows this pattern:

```
http://SERVER:PORT/riak/BUCKET/KEY
```

A straightforward way of populating a Riak bucket is to know your key in advance. We'll first add *Ace, The Wonder Dog* and give him the key ace with the value {"nickname" : "The Wonder Dog", "breed" : "German Shepherd"}. You don't need to explicitly create a bucket—putting a first value into a bucket name will create that bucket.

```
$ curl -v -X PUT http://localhost:8091/riak/animals/ace \
  -H "Content-Type: application/json" \
  -d '{"nickname" : "The Wonder Dog", "breed" : "German Shepherd"}'
```

Putting a new value returns a 204 code. The -v (verbose) attribute in the curl command outputs this header line.

```
< HTTP/1.1 204 No Content
```

We can view our list of buckets that have been created.

```
$ curl -X GET http://localhost:8091/riak?buckets=true
{"buckets":["favs","animals"]}
```

Optionally, you can return the set results with the ?returnbody=true parameter, which we'll test by adding another animal, Polly:

```
$ curl -v -X PUT http://localhost:8091/riak/animals/polly?returnbody=true \
  -H "Content-Type: application/json" \
  -d '{"nickname" : "Sweet Polly Purebred", "breed" : "Purebred"}'
```

This time you'll see a 200 code.

```
< HTTP/1.1 200 OK
```

If we aren't picky about our key name, Riak will generate one when using POST.

```
$ curl -i -X POST http://localhost:8091/riak/animals \
  -H "Content-Type: application/json" \
  -d '{"nickname" : "Sergeant Stubby", "breed" : "Terrier"}'
```

The generated key will be in the header under Location—also note the 201 success code in the header.

```
HTTP/1.1 201 Created
Vary: Accept-Encoding
Server: MochiWeb/1.1 WebMachine/1.7.3 (participate in the frantic)
Location: /riak/animals/6VZc2o7zKxq2B34kJrm1S0ma3PO
Date: Tue, 05 Apr 2011 07:45:33 GMT
Content-Type: application/json
Content-Length: 0
```

A GET request (cURL's default if left unspecified) to that location will retrieve the value.

```
$ curl http://localhost:8091/riak/animals/6VZc2o7zKxq2B34kJrm1S0ma3PO
```

DELETE will remove it.

```
$ curl -i -X DELETE http://localhost:8091/riak/animals/6VZc2o7zKxq2B34kJrm1S0ma3PO
HTTP/1.1 204 No Content
Vary: Accept-Encoding
Server: MochiWeb/1.1 WebMachine/1.7.3 (participate in the frantic)
Date: Mon, 11 Apr 2011 05:08:39 GMT
Content-Type: application/x-www-form-urlencoded
Content-Length: 0
```

DELETE won't return any body, but the HTTP code will be 204 if successful. Otherwise, as you'd expect, it returns a 404.

If we've forgotten any of our keys in a bucket, we can get them all with keys=true.

```
$ curl http://localhost:8091/riak/animals?keys=true
```

You can also get them as a stream with keys=stream, which can be a safer choice for huge datasets—it just keeps sending chunks of keys array objects and ends with an empty array.

Links

Links are metadata that associate one key to other keys. The basic structure is this:

```
Link: </riak/bucket/key>; riaktag=\"whatever\"
```

The key to where this value links is in pointy brackets (<...>), followed by a semicolon and then a tag describing how the link relates to this value (it can be whatever string we like).

Link Walking

Our little dog hotel has quite a few (large, comfortable, and humane) cages. To keep track of which animal is in what cage, we'll use a link. Cage 1 contains Polly by linking to her key (this also creates a new bucket named cages). The cage is installed in room 101, so we set that value as JSON data.

```
$ curl -X PUT http://localhost:8091/riak/cages/1 \
  -H "Content-Type: application/json" \
  -H "Link: </riak/animals/polly>; riaktag=\"contains\"" \
  -d '{"room" : 101}'
```

Note that this link relationship is one-directional. In effect, the cage we've just created knows that Polly is inside it, but no changes have been made to Polly. We can confirm this by pulling up Polly's data and checking that there have been no changes to the Link headers.

```
$ curl -i http://localhost:8091/riak/animals/polly
```

```
HTTP/1.1 200 OK
X-Riak-Vclock: a85hYGBgzGDKBVIcypz/fvrde/U5gymRMY+VwZw35gRfFgA=
Vary: Accept-Encoding
Server: MochiWeb/1.1 WebMachine/1.9.0 (participate in the frantic)
Link: </riak/animals>; rel="up"
Last-Modified: Tue, 13 Dec 2011 17:53:59 GMT
ETag: "VD0ZAfOTsIHsgG5PM3YZW"
Date: Tue, 13 Dec 2011 17:54:51 GMT
Content-Type: application/json
Content-Length: 59

{"nickname" : "Sweet Polly Purebred", "breed" : "Purebred"}
```

You can have as many metadata Links as necessary, separated by commas. We'll put Ace in cage 2 and also point to cage 1 tagged with *next_to* so we know that it's nearby.

```
$ curl -X PUT http://localhost:8091/riak/cages/2 \
-H "Content-Type: application/json" \
-H "Link:</riak/animals/ace>;riaktag=\"contains\"",
  </riak/cages/1>;riaktag=\"next_to\"" \
-d '{"room" : 101}'
```

What makes Links special in Riak is *link walking* (and a more powerful variant, linked mapreduce queries, which we investigate tomorrow). Getting the linked data is achieved by appending a *link spec* to the URL that is structured like this: /_,_,_. The underscores (_) in the URL represent wildcards to each of the link criteria: bucket, tag, keep. We'll explain those terms shortly. First let's retrieve all links from cage 1.

```
$ curl http://localhost:8091/riak/cages/1/_,_,_

--4PYi9DW8iJK5aCvQQrrP7mh7jZs
Content-Type: multipart/mixed; boundary=Av1fawIA4WjypRlz5gHJtrRqklD

--Av1fawIA4WjypRlz5gHJtrRqklD
X-Riak-Vclock: a85hYGBgzGDKBVIcypz/fvrde/U5gymRMY+VwZw35gRfFgA=
Location: /riak/animals/polly
Content-Type: application/json
Link: </riak/animals>; rel="up"
Etag: VD0ZAfOTsIHsgG5PM3YZW
Last-Modified: Tue, 13 Dec 2011 17:53:59 GMT

{"nickname" : "Sweet Polly Purebred", "breed" : "Purebred"}
--Av1fawIA4WjypRlz5gHJtrRqklD--

--4PYi9DW8iJK5aCvQQrrP7mh7jZs--
```

It returns a multipart/mixed dump of headers plus bodies of all linked keys/values. It's also a headache to look at. Tomorrow we'll find a more powerful way to get link-walked data that also happens to return nicer values—but today we'll dig a bit more into this syntax.

If you're not familiar with reading the multipart/mixed MIME type, the Content-Type definition describes a boundary string, which denotes the beginning and end of some HTTP header and body data.

```
--BcOdSWMLuhkisryp0GidDLqeA64
some HTTP header and body data
--BcOdSWMLuhkisryp0GidDLqeA64--
```

In our case, the data is what cage 1 links to: Polly Purebred. You may have noticed that the headers returned don't actually display the link information. This is OK; that data is still stored under the linked-to key.

When link walking, we can replace the underscores in the link spec to filter only values we want. Cage 2 has two links, so performing a link spec request will return both the animal Ace contained in the cage and the cage 1 next_to it. To specify only following the animals bucket, replace the first underscore with the bucket name.

```
$ curl http://localhost:8091/riak/cages/2/animals,_,_
```

Or follow the cages *next to* this one by populating the tag criteria.

```
$ curl http://localhost:8091/riak/cages/2/_,next_to,_
```

The final underscore—keep—accepts a 1 or 0. keep is useful when following second-order links, or links following other links, which you can do by just appending another link spec. Let's follow the keys next_to cage 2, which will return cage 1. Next, we walk to the animals linked to cage 1. Since we set keep to 0, Riak will not return the intermediate step (the cage 1 data). It will return only Polly's information, who is next to Ace's cage.

```
$ curl http://localhost:8091/riak/cages/2/_,next_to,0/animals,_,_
```

```
--6mBdsboQ8kTT6MlUHg0rgvbLhzd
Content-Type: multipart/mixed; boundary=EZYdVz90x4xzR4jx1I2ugUFFiZh

--EZYdVz90x4xzR4jx1I2ugUFFiZh
X-Riak-Vclock: a85hYGBgzGDKBVIcypz/fvrde/U5gymRMY+VwZw35gRfFgA=
Location: /riak/animals/polly
Content-Type: application/json
Link: </riak/animals>; rel="up"
Etag: VD0ZAfOTsIHsgG5PM3YZW
Last-Modified: Tue, 13 Dec 2011 17:53:59 GMT

{"nickname" : "Sweet Polly Purebred", "breed" : "Purebred"}
--EZYdVz90x4xzR4jx1I2ugUFFiZh--

--6mBdsboQ8kTT6MlUHg0rgvbLhzd--
```

If we want Polly's information and cage 1, set keep to 1.

```
$ curl http://localhost:8091/riak/cages/2/_,next_to,1/_,_,_
```

```
--PDVOEl7Rh1AP90jGln1mhz7x8r9
Content-Type: multipart/mixed; boundary=YliPQ9LPNEoAnDeAMiRkAjCbmed

--YliPQ9LPNEoAnDeAMiRkAjCbmed
X-Riak-Vclock: a85hYGBgzGDKBVIcypz/fvrde/U5gymRKY+VIYo35gRfFgA=
```

```
Location: /riak/cages/1
Content-Type: application/json
Link: </riak/animals/polly>; riaktag="contains", </riak/cages>; rel="up"
Etag: 6LYhRnMRrGIqsTmpE55PaU
Last-Modified: Tue, 13 Dec 2011 17:54:34 GMT

{"room" : 101}
--YliPQ9LPNEoAnDeAMiRkAjCbmed--

--PDVOEl7Rh1AP90jGln1mhz7x8r9
Content-Type: multipart/mixed; boundary=GS9J6KQLsI8zzMxJluDITfwiUKA

--GS9J6KQLsI8zzMxJluDITfwiUKA
X-Riak-Vclock: a85hYGBgzGDKBVIcypz/fvrde/U5gymRMY+VwZw35gRfFgA=
Location: /riak/animals/polly
Content-Type: application/json
Link: </riak/animals>; rel="up"
Etag: VD0ZAfOTsIHsgG5PM3YZW
Last-Modified: Tue, 13 Dec 2011 17:53:59 GMT

{"nickname" : "Sweet Polly Purebred", "breed" : "Purebred"}
--GS9J6KQLsI8zzMxJluDITfwiUKA--

--PDVOEl7Rh1AP90jGln1mhz7x8r9--
```

This returns the objects in the path to the final result. In other words, *keep* the step.

Beyond Links

Along with Links, you can store arbitrary metadata by using the X-Riak-Meta- header prefix. If we wanted to keep track of the color of a cage but it wasn't necessarily important in the day-to-day cage-managing tasks at hand, we could mark cage 1 as having the color pink. Getting the URL's header (the -I flag) will return your metadata name and value.

```
$ curl -X PUT http://localhost:8091/riak/cages/1 \
  -H "Content-Type: application/json" \
  -H "X-Riak-Meta-Color: Pink" \
  -H "Link: </riak/animals/polly>; riaktag=\"contains\"" \
  -d '{"room" : 101}'
```

MIME Types in Riak

Riak stores everything as a binary-encoded value, just like normal HTTP. The MIME type gives the binary data context—we've been dealing only with plain text up until now. MIME types are stored on the Riak server but are really just a flag to the client so that when it downloads the binary data, it knows how to render it.

We'd like our dog hotel to keep images of our guests. We need only use the data-binary flag on the curl command to upload an image to the server and specify the MIME type as image/jpeg. We'll add a link back to the /animals/polly key so we know who we are looking at.

First, create an image called polly_image.jpg and place it in the same directory you've been using to issue the curl commands.

```
$ curl -X PUT http://localhost:8091/riak/photos/polly.jpg \
  -H "Content-type: image/jpeg" \
  -H "Link: </riak/animals/polly>; riaktag=\"photo\"" \
  --data-binary @polly_image.jpg
```

Now visit the URL in a web browser, which will be delivered and rendered exactly as you'd expect any web client-server request to function.

```
http://localhost:8091/riak/photos/polly.jpg
```

Since we pointed the image to /animals/polly, we could link walk from the image key *to* Polly but not vice versa. Unlike a relational database, there is no "has a" or "is a" rule concerning links. You link the direction you need to walk. If we believe our use case will require accessing image data from the animals bucket, a link should exist on that object instead (or in addition).

Day 1 Wrap-Up

We hope you're seeing a glimmer of Riak's potential as a flexible storage option. So far, we've covered only standard key-value practice with some links thrown in. When designing a Riak schema, think somewhere in between a caching system and PostgreSQL. You will break up your data into different logical classifications (buckets), and values can tacitly relate to each other. But you will not go so far as to normalize into fine components like you would in a relational database, since Riak performs no sense of relational joins to recompose values.

Day 1 Homework

Find

1. Bookmark the online Riak project documentation and discover the REST API documentation.

2. Find a good list of browser-supported MIME types.

3. Read the example Riak config dev/dev1/etc/app.config, and compare it to the other dev configurations.

Do

1. Using PUT, update animals/polly to have a Link pointing to photos/polly.jpg.

2. POST a file of a MIME type we haven't tried (such as application/pdf), find the generated key, and hit that URL from a web browser.

3. Create a new bucket type called *medicines*, PUT a JPEG image value (with the proper MIME type) keyed as *antibiotics*, and link to the animal Ace (poor, sick puppy).

3.3 Day 2: Mapreduce and Server Clusters

Today we'll dive into the mapreduce framework to perform more powerful queries than the standard key-value paradigm can normally provide. We'll then expand on this power by including link walking with mapreduce. Finally, we will investigate the server architecture of Riak and how it uses a novel server layout to provide flexibility in consistency or availability, even in the face of network partitions.

Population Script

We'll need a bit more data in this section. To achieve that, we'll switch to an example using a different kind of hotel, one for people and not pets. A quick populator script in Ruby will create data for a gigantic 10,000-room hotel.

If you are not familiar with Ruby, it is a popular general-purpose programming language. It's quite useful for writing quick scripts in a straightforward and readable manner. You can learn more about Ruby in *Programming Ruby: The Pragmatic Programmer's Guide [TH01]* by Dave Thomas and Andy Hunt, as well as online.[4]

You'll also need Ruby's package manager called RubyGems.[5] With Ruby and RubyGems installed, next install the Riak driver.[6] You may also require the json driver and can run both to make sure.

```
$ gem install riak-client json
```

Each room in our hotel will have a random capacity from one to eight people and be of a random style such as a single room or a suite.

---

4. http://ruby-lang.org
5. http://rubygems.org
6. http://rubygems.org/gems/riak-client

```
riak/hotel.rb
# generate loads and loads of rooms with random styles and capacities
require 'rubygems'
require 'riak'
STYLES = %w{single double queen king suite}

client = Riak::Client.new(:http_port => 8091)
bucket = client.bucket('rooms')
# Create 100 floors to the building
for floor in 1..100
  current_rooms_block = floor * 100
  puts "Making rooms #{current_rooms_block} - #{current_rooms_block + 100}"
  # Put 100 rooms on each floor (huge hotel!)
  for room in 1...100
    # Create a unique room number as the key
    ro = Riak::RObject.new(bucket, (current_rooms_block + room))
    # Randomly grab a room style, and make up a capacity
    style = STYLES[rand(STYLES.length)]
    capacity = rand(8) + 1
    # Store the room information as a JSON value
    ro.content_type = "application/json"
    ro.data = {'style' => style, 'capacity' => capacity}
    ro.store
  end
end
```

```
$ ruby hotel.rb
```

We've now populated a human hotel we'll mapreduce against.

Introducing Mapreduce

One of Google's greatest lasting contributions to computer science is the popularization of mapreduce as an algorithmic framework for executing jobs in parallel over several nodes. It is described in Google's seminal paper[7] on the topic and has become a valuable tool for executing custom queries in the class of partition-tolerant datastores.

Mapreduce breaks down problems into two parts. Part 1 is to convert a list of data into another type of list by way of a map() function. Part 2 is to convert this second list to one or more scalar values by way of a reduce() function. Following this pattern allows a system to divide tasks into smaller components and run them across a massive cluster of servers in parallel. We could count up all Riak values containing {country : 'CA'} by mapping each matching document to {count : 1} and reducing the sum of all of these counts.

---

7.   http://research.google.com/archive/mapreduce.html

If there were 5,012 Canadian values in our dataset, the reduce result would be {count : 5012}.

```
map = function(v) {
  var parsedData = JSON.parse(v.values[0].data);
  if(parsedData.country === 'CA')
    return [{count : 1}];
  else
    return [{count : 0}];
}

reduce = function(mappedVals) {
  var sums = {count : 0};
  for (var i in mappedVals) {
    sums[count] += mappedVals[i][count];
  }
  return [sums];
}
```

In one way, mapreduce is the opposite of how we normally run queries. A Ruby on Rails system might grab data like this (via its ActiveRecord interface):

```
# Construct a Hash to store room capacity count keyed by room style
capacity_by_style = {}
rooms = Room.all
for room in rooms
  total_count = capacity_by_style[room.style]
  capacity_by_style[room.style] = total_count.to_i + room.capacity
end
```

Room.all runs an SQL query against the backing database similar to this:

```
SELECT * FROM rooms;
```

The database sends all of the results to the app server, and the app server code performs some action on that data. In this case, we're looping through each room in the hotel and then counting the total capacity for each room style (for example, the capacity of all the suites in the hotel may be 448 guests). This is acceptable for small datasets. But as room count grows, the system slows as the database continues to stream each room's data to the application.

Mapreduce runs in an inverse manner. Rather than grabbing data from the database and running it on a client (or app server), mapreduce is a pattern to pass an algorithm to all of the database nodes, which are then each responsible for returning a result. *Each object on the server is "mapped" to some common key that groups the data together, and then all matching keys are "reduced" into some single value.*

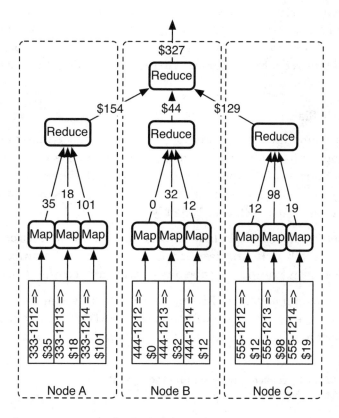

The map function outputs feed into the reduce outputs and then to other reducers.

Figure 7—The map function outputs

For Riak, that means the database servers are responsible for mapping and reducing the values on each node. Those reduced values are passed around, where some other server (usually the requesting server) reduces those values further, until a final result is passed to the requesting client (or Rails application server, as the case may be).

This simple reversal is a powerful way to allow complex algorithms to run locally on each server and return a very small result to the calling client. *It's faster to send the algorithm to the data and then send the data to the algorithm.* In Figure 7, *The map function outputs*, on page 65, we can see how a bucket of phone bills keyed by phone number may calculate the total charged against all numbers across three servers, where each server contains all numbers with a similar prefix.

The results of map functions will populate reduce functions; however, a combination of the results of map *and* previous reduce function calls populate successive reduce functions. We'll revisit this idea in later chapters because it's an important yet subtle component to the art of writing effective mapreduce queries.

Mapreduce in Riak

Let's create mapreduce functions for our Riak dataset that work like the previous hotel capacity counter. A neat feature of Riak's mapreduce is that you can run the map() function alone and see what all the results are mid-run (assuming you even want to run a reduce). Let's take it slow and look at the results for rooms 101, 102, and 103 only.

The map setting needs the language we're using and the source code; only then do we actually write the JavaScript map function (the function is just a string, so we always need to escape any characters accordingly).

Using the @- command in cURL keeps the console's standard input open until receiving CTRL+D. This data will populate the HTTP body sent to the URL, which we post to the /mapred command (look carefully—the URL is /mapred, not /riak/mapred).

```
$ curl -X POST -H "content-type:application/json" \
http://localhost:8091/mapred --data @-
{
  "inputs":[
    ["rooms","101"],["rooms","102"],["rooms","103"]
  ],
  "query":[
    {"map":{
      "language":"javascript",
      "source":
        "function(v) {
          /* From the Riak object, pull data and parse it as JSON */
          var parsed_data = JSON.parse(v.values[0].data);
          var data = {};
          /* Key capacity number by room style string */
          data[parsed_data.style] = parsed_data.capacity;
          return [data];
        }"
    }}
  ]
}
CTRL-D
```

The /mapred command expects valid JSON, and here we specified the form of our mapreduce commands. We choose the three rooms we want by setting the "inputs" value to be an array containing [bucket, key] pairs. But the real meat of the settings is under the *query* value, which accepts an array of JSON objects containing objects, keyed by *map*, *reduce*, and/or *links* (more on links later).

All this does is dig down into the data (v.values[0].data), parse the value as a JSON object (JSON.parse(...)), and return the capacity (parsed_data.capacity) keyed by room style (parsed_data.style). You'll get a result like this:

```
[{"suite":6},{"single":1},{"double":1}]
```

It's just the three objects' JSON data from rooms 101, 102, and 103.

We didn't need to simply output the data as JSON. We could have converted the value of each key value into anything we wanted. We dug into the body data only but could have retrieved metadata, link information, the key, or data. Anything is possible after that—we are mapping each key value into some other value.

If you feel up to it, you can return the maps of all 10,000 rooms by replacing the input-specific [bucket, key] arrays with the rooms bucket name, like this:

```
"inputs":"rooms"
```

Fair warning: it will dump a lot of data. Finally, it's worth mentioning that since Riak version 1.0, mapreduce functions are handled by a subsystem called Riak Pipe. Any older systems will use the legacy mapred_system. This should not affect you much as an end user, but it's certainly a boost in speed and stability.

Stored Functions

Another option Riak provides us with is to store the map function in a bucket value. This is another example of moving the algorithm to the database. This is a stored procedure or, more specifically, a user-defined function—of similar philosophy to those used in relational databases for years.

```
$ curl -X PUT -H "content-type:application/json" \
http://localhost:8091/riak/my_functions/map_capacity --data @-
function(v) {
  var parsed_data = JSON.parse(v.values[0].data);
  var data = {};
  data[parsed_data.style] = parsed_data.capacity;
  return [data];
}
```

With your function safely stored, we'll run the function by pointing to the new bucket and key containing the function.

```
$ curl -X POST -H "content-type:application/json" \
http://localhost:8091/mapred --data @-
{
  "inputs":[
    ["rooms","101"],["rooms","102"],["rooms","103"]
  ],
  "query":[
    {"map":{
      "language":"javascript",
      "bucket":"my_functions",
      "key":"map_capacity"
    }}
  ]
}
```

You should receive the same results you received by putting the JavaScript source inline.

Built-in Functions

You can use some of Riak's built-in functions attached to the JavaScript object Riak. If you run the following code, your room objects will map the values into JSON and return them. The Riak.mapValuesJson function returns values as JSON.

```
curl -X POST http://localhost:8091/mapred \
-H "content-type:application/json" --data @-
{
  "inputs":[
    ["rooms","101"],["rooms","102"],["rooms","103"]
  ],
  "query":[
    {"map":{
      "language":"javascript",
      "name":"Riak.mapValuesJson"
    }}
  ]
}
```

Riak provides more of these in a file named mapred_builtins.js, which you can find online (or, deep in the code). You can also use this syntax to call your own built-in functions, which is something we'll investigate tomorrow.

Reducing

Mapping is useful, but you're limited to converting individual values into other individual values. Performing some sort of analysis over that set of data, even something as simple as counting the records, requires another step. This is where reduce comes into play.

The SQL/Ruby example that we looked at earlier (in *Introducing Mapreduce,* on page 63) showed how each value could be iterated over and how capacity was totaled for each style of room. We will perform this in our reduce function in JavaScript.

Most of the command we pass to /mapred will be the same. This time, we add the reduce function.

```
$ curl -X POST -H "content-type:application/json" \
http://localhost:8091/mapred --data @-
{
  "inputs":"rooms",
  "query":[
    {"map":{
      "language":"javascript",
      "bucket":"my_functions",
      "key":"map_capacity"
    }},
    {"reduce":{
      "language":"javascript",
      "source":
        "function(v) {
          var totals = {};
          for (var i in v) {
            for(var style in v[i]) {
              if( totals[style] ) totals[style] += v[i][style];
              else                totals[style] = v[i][style];
            }
          }
          return [totals];
        }"
    }}
  ]
}
```

Running this on all rooms should return total counts of capacity, keyed by room style.

```
[{"single":7025,"queen":7123,"double":6855,"king":6733,"suite":7332}]
```

Your totals won't match the previous exactly, since we randomly generated room data.

Key Filters

A rather recent addition to Riak is the concept of key filters. A key filter is a collection of commands that process each key before executing mapreduce

Reducer Patterns

It's easier to write a reduce function if it follows the same pattern as your map function. Meaning, if you map a single value as…

```
[{name:'Eric', count:1}]
```

…then the result of reduce should be like this:

```
[{name:'Eric', count:105}, {name:'Jim', count:215}, …]
```

This certainly isn't a requirement; it's just practical. Since reducers can feed into other reducers, you don't know whether the values you receive on any particular reduce function call will be populated by map output, reduce output, or a combination of both. However, if they follow the same object pattern, you don't need to care; they're all the same! Otherwise, your reduce function must always check for the type of data it's receiving and make a decision accordingly.

on it. This shortcut saves the operation the pain of loading unwanted values. In the following example, we'll convert each room number key into an integer and check that it's less than 1,000 (one of the first ten floors; any room over the tenth floor will be ignored).

In our mapreduce to return room capacity, replace "inputs":"rooms", with the following block (it must end with a comma):

```
"inputs":{
  "bucket":"rooms",
  "key_filters":[["string_to_int"], ["less_than", 1000]]
},
```

You should notice two things: the query ran much faster (since we processed only the values we needed), and the totals were fewer (since we added only the first ten floors).

Mapreduce is a powerful tool for bundling data and performing some overarching analysis on it. It's a concept we'll revisit often in this book, but the core concept is the same. Riak has one slight tweak to the basic mapreduce form, and that's the addition of links.

Link Walking with Mapreduce

Yesterday we introduced link walking. Today we'll look at how to do the same thing using mapreduce. The query section has one more value option along with map and reduce. It's link.

Let's return to our cages bucket from yesterday's dog hotel example and write a mapper that returns only cage 2 (remember, the one housing Ace the dog).

```
$ curl -X POST -H "content-type:application/json" \
http://localhost:8091/mapred --data @-
{
  "inputs":{
    "bucket":"cages",
    "key_filters":[["eq", "2"]]
  },
  "query":[
    {"link":{
      "bucket":"animals",
      "keep":false
    }},
    {"map":{
      "language":"javascript",
      "source":
        "function(v) { return [v]; }"
    }}
  ]
}
```

Although we ran the mapreduce query against the cages bucket, this will
return *Ace the dog*'s information, because he was linked to cage 2.

```
[{
  "bucket":"animals",
  "key":"ace",
  "vclock":"a85hYGBgzmDKBVIsrDJPfTKYEhnzWBn6LfiP80GFWVZay0KF5yGE2ZqTGPmCLiJLZAEA",
  "values":[{
    "metadata":{
      "Links":[],
      "X-Riak-VTag":"4JVlDcEYRIKuyUhw8OUYJS",
      "content-type":"application/json",
      "X-Riak-Last-Modified":"Tue, 05 Apr 2011 06:54:22 GMT",
      "X-Riak-Meta":[]},
    "data":"{\"nickname\" : \"The Wonder Dog\", \"breed\" : \"German Shepherd\"}"
  }]
}]
```

Both data and metadata (which would normally be returned in the HTTP
header) appear under a values array.

Put map, reduce, link walking, and key filters together, and you can execute
arbitrary queries on a wide array of Riak keys. It's considerably more efficient
than scanning all data from a client. Since these queries are generally run
across several servers simultaneously, you should never have to wait long.
But if you really cannot wait, a query has one more option: timeout. Set timeout
to a value in milliseconds (the default is "timeout": 60000, or 60 seconds), and
if the query does not complete in the allotted time, it will abort.

Of Consistency and Durability

Riak server architecture removes single points of failure (all nodes are peers) and allows you to grow or shrink the cluster at will. This is important when dealing with large-scale deployments, since it allows your database to remain available even if several nodes fail or are otherwise unresponsive.

Distributing data across several servers is saddled with an inherent problem. If you want your database to continue running when a network partition occurs (meaning, some messages were lost), it means you must make a trade-off. Either you can remain *available* to server requests or you can refuse requests and ensure the *consistency* of your data. It is not possible to create a distributed database that is fully consistent, available, and partition tolerant. You can have only two (partition tolerant and consistent, partition tolerant and available, or consistent and available but not distributed). This is known as the CAP theorem (Consistency, Availability, Partition tolerance). See Appendix 2, *The CAP Theorem*, on page 317 for more details, but suffice to say it is a problem in system design.

But the theorem has a loophole. The reality is that at *any moment in time* you cannot be consistent, available, and partition tolerant. Riak takes advantage of this fact by allowing you to trade availability for consistency on a per-request basis. We'll first look at how Riak clusters its servers and then how to tune reads and writes to interact with the cluster.

The Riak Ring

Riak divides its server configuration into partitions denoted by a 160-bit number (that's 2^{160}). The Riak team likes to represent this massive integer as a circle, which they call the *ring*. When a key is hashed to a partition, the ring helps direct which Riak servers store the value.

One of the first decisions you'll make when setting up a Riak cluster is how many partitions you'd like. Let's consider the case where you have 64 partitions (Riak's default). If you divide those sixty-four partitions across three nodes (or, servers), then Riak will give each node twenty-one or twenty-two partitions (64 / 3). Each partition is called a virtual node, or *vnode*. Each Riak service counts around the ring on boot, claiming partitions in turn until all vnodes are claimed, as shown in Figure 8, *"The Riak ring" of sixty-four vnodes, assigned across three physical nodes*, on page 73.

Node A manages vnodes 1, 4, 7, 10...63. These vnodes are mapped to partitions of the 160-bit ring. If you view the status of your three development servers

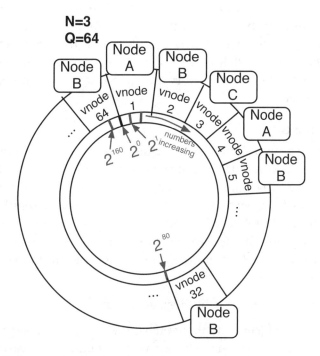

Figure 8—"The Riak ring" of sixty-four vnodes, assigned across three physical nodes

(remember `curl -H "Accept: text/plain" http://localhost:8091/stats` from yesterday), you can see a line like this:

```
"ring_ownership": \
"[{'dev3@127.0.0.1',21},{'dev2@127.0.0.1',21},{'dev1@127.0.0.1',22}]"
```

The second number of each object is the number of vnodes each node owns. They will total sixty-four (21 + 21 + 22).

Each vnode represents a range of hashed keys. When we insert the room data for key *101*, it may get hashed into the vnode 2 range, so then the key-value object gets stored onto Node B. The benefit is that if we need to find which server the key lives on, Riak just hashes the key to find the corresponding vnode. Specifically, Riak will convert the hash into a list of potential vnodes and use the first value.

Nodes/Writes/Reads

Riak allows us to control reads and writes into the cluster by altering three values: N, W, and R. *N* is the number of nodes a write ultimately replicates to, in other words, the number of copies in the cluster. *W* is the number of nodes that must be successfully written to before a successful response. If W is less than N, a write will be considered successful even while Riak is still copying the value. Finally, *R* is the number of nodes required to read a value successfully. If R is greater than the number of copies available, the request will fail.

Let's investigate each of these in more detail.

When we write an object in Riak, we have the choice to replicate that value across multiple nodes. The benefit here is that if one server goes down, then a copy is available on another. The n_val bucket property stores the number of nodes to replicate a value to (the N value); it's 3 by default. We can alter a bucket's properties by putting a new value in the props object. Here we set animals to have an n_val of 4:

```
$ curl -X PUT http://localhost:8091/riak/animals \
  -H "Content-Type: application/json" \
  -d '{"props":{"n_val":4}}'
```

N is simply the total number of nodes that will *eventually* contain the correct value. This doesn't mean we must wait for the value to replicate to *all* of those nodes in order to return. Sometimes we just want our client to return immediately and let Riak replicate in the background. Or sometimes we want to wait until Riak has replicated to all *N* nodes (just to be safe) before returning.

We can set the *W* value to the number of successful writes that must occur before our operation is considered a success. Although we're writing to four nodes eventually, if we set W to 2, a write operation will return after only two copies are made. The remaining two will replicate in the background.

```
curl -X PUT http://localhost:8091/riak/animals \
  -H "Content-Type: application/json" \
  -d '{"props":{"w":2}}'
```

Finally, we can use the *R* value. *R* is the number of nodes that must be read in order to be considered a successful read. You can set a default *R* like we did earlier with n_val and w.

```
curl -X PUT http://localhost:8091/riak/animals \
  -H "Content-Type: application/json" \
  -d '{"props":{"r":3}}'
```

But Riak provides a more flexible solution. We may choose the number of nodes we want to read by setting an r parameter in the URL *per request.*

```
curl http://localhost:8091/riak/animals/ace?r=3
```

You may be asking yourself why we would ever need to read from more than one node. After all, values we write will eventually be replicated to *N* nodes, and we can read from any of them. We find the idea is easier to visualize.

Let's say we set our NRW values to {"n_val":3, "r":2, "w":1}, like Figure 9, *Eventual consistency: W+R <= N,* on page 76. This makes our system more responsive on writes, since only one node needs to be written before returning. But there is a chance that another operation could perform a read before the nodes had a chance to synchronize. Even if we read from two nodes, it's possible we could receive an old value.

One way to be certain we have the most current value is to set W=N and R=1 like this: {"n_val":3, "r":1, "w":3} (see Figure 10, *Consistency by writes: W=N, R=1,* on page 76). In essence, this is what relational databases do; they enforce consistency by ensuring a write is complete before returning. We can certainly read faster, since we need to access only one node. But this can really slow down writes.

Or you could just write to a single node but read from all of them. This would be setting W=1 and R=N like this: {"n_val":3, "r":3, "w":1} (see Figure 11, *Consistency by reads: W=1, R=N,* on page 76). Although you may read a few old values, you are guaranteed to retrieve the most recent value, too. You'll just have to resolve which one that is (using a vector clock, which we'll cover tomorrow). Of course, this has the opposite problem as shown earlier and slows down reads.

Or you could set W=2 and R=2 as {"n_val":3, "r":2, "w":2} (see Figure 12, *Consistency by quorum: W+R > N,* on page 77). This way, you need only write to more than half of the nodes and read from more than half, but you still get the benefits of consistency while sharing the time delays between reads and writes. This is called a *quorum* and is the minimum amount to keep consistent data.

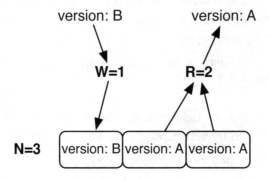

Figure 9—Eventual consistency: W+R <= N

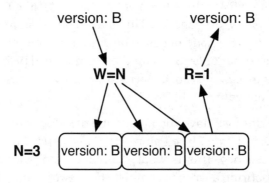

Figure 10—Consistency by writes: W=N, R=1

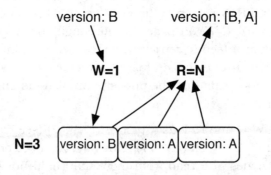

Figure 11—Consistency by reads: W=1, R=N

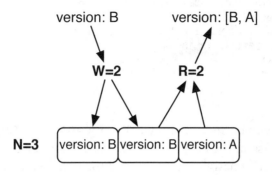

Figure 12—Consistency by quorum: W+R > N

You are free to set your R or W to any values between 1 and N but will generally want to stick with one, all, or a quorum. These are such common values that R and W can accept string values representing them, defined in the following table:

Term	Definition
One	This is just the value 1. Setting W or R means only one node need respond for the request to succeed.
All	This is the same value as N. Setting W or R to this means all replicated nodes must respond.
Quorum	This equals setting the value to N/2+1. Setting W or R means most nodes must respond to succeed.
Default	Whatever the W or R value is set for the bucket. Generally defaults to 3.

In addition to the previous values as valid bucket properties, you can also use them as query parameter values.

```
curl http://localhost:8091/riak/animals/ace?r=all
```

The danger with requiring reading from all nodes is that if one goes down, Riak may be unable to fulfill your request. As an experiment, let's shut down dev server 3.

```
$ dev/dev3/bin/riak stop
```

Now if we attempt to read from all nodes, there's a good chance our request will fail (if it doesn't, try shutting down dev2 as well, or possibly shut down dev1 and read from port 8092 or 8093; we cannot control what vnodes Riak writes to).

```
$ curl -i http://localhost:8091/riak/animals/ace?r=all
HTTP/1.1 404 Object Not Found
Server: MochiWeb/1.1 WebMachine/1.7.3 (participate in the frantic)
Date: Thu, 02 Jun 2011 17:18:18 GMT
Content-Type: text/plain
Content-Length: 10

not found
```

If your request cannot be fulfilled, you'll get a 404 code (Object Not Found), which makes sense in the scope of the request. That object cannot be found, because there aren't enough copies to fulfill the URL request. This isn't a good thing, of course, so this kicks Riak to do a *read repair*: to request *N* replications of the key across the servers still available. If you attempt to access the same URL again, you'll get the key's value rather than another 404. The online Riak docs have an excellent example[8] using Erlang.

But a safer play is to require a quorum (data from most, but not all, vnodes).

```
curl http://localhost:8091/riak/animals/polly?r=quorum
```

As long as you write to a quorum, which you can force on a per-write basis, your reads should be consistent. Another value you can set on-the-fly is W. If you don't want to wait for Riak to write to any nodes, you can set W to 0 (zero), which means "I trust you'll write it, Riak; just return."

```
curl -X PUT http://localhost:8091/riak/animals/jean?w=0 \
-H "Content-Type: application/json" \
-d '{"nickname" : "Jean", "breed" : "Border Collie"}' \
```

All this power aside, much of the time you'll want to stick with the default values unless you have a good reason. Logs are great for setting W=0, and you can set W=N and R=1 for seldom written data for extra-fast reads.

Writes and Durable Writes

We've been keeping a secret from you. Writes in Riak aren't necessarily durable, meaning they aren't immediately written to disk. Although a *node write* may be considered successful, it's still possible that a failure could occur where a node loses data; even if W=N, servers may fail and lose data. A write is buffered in memory for a moment before being stored on disk, and that split millisecond is a danger zone.

That's the bad news. The good news is Riak has provided us with a separate setting named DW for *durable write*. This is slower but further reduces risk,

---

8.   http://wiki.basho.com/Replication.html

since Riak will not return a success until after the object is written to disk on the given number of nodes. Just like we did with writes, you can set this property on the bucket. Here we're setting `dw` to be `one` to be certain at least one node has stored our data.

```
$ curl -X PUT http://localhost:8091/riak/animals \
-H "Content-Type: application/json" \
-d '{"props":{"dw":"one"}}'
```

Or, if you like, you can override this on a per-write basis using the `dw` query parameter in the URL.

A Note on Hinted Handoff

Attempting to write to nodes that aren't available still succeeds with a "204 No Content." This is because Riak will write the value to a nearby node that holds that data until such a time that it can hand it to the unavailable node. This is a fantastic safety net in the short-term, since if a server goes down, another Riak node will take over. Of course, if all of server A's requests get routed to server B, then server B is now dealing with double the load. There is a danger this will cause B to fail, which might spread to C and D, and so on. This is known as a *cascading failure*, and it's rare but possible. Consider this a fair warning not to tax every Riak server at full capacity, since you never know when one will have to pick up the slack.

Day 2 Wrap-Up

Today you saw two of the biggest topics in Riak: the powerful mapreduce method and its flexible server clustering ability. Mapreduce is used by many of the other databases in this book, so if you still have any questions about it, we recommend rereading the first part of Day 2 and checking out the Riak online documentation[9] and Wikipedia[10] articles.

Day 2 Homework

Find

1. Read the online Riak mapreduce documentation.

2. Find the Riak contrib functions repository, with lots of prebuilt mapreduce functions.

3. Find the online documentation for a complete list of key filters, which range from converting strings to_upper to finding numerical values between

---

9.   http://wiki.basho.com/MapReduce.html
10.   http://en.wikipedia.org/wiki/MapReduce

some range to even some simple Levenshtein distance string matches and logical and/or/not operations.

Do

1. Write map and reduce functions against the rooms bucket to find the total guest capacity per floor.

2. Extend the previous function with a filter to find the capacities only for rooms on floors 42 and 43.

3.4 Day 3: Resolving Conflicts and Extending Riak

Today we delve into some of the edges of Riak. We've seen how Riak is a simple key-value database across a cluster of servers. When dealing with multiple nodes, data conflicts can occur, and sometimes we have to resolve them. Riak provides a mechanism to sort out which writes happened most recently by way of vector clocks and sibling resolution.

We'll also see how we can validate incoming data by way of pre- and post-commit hooks. We'll extend Riak into our own personal search engine with Riak search (with the SOLR interface) and faster queries with secondary indexing.

Resolving Conflicts with Vector Clocks

A *vector clock*[11] is a token that distributed systems like Riak use to keep the order of conflicting key-value updates intact. It's important to keep track of which updates happen in what order, since several clients may connect to different servers, and while one client updates one server, another client updates another server (you can't control which server you write to).

You may think "just timestamp the values and let the last value win," but in a server cluster this works only if all server clocks are perfectly synchronous. Riak makes no such requirement, since keeping clocks synchronized is at best difficult and in many cases an impossible requirement. Using a centralized clock system would be anathema to the Riak philosophy, since it presents a single point of failure.

Vector clocks help by tagging each key-value event (create, update, or delete) with which client made the change, in which order. This way, the clients, or application developer, can decide who wins in the case of conflict. If you are

---

11. http://en.wikipedia.org/wiki/Vector_clock

familiar with version control systems like Git or Subversion, this is not dis-similar to resolving version conflicts when two people change the same file.

Vector Clocks in Theory

Let's say that your dog hotel is doing well so you must start being more selective of the clientele. To help make the best decision, you've gathered a panel of three animal experts to help decide which new dogs are a good fit. They give each dog a score from 1 (not a good fit) to 4 (a perfect candidate). All of these panelists—named Bob, Jane, and Rakshith—must reach a unanimous decision.

Each panelist has their own client connecting to a database server, and each client stamps a unique client ID onto each request. This client ID is used to build the vector clock, as well as keep track of the last updating client in the object header. Let's look at a simple pseudocode example and later try the example in Riak.

Bob creates the object first, with a respectable score of 3 for a new puppy named Bruiser. The vector clock encodes his name and the version 1.

```
vclock: bob[1]
value:  {score : 3}
```

Jane pulls this record and gives Bruiser a score of 2. The vclock created for her update succeeded Bob's, so her version 1 is added to the end of the vector.

```
vclock: bob[1], jane[1]
value:  {score : 2}
```

Simultaneously, Rakshith pulled the version that Bob created but not Jane's. He loved Bruiser and set a score of 4. Just like Jane's, his client name is appended to the end of the vector clock as version 1.

```
vclock: bob[1], rakshith[1]
value:  {score : 4}
```

Later that day, Jane (as the panel chair) rechecks the scores. Since Rakshith's update vector did not occur after Jane's but rather alongside hers, the updates are in conflict and need to be resolved. She receives both values, and it's up to her to resolve them.

```
vclock: bob[1], jane[1]
value:  {score : 2}
---
vclock: bob[1], rakshith[1]
value:  {score : 4}
```

She chooses a middle value so updates the score to 3.

```
vclock: bob[1], rakshith[1], jane[2]
value:  {score : 3}
```

Having been resolved, anyone who pulls a request after this point will get this most recent value.

Vector Clocks in Practice

Let's run through the previous example scenario using Riak.

For this example we want to see all conflicting versions so we can resolve them manually. Let's keep multiple versions by setting the allow_mult property on the animals bucket. Any key with multiple values are called *sibling* values.

```
$ curl -X PUT http://localhost:8091/riak/animals \
  -H "Content-Type: application/json" \
  -d '{"props":{"allow_mult":true}}'
```

Here, Bob puts Bruiser in the system with his chosen score of 3 and a client ID of *bob*.

```
$ curl -i -X PUT http://localhost:8091/riak/animals/bruiser \
  -H "X-Riak-ClientId: bob" \
  -H "Content-Type: application/json" \
  -d '{"score" : 3}'
```

Jane and Rakshith both pull Bruiser's data that Bob created (you'll have much more header information; we're just showing the vector clock here).

Note that Riak encoded Bob's vclock, but under the covers it's a client and a version (and timestamp, so yours will be different from the one shown).

```
$ curl -i http://localhost:8091/riak/animals/bruiser?return_body=true
X-Riak-Vclock: a85hYGBgzGDKBVIs7NtEXmUwJTLmsTI8FMs5zpcFAA==

{"score" : 3}
```

Jane makes her update to score 2 and includes the most recent vector clock she received from Bob's version. This is a signal to Riak that her value is an update of Bob's version.

```
$ curl -i -X PUT http://localhost:8091/riak/animals/bruiser \
  -H "X-Riak-ClientId: jane" \
  -H "X-Riak-Vclock: a85hYGBgzGDKBVIs7NtEXmUwJTLmsTI8FMs5zpcFAA==" \
  -H "Content-Type: application/json" \
  -d '{"score" : 2}'
```

Since Jane and Rakshith pulled Bob's data at the same time, he also submits an update (of score 4) using Bob's vector clock.

```
$ curl -i -X PUT http://localhost:8091/riak/animals/bruiser \
  -H "X-Riak-ClientId: rakshith" \
  -H "X-Riak-Vclock: a85hYGBgzGDKBVIs7NtEXmUwJTLmsTI8FMs5zpcFAA==" \
  -H "Content-Type: application/json" \
  -d '{"score" : 4}'
```

When Jane rechecks the score, she sees not a value, as expected, but rather an HTTP code for multiple choices and a body containing two "sibling" values.

```
$ curl http://localhost:8091/riak/animals/bruiser?return_body=true
Siblings:
637aZSiky628lx1YrstzH5
7F85FBAIW8eiD9ubsBAeVk
```

Riak stored these versions in a multipart format, so she can retrieve the entire object by accepting that MIME type.

```
$ curl -i http://localhost:8091/riak/animals/bruiser?return_body=true \
  -H "Accept: multipart/mixed"

HTTP/1.1 300 Multiple Choices
X-Riak-Vclock: a85hYGBgyWDKBVHs20Re...OYn9XY4sskQUA
Content-Type: multipart/mixed; boundary=1QwWn1ntX3gZmYQVBG6mAZRVXlu
Content-Length: 409

--1QwWn1ntX3gZmYQVBG6mAZRVXlu
Content-Type: application/json
Etag: 637aZSiky628lx1YrstzH5

{"score" : 4}
--1QwWn1ntX3gZmYQVBG6mAZRVXlu
Content-Type: application/json
Etag: 7F85FBAIW8eiD9ubsBAeVk

{"score" : 2}
--1QwWn1ntX3gZmYQVBG6mAZRVXlu--
```

Notice that the "siblings" shown earlier are HTTP etags (which Riak called vtags) to specific values. As a side note, you can use the vtag parameter in the URL to retrieve only that version: curl http://localhost:8091/riak/animals/bruiser?vtag=7F85FBAIW8eiD9ubsBAeVk will return {"score" : 2}. Jane's job now is to use this information to make a reasonable update. She decides to average the two scores and update to 3, using the vector clock given to resolve the conflict.

```
$ curl -i -X PUT http://localhost:8091/riak/animals/bruiser?return_body=true \
-H "X-Riak-ClientId: jane" \
-H "X-Riak-Vclock: a85hYGBgyWDKBVHs20Re...OYn9XY4sskQUA" \
-H "Content-Type: application/json" \
-d '{"score" : 3}'
```

Now when Bob and Rakshith retrieve bruiser's information, they'll get the resolved score.

```
$ curl -i http://localhost:8091/riak/animals/bruiser?return_body=true
HTTP/1.1 200 OK
X-Riak-Vclock: a85hYGBgyWDKBVHs20Re...CpQmAkonCcHFM4CAA==

{"score" : 3}
```

Any future requests will receive score 3.

Time Keeps on Growing

You may have noticed that the vector clock keeps growing as more clients update values. This is a fundamental problem with vector clocks, which the Riak developers understood. They extended vector clocks to be "pruned" over time, thus keeping their size small. The rate at which Riak prunes old vector clock values are bucket properties, which can be viewed (along with all other properties) by reading the bucket.

```
$ curl http://localhost:8091/riak/animals
```

You'll see some of the following properties, which dictate how Riak will prune the clock before it gets too large.

```
"small_vclock":10,"big_vclock":50,"young_vclock":20,"old_vclock":86400
```

small_vclock and *big_vclock* determine the minimum and maximum length of the vector, while *young_vclock* and *old_vclock* describe the minimum and maximum age of a vclock before pruning happens.

You can read more about vector clocks and pruning online.[12]

Pre/Post-commit Hooks

Riak can transform data before or after saving an object, by way of hooks. Pre- and post-commit hooks are simply JavaScript (or Erlang) functions that get executed before or after a commit occurs. Pre-commit functions can modify the incoming object in some way (and even cause it to fail), while post-commits can respond to a successful commit (such as writing to a log or sending an email to something).

Each server has an app.config file, which needs to reference the location of any custom JavaScript code. First open your file for server dev1, under dev/dev1/etc/app.config, and find the line containing js_source_dir. Replace it with any directory path you want (note that the line may be commented out with

---

12. http://wiki.basho.com/Vector-Clocks.html

a % character, so uncomment it first by removing the character). Our line looks like this:

```
{js_source_dir, "~/riak/js_source"},
```

You'll need to make this change in triplicate, once for each dev server.

Let's create a validator that runs pre-commit to parse incoming data, ensures that a score exists, and ensures that the score is between 1 and 4. If any of those criteria fail, an error will be thrown, and our validator will return the JSON object containing only {"fail" : message}, where message is whatever we want to relay to the user. If the data is as expected, you need return only the object, and Riak will store the value.

```
riak/my_validators.js
function good_score(object) {
  try {
    /* from the Riak object, pull data and parse it as JSON */
    var data = JSON.parse( object.values[0].data );
    /* if score is not found, fail here */
    if( !data.score || data.score === '' ) {
      throw( 'Score is required' );
    }
    /* if score is not within range, fail here */
    if( data.score < 1 || data.score > 4 ) {
      throw( 'Score must be from 1 to 4' );
    }
  } catch( message ) {
    /* Riak expects the following JSON if a failure occurs */
    return { "fail" : message };
  }
  /* No problems found, so continue */
  return object;
}
```

Store this file in the js_source_dir directory you set. Since we're making core server changes, we need to restart all of the development servers using the restart argument.

```
$ dev/dev1/bin/riak restart
$ dev/dev2/bin/riak restart
$ dev/dev3/bin/riak restart
```

Riak will scan for any files ending in .js and load those into memory. You can now set a bucket's precommit property to use the JavaScript *function* name (not the filename).

```
curl -X PUT http://localhost:8091/riak/animals \
-H "content-type:application/json" \
-d '{"props":{"precommit":[{"name" : "good_score"}]}}'
```

Let's test our new hook by setting a score greater than 4. Our pre-commit hook enforces that a score must be from 1 to 4, so the following will fail:

```
curl -i -X PUT http://localhost:8091/riak/animals/bruiser \
-H "Content-Type: application/json" -d '{"score" : 5}'
HTTP/1.1 403 Forbidden
Content-Type: text/plain
Content-Length: 25

Score must be 1 to 4
```

You'll get a 403 Forbidden code, as well as a plain-text error message that was returned under the "fail" field. If you GET the bruiser value, its score remains 3. Try setting the score to 2, and you'll have more success.

Post-commit is similar to pre-commit but happens after the commit is successful. We're skipping it here, since you can write postcommit hooks only in Erlang. If you're an Erlang developer, the online docs can help guide you through installing your own modules. In fact, you can write Erlang mapreduce functions, too. But our Riak journey continues to other prebuilt modules and extensions.

Extending Riak

Riak ships with several extensions that are turned off by default yet add new behaviors you may find useful.

Searching Riak

Riak search scans data inside your Riak cluster and builds an inverted index against it. You may recall the term *inverted index* from the PostgreSQL chapter (the GIN index stands for Generalized Inverted Index). Just like GIN, the Riak index exists to make many varieties of string searching fast and efficient but in a distributed manner.

Using Riak search requires enabling it in your app.config files and setting the Riak search config to enabled, true.

```
%% Riak Search Config
{riak_search, [
  %% To enable Search functionality set this 'true'.
  {enabled, true}
]},
```

If you're familiar with search engine solutions such as Lucene, this part should be a cakewalk. If not, it's easy to get the hang of it.

We need to let the search know when we change values in the database by way of a pre-commit hook. You can install riak_search_kv_hook, Erlang module's precommit function, in a new animals bucket with the following command:

```
$ curl -X PUT http://localhost:8091/riak/animals \
-H "Content-Type: application/json" \
-d '{"props":{"precommit":
[{"mod": "riak_search_kv_hook","fun":"precommit"}]}}'
```

Calling curl http://localhost:8091/riak/animals will show that the hook has been added to the animals bucket's precommit property. Now, when you put data that is encoded as JSON or XML into the animals bucket, Riak search will index the field names and values. Let's upload a few animals.

```
$ curl -X PUT http://localhost:8091/riak/animals/dragon \
-H "Content-Type: application/json" \
-d '{"nickname" : "Dragon", "breed" : "Briard", "score" : 1 }'
$ curl -X PUT http://localhost:8091/riak/animals/ace \
-H "Content-Type: application/json" \
-d '{"nickname" : "The Wonder Dog", "breed" : "German Shepherd", "score" : 3 }'
$ curl -X PUT http://localhost:8091/riak/animals/rtt \
-H "Content-Type: application/json" \
-d '{"nickname" : "Rin Tin Tin", "breed" : "German Shepherd", "score" : 4 }'
```

There are several options for querying this data, but let's use Riak's HTTP Solr interface (which implements the Apache Solr[13] search interface). To search /animals, we access /solr, followed by the bucket name /animals and the /select command. The parameters specify the search terms. Here we select any *breed* that contains the word *Shepherd*.

```
$ curl http://localhost:8091/solr/animals/select?q=breed:Shepherd
<?xml version="1.0" encoding="UTF-8"?>
<response>
  <lst name="responseHeader">
    <int name="status">0</int>
    <int name="QTime">1</int>
    <lst name="params">
      <str name="indent">on</str>
      <str name="start">0</str>
      <str name="q">breed:Shepherd</str>
      <str name="q.op">or</str>
      <str name="df">value</str>
      <str name="wt">standard</str>
      <str name="version">1.1</str>
      <str name="rows">2</str>
    </lst>
  </lst>
```

---

13. http://lucene.apache.org/solr/

```
<result name="response" numFound="2" start="0" maxScore="0.500000">
  <doc>
    <str name="id">ace</str>
    <str name="breed">German Shepherd</str>
    <str name="nickname">The Wonder Dog</str>
    <str name="score">3</str>
  </doc>
  <doc>
    <str name="id">rtt</str>
    <str name="breed">German Shepherd</str>
    <str name="nickname">Rin Tin Tin</str>
    <str name="score">4</str>
  </doc>
</result>
</response>
```

If you prefer that the query returns JSON, add the parameter wt=json. You can combine multiple parameters in the query by separating them with a space (or %20 in URL-encoded form) and setting the q.op parameter with the value and. To find a breed with a nickname containing the word *rin* and a breed of shepherd, perform the following:

```
$ curl http://localhost:8091/solr/animals/select\
?wt=json&q=nickname:rin%20breed:shepherd&q.op=and
```

Riak search allows for more colorful query syntaxes, such as wildcards (using * to match multiple characters and using ? to match one character), though only at the end of the term. The query nickname:Drag* would match Dragon, but nickname:*ragon would not match. Range searches are also nice options:

```
nickname:[dog TO drag]
```

More-complex queries based on boolean operators, grouping, and proximity searches are available. Beyond that, you can specify custom data encodings, create custom indexes, and even choose between them when you search. You can find other URL parameters in the following table:

Param	Description	Default
q	The given query string	
q.op	Query terms are either and or or	or
sort	Field name to sort by	none
start	The first object in the matching list to return	0
rows	The max number of results to return	20
wt	Output either xml or json	xml
index	Specifies the index to use	

There is plenty more to learn about the Riak search extension, far more than we can reasonably cover here. Ideally you've gotten a feel for its power. It's a clear choice if you plan to provide search functionality for a large web application, but it also deserves a second look if you need a lot of simple ad hoc querying.

Indexing Riak

As of version 1.0, Riak supports secondary indexes. These are similar to the indexes we saw in PostgreSQL but with a slight twist. Rather than indexing on a specific column or columns of data, Riak allows you to index on metadata attached to the header of the object.

Once again, we must make a change to the app.config file. Switch the storage back end from bitcask to eLevelDB, as shown here, and then restart the servers:

```
{riak_kv, [
  %% Storage_backend specifies the Erlang module defining the
  %% storage mechanism that will be used on this node.
  {storage_backend, riak_kv_eleveldb_backend},
```

eLevelDB is an Erlang implementation of the Google key-value store called LevelDB.[14] This new back-end implementation allowed for secondary indexing in Riak to take place.

With our system ready to go, we can index any object with any number of header tags known as an *index entries* that define how an object is indexed. The field names begin with x-riak-index- and end with either _int or _bin for integer or binary (anything not an integer) values, respectively.

To add Blue II, the Butler Bulldogs mascot, we'd like to index by the university name that this dog is a mascot for (butler), as well as the version number (Blue 2 is the second bulldog mascot).

```
$ curl -X PUT http://localhost:8098/riak/animals/blue
-H "x-riak-index-mascot_bin: butler"
-H "x-riak-index-version_int: 2"
-d '{"nickname" : "Blue II", "breed" : "English Bulldog"}'
```

You may have noticed that the indexes have nothing to do with the value stored in the key. This is actually a powerful feature, since it allows us to index data orthogonal to any data we may store. If you want to store a video as a value, you may still index it.

---

14. http://code.google.com/p/leveldb/

Getting the value by the index is fairly straightforward.

```
$ curl http://localhost:8098/riak/animals/index/mascot_bin/butler
```

Though secondary indexing in Riak is a big step in the right direction, it still has a way to go. If you want to index dates, for example, you must store a string that can be sorted in order—such as "YYYYMMDD". Storing any floating digits requires to you first multiply the float by some significant precision multiple of 10 and then store it as an integer—such as 1.45 * 100 == 145. Your client is responsible for doing this conversion. But between mapreduce, Riak search, and now secondary indexing, Riak is providing many tools to loosen up the classic constraints of the key-value store design by other means of value access beyond simple keys.

Day 3 Wrap-Up

We finished Riak with some of its more advanced concepts: how to deal with version conflicts by using vector clocks and how to ensure or modify incoming data with commit hooks. We also dug into using a couple Riak extensions: activating Riak search and indexing data to allow for a little more query flexibility.

Using these concepts along with mapreduce from Day 2 and Links from Day 1, you can create a flexible combination of tools far beyond your standard key-value store.

Day 3 Homework

Find

1. Find the Riak function contrib list repository (hint: it's in GitHub).
2. Read more about vector clocks.
3. Learn to create your own index configuration.

Do

1. Create your own index that defines the animals schema. Specifically, set the score field to integer type, and query it as a range.

2. Start up a small cluster of three servers (such as three laptops or EC2[15] instances), and install Riak on each. Set up the servers as a cluster. Install the Google stock dataset, located on the Basho website.[16]

---

15. http://aws.amazon.com/ec2/
16. http://wiki.basho.com/Loading-Data-and-Running-MapReduce-Queries.html

3.5   Wrap-Up

Riak is the first NoSQL style database we've covered. It is a distributed, data-replicating, enhanced key-value store without a single point of failure.

If your experience with databases until now has been only relational, Riak may seem like an alien beast. There are no transactions, no SQL, no schema. There are keys, but linking between buckets is not at all like a table join, and mapreduce can be a daunting methodology to grok.

The trade-offs, however, are worth it for a certain class of problems. Riak's ability to scale out with more servers (rather than scale up with larger single servers) and its ease of use are excellent attempts at solving the unique scalability problems of the Web. And rather than reinventing the wheel, Riak piggybacks on the HTTP structure, allowing maximum flexibility for any framework or web-enabled system.

Riak's Strengths

If you want to design a large-scale ordering system a la Amazon, or in any situation where high availability is your paramount concern, you should consider Riak. Hands down, one of Riak's strengths lies in its focus on removing single points of failure in an attempt to support maximum uptime and grow (or shrink) to meet changing demands. If you do not have complex data, Riak keeps things simple but still allows for some pretty sophisticated data diving should you need it. There is currently support for about a dozen languages (which you can find on the Riak website) but is extendable to its core if you like to write in Erlang. And if you require more speed than HTTP can handle, you can also try your hand at communicating via Protobuf,[17] which is a more efficient binary encoding and transport protocol.

Riak's Weaknesses

If you require simple queryability, complex data structures, or a rigid schema or if you have no need to scale horizontally with your servers, Riak is probably not your best choice. One of our major gripes about Riak is it still lags in terms of an easy and robust ad hoc querying framework, although it is certainly on the right track. Mapreduce provides fantastic and powerful functionality, but we'd like to see more built-in URL-based or other PUT query actions. The addition of indexing was a major step in the right direction and a concept we'd love to see expanded upon. Finally, if you don't want to write

---

17. http://code.google.com/p/protobuf/

Erlang, you may see a few limitations using JavaScript, such as the unavail-ability of post-commit or slower mapreduce execution. However, the Riak team is working on these relatively minor hiccups.

Riak on CAP

Riak provides a clever way of circumventing the constraints that CAP places on all distributed databases. How it dances around the problem is astounding, compared to a system like PostgreSQL that can (largely) only support strong write consistency. Riak leverages the Amazon Dynamo paper's insight that CAP can be changed on a per-bucket, or per-request, basis. It's a big step forward for robust and flexible open source database systems. As you read about other databases in this book, keep Riak in mind, and you'll continue to be impressed by its flexibility.

Parting Thoughts

If you need to store a huge catalog of data, you could do worse than Riak. Though relational databases have been researched and tweaked for more than forty years, not every problem needs ACID compliance or the ability to enforce a schema. If you want to embed a database into a device or handle financial transactions, you should avoid Riak. If you want to scale out or serve up loads of data on the Web, take a look.

## CHAPTER 4

HBase

Apache HBase is made for big jobs, like a nail gun. You would never use HBase to catalog your corporate sales list, just like you'd never use a nail gun to build a dollhouse. If your data is not measured by many gigabytes, you probably need a smaller tool.

HBase, at first glance, looks a lot like a relational database—so much so that if you didn't know any better, you might think that it is one. The most challenging part of learning HBase isn't the technology; it's that many of the words used in HBase are coaxingly, deceptively familiar. For example, HBase stores data in buckets it calls *tables*, which contain *cells* that appear at the intersection of *rows* and *columns*. So far so good, right?

Wrong! In HBase, tables don't behave like relations, rows don't act like records, and columns are completely variable (not enforced by a schema description). Schema design is still important, since it informs the performance characteristics of the system, but it won't keep your house in order. HBase is the evil twin, the bizarro, if you will, of RDBMS.

So, why would you use this database? Aside from scalability, there are a few reasons. First, HBase has some built-in features that other databases lack, such as versioning, compression, garbage collection (for expired data), and in-memory tables. Having these features available right out of the box means less code that you have to write when your requirements demand them. HBase also makes strong consistency guarantees, making it easier to transition from relational databases.

For all of these reasons, HBase really shines as the cornerstone of an online analytics processing system. While individual operations may be slower than equivalent operations in other databases, scanning through enormous datasets is something HBase takes to with relish. So, for genuinely big queries, HBase often outpaces other databases. This also explains why HBase is often employed at big companies to back logging and search systems.

4.1 Introducing HBase

HBase is a *column-oriented* database that prides itself on consistency and scaling out. It is based on BigTable, a high-performance, proprietary database developed by Google and described in the 2006 white paper "Bigtable: A Distributed Storage System for Structured Data."[1] Initially created for natural-language processing, HBase started life as a contrib package for Apache Hadoop. Since then, it has become a top-level Apache project.

On the architecture front, HBase is designed to be fault tolerant. Hardware failures may be uncommon for individual machines, but in a large cluster, node failure is the norm. By using write-ahead logging and distributed config-uration, HBase can quickly recover from individual server failures.

Additionally, HBase lives in an ecosystem that has its own complementary benefits. HBase is built on Hadoop—a sturdy, scalable computing platform that provides a distributed file system and mapreduce capabilities. Wherever you find HBase, you'll find Hadoop and other infrastructural components that you can lever in your own applications.

It is actively used and developed by a number of high-profile companies for their "Big Data" problems. Notably, Facebook chose HBase as a principal component of its new messaging infrastructure announced in November 2010. Stumbleupon has been using HBase for real-time data storage and analytics for several years, serving various site features directly from HBase. Twitter uses HBase extensively, ranging from data generation (for applications such as people search) to storing monitoring/performance data. The parade of companies using HBase also includes the likes of eBay, Meetup, Ning, Yahoo!, and many others.

With all of this activity, new versions of HBase are coming out at a fairly rapid clip. At the time of this writing, the current stable version is 0.90.3, so that's what we'll be using. Go ahead and download HBase, and we'll get started.

4.2 Day 1: CRUD and Table Administration

Today's goal is to learn the nuts and bolts of working with HBase. We'll get a local instance of HBase running in stand-alone mode, and then we'll use

1. http://research.google.com/archive/bigtable.html

the HBase shell to create and alter tables and to insert and modify data using basic commands. After that, we'll explore how to perform some of those operations programmatically by using the HBase Java API in JRuby. Along the way, we'll uncover some HBase architectural concepts, such as the relationship between rows, column families, columns, and values in a table.

A fully operational, production-quality HBase cluster should really consist of no fewer than five nodes, or so goes the conventional wisdom. Such a setup would be overkill for our needs. Fortunately, HBase supports three running modes:

- Stand-alone mode is a single machine acting alone.
- Pseudodistributed mode is a single node pretending to be a cluster.
- Fully distributed mode is a cluster of nodes working together.

For most of this chapter, we'll be running HBase in stand-alone mode. Even that can be a bit of a challenge, so although we won't cover every aspect of installation and administration, we'll give some relevant troubleshooting tips where appropriate.

Configuring HBase

Before using HBase, it has to be configured. Configuration settings for HBase are kept in a file called hbase-site.xml, which can be found in the ${HBASE_HOME}/conf/ directory. Note that HBASE_HOME is an environment variable pointing to the directory where HBase has been installed.

Initially, this file contains just an empty <configuration> tag. You can add any number of property definitions to your configuration using this format:

```
<property>
  <name>some.property.name</name>
  <value>A property value</value>
</property>
```

A full list of available properties, along with default values and descriptions, is available in hbase-default.xml under ${HBASE_HOME}/src/main/resources.

By default, HBase uses a temporary directory to store its data files. This means you'll lose *all your data* whenever the operating system decides to reclaim the disk space.

To keep your data around, you should specify an involatile storage location. Set the hbase.rootdir property to an appropriate path like so:

```
<property>
  <name>hbase.rootdir</name>
  <value>file:///path/to/hbase</value>
</property>
```

To start HBase, open a terminal (command prompt) and run this command:

```
${HBASE_HOME}/bin/start-hbase.sh
```

To shut down HBase, use the stop-hbase.sh command in the same directory.

If anything goes wrong, take a look at the most recently modified files in the ${HBASE_HOME}/logs directory. On *nix-based systems, the following command will pipe the latest log data to the console as it's written:

```
cd ${HBASE_HOME}
find ./logs -name "hbase-*.log" -exec tail -f {} \;
```

The HBase Shell

The HBase shell is a JRuby-based command-line program you can use to interact with HBase. In the shell, you can add and remove tables, alter table schema, add or delete data, and do a bunch of other tasks. Later we'll explore other means of connecting to HBase, but for now the shell will be our home.

With HBase running, open a terminal and fire up the HBase shell:

```
${HBASE_HOME}/bin/hbase shell
```

To confirm that it's working properly, try asking it for version information.

```
hbase> version
0.90.3, r1100350, Sat May  7 13:31:12 PDT 2011
```

You can enter help at any time to see a list of available commands or to get usage information about a particular command.

Next, execute the status command to see how your HBase server is holding up.

```
hbase> status
1 servers, 0 dead, 2.0000 average load
```

If an error occurs for any of these commands or if the shell hangs, it could be a connection problem. HBase does its best to automatically configure its services based on your network setup, but sometimes it gets it wrong. If you're seeing these symptoms, check out *HBase Network Settings*, on page 97.

Creating a Table

A map is a key-value pair, like a hash in Ruby or a hashmap in Java. A table in HBase is basically a big map. Well, more accurately, it's a map of maps.

HBase Network Settings

By default, HBase tries to make its services available to external clients, but in our case, we simply need to connect from the same machine. So, it might help to add some or all of the following properties to your hbase-site.xml file (your mileage may vary). Note that the values in the following table will help only if you plan to connect locally and not remotely:

property name	value
hbase.master.dns.interface	lo
hbase.master.info.bindAddress	127.0.0.1
hbase.regionserver.info.bindAddress	127.0.0.1
hbase.regionserver.dns.interface	lo
hbase.zookeeper.dns.interface	lo

The properties tell HBase how to establish connections for the master server and region servers (both of which we'll discuss later) and the zookeeper configuration service. The properties with the value "lo" refer to the so-called loopback interface. On *nix systems, the loopback interface is not a real network interface (like your Ethernet or wireless cards) but rather a software-only interface for the computer to use to connect to itself. The bindAddress properties tell HBase what IP address to try to listen on.

In an HBase table, keys are arbitrary strings that each map to a *row* of data. A row is itself a map, in which keys are called *columns* and values are uninterpreted arrays of bytes. Columns are grouped into *column families*, so a column's full name consists of two parts: the column family name and the *column qualifier*. Often these are concatenated together using a colon (for example, 'family:qualifier').

To illustrate these concepts, take a look at Figure 13, *HBase tables consist of rows, keys, column families, columns, and values*, on page 98.

In this figure, we have a hypothetical table with two column families: color and shape. The table has two rows—denoted by dashed boxes—identified by their row keys: first and second. Looking at just the first row, we see that it has three columns in the color column family (with qualifiers red, blue, and yellow) and one column in the shape column family (square). The combination of row key and column name (including both family and qualifier) creates an address for locating data. In this example, the tuple first/color:red points us to the value '#F00'.

Now let's take what we've learned about table structure and use it to do something fun—we're going to make a wiki!

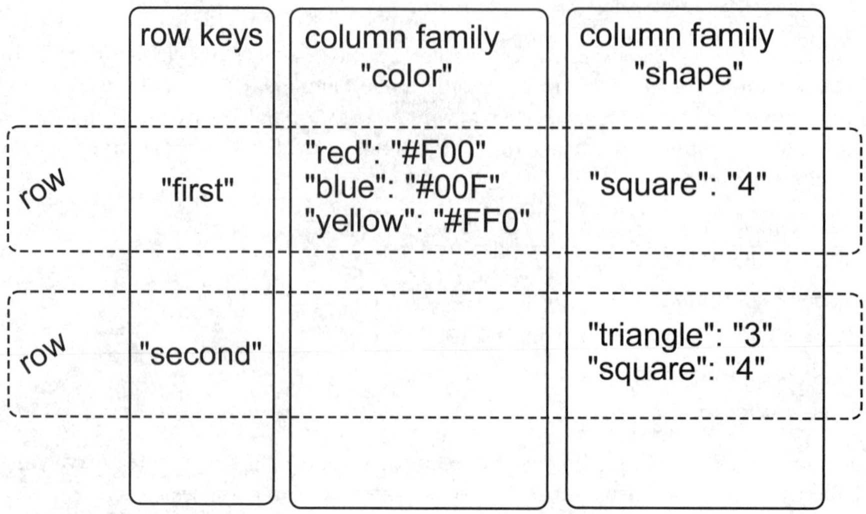

	row keys	column family "color"	column family "shape"
row	"first"	"red": "#F00" "blue": "#00F" "yellow": "#FF0"	"square": "4"
row	"second"		"triangle": "3" "square": "4"

Figure 13—HBase tables consist of rows, keys, column families, columns, and values.

There are lots of juicy info bits we might want to associate with a wiki, but we'll start with the bare minimum. A wiki contains pages, each of which has a unique title string and contains some article text.

Use the create command to make our wiki table:

```
hbase> create 'wiki', 'text'
0 row(s) in 1.2160 seconds
```

Here, we're creating a table called wiki with a single column family called text. The table is currently empty; it has no rows and thus no columns. Unlike a relational database, in HBase a column is specific to the row that contains it. When we start adding rows, we'll add columns to store data at the same time.

Visualizing our table architecture, we arrive at something like Figure 14, *The wiki table has one column family*, on page 99. By our own convention, we expect each row to have exactly one column within the text family, qualified by the empty string ("). So, the full column name containing the text of a page will be 'text:'.

Of course, for our wiki table to be useful, it's going to need content. Let's add some!

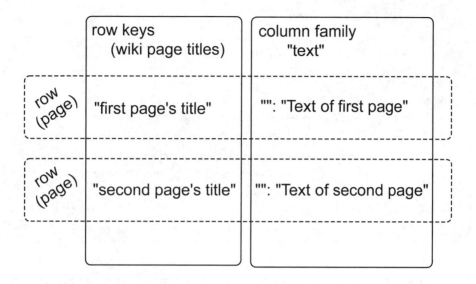

Figure 14—The wiki table has one column family.

Inserting, Updating, and Retrieving Data

Our wiki needs a Home page, so we'll start with that. To add data to an HBase table, use the put command:

```
hbase> put 'wiki', 'Home', 'text:', 'Welcome to the wiki!'
```

This command inserts a new row into the wiki table with the key 'Home', adding 'Welcome to the wiki!' to the column called 'text:'.

We can query the data for the 'Home' row using get, which requires two parameters: the table name and the row key. You can optionally specify a list of columns to return.

```
hbase> get 'wiki', 'Home', 'text:'
COLUMN      CELL
 text:      timestamp=1295774833226, value=Welcome to the wiki!
1 row(s) in 0.0590 seconds
```

Notice the timestamp field in the output. HBase stores an integer timestamp for all data values, representing time in milliseconds since the epoch (00:00:00 UTC on January 1, 1970). When a new value is written to the same cell, the old value hangs around, indexed by its timestamp. This is a pretty awesome feature. Most databases require you to specifically handle historical data yourself, but in HBase, versioning is baked right in!

Case Study: Facebook's Messaging Index Table

Facebook uses HBase as a principal component of its messaging infrastructure, both for storing message data and for maintaining an inverted index for search.

In its index table schema:

- The row keys are user IDs.
- Column qualifiers are words that appear in that user's messages.
- Timestamps are message IDs of messages that contain that word.

Since messages between users are immutable, the index entries for a message are static as well. The concept of versioned values doesn't make sense.

For Facebook, manipulating the timestamp to match message IDs gives them another dimension for storing data.

Put and Get

The put and get commands allow you to specify a timestamp explicitly. If using milliseconds since the epoch doesn't strike your fancy, you can specify another integer value of your choice. This gives you an extra dimension to work with if you need it. If you don't specify a timestamp, HBase will use the current time when inserting, and it will return the most recent version when reading.

For an example of how one company chose to overload the timestamp field, see *Case Study: Facebook's Messaging Index Table*, on page 100. In the rest of this chapter, we'll continue to use the default timestamp interpretation.

Altering Tables

So far, our wiki schema has pages with titles, text, and an integrated version history but nothing else. Let's expand our requirements to include the following:

- In our wiki, a page is uniquely identified by its title.
- A page can have unlimited revisions.
- A revision is identified by its timestamp.
- A revision contains text and optionally a commit comment.
- A revision was made by an author, identified by name.

Visually, our requirements can be sketched, like in Figure 15, *Requirements for a wiki page (including time dimension)*, on page 102. In this abstract representation of our requirements for a page, we see that each revision has an author, a commit comment, some article text, and a timestamp. The title of a page is not part of a revision, because it's the identifier we use to denote revisions belonging to the same page.

Mapping our vision to an HBase table takes a somewhat different form, as illustrated in Figure 16, *Updated wiki table architecture (time dimension not shown)*, on page 102. Our wiki table uses the title as the row key and will group other page data into two column families called text and revision. The text column family is the same as before; we expect each row to have exactly one column, qualified by the empty string ("), to hold the article contents. The job of the revision column family is to hold other revision-specific data, such as the author and commit comment.

Defaults

We created the wiki table with no special options, so all the HBase default values were used. One such default value is to keep only three VERSIONS of column values, so let's increase that. To make schema changes, first we have to take the table offline with the disable command.

```
hbase> disable 'wiki'
0 row(s) in 1.0930 seconds
```

Now we can modify column family characteristics using the alter command.

```
hbase> alter 'wiki', { NAME => 'text', VERSIONS =>
hbase*    org.apache.hadoop.hbase.HConstants::ALL_VERSIONS }
0 row(s) in 0.0430 seconds
```

Here, we're instructing HBase to alter the text column family's VERSIONS attribute. There are a number of other attributes we could have set, some of which we'll discuss in Day 2. The hbase* line means that it's a continuation of the previous line.

Altering a Table

Operations that alter column family characteristics can be very expensive because HBase has to create a new column family with the chosen specifications and then copy all the data over. In a production system, this may incur significant downtime. For this reason, settling on column family options up front is a good thing.

With the wiki table still disabled, let's add the revision column family, again using the alter command:

```
hbase> alter 'wiki', { NAME => 'revision', VERSIONS =>
hbase*    org.apache.hadoop.hbase.HConstants::ALL_VERSIONS }
0 row(s) in 0.0660 seconds
```

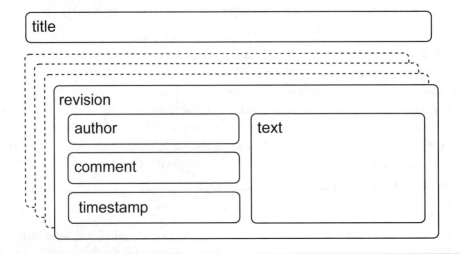

Figure 15—Requirements for a wiki page (including time dimension)

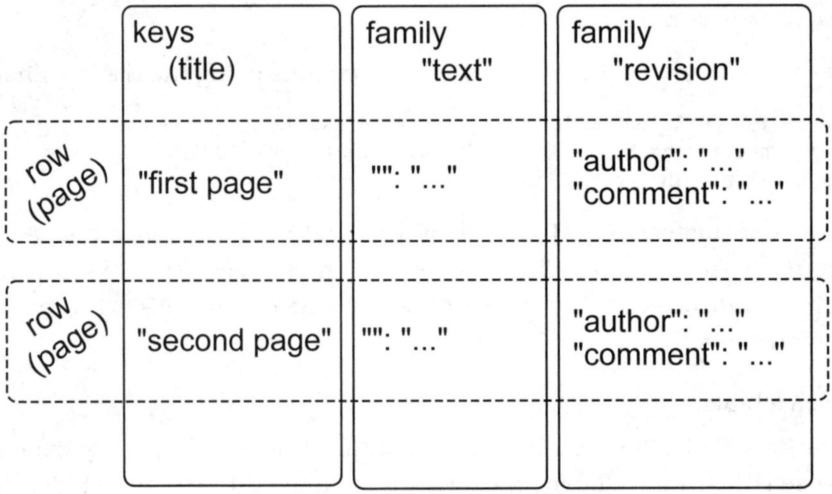

keys (title)	family "text"	family "revision"
row (page)	"first page"	"": "..."	"author": "..." "comment": "..."
row (page)	"second page"	"": "..."	"author": "..." "comment": "..."

Figure 16—Updated wiki table architecture (time dimension not shown)

Just as before, with the text family, we're only adding a revision *column family* to the table schema, not individual *columns*. Though we expect each row to eventually contain a revision:author and revision:comment, it's up to the client to honor this expectation; it's not written into any formal schema. If someone wants to add a revision:foo for a page, HBase won't stop them.

Moving On

With these additions in place, let's reenable our wiki:

```
hbase> enable 'wiki'
0 row(s) in 0.0550 seconds
```

Now that our wiki table has been modified to support our growing requirements list, we can start adding data to columns in the revision column family.

Adding Data Programmatically

As we've seen, the HBase shell is great for tasks such as manipulating tables. Sadly, the shell's data insertion support isn't the best. The put command only allows setting one column value at a time, and in our newly updated schema, we need to add multiple column values simultaneously so they all share the same timestamp. We're going to need to start scripting.

The following script can be executed directly in the HBase shell, since the shell is also a JRuby interpreter. When run, it adds a new version of the text for the Home page, setting the author and comment fields at the same time. JRuby runs on the Java virtual machine (JVM), giving it access to the HBase Java code. These examples will not work with non-JVM Ruby.

hbase/put_multiple_columns.rb
```ruby
import 'org.apache.hadoop.hbase.client.HTable'
import 'org.apache.hadoop.hbase.client.Put'

def jbytes( *args )
  args.map { |arg| arg.to_s.to_java_bytes }
end

table = HTable.new( @hbase.configuration, "wiki" )

p = Put.new( *jbytes( "Home" ) )

p.add( *jbytes( "text", "", "Hello world" ) )
p.add( *jbytes( "revision", "author", "jimbo" ) )
p.add( *jbytes( "revision", "comment", "my first edit" ) )

table.put( p )
```

The import lines bring references to useful HBase classes into the shell. This saves us from having to write out the full namespace later. Next, the jbytes() function takes any number of arguments and returns an array converted to Java byte arrays, as the HBase API methods demand.

After that, we create a local variable (table) pointing to our wiki table, using the @hbase administration object for configuration information.

Next we stage a commit operation by creating and preparing a new instance of Put, which takes the row to be modified. In this case, we're sticking with the Home page we've been working with thus far. Finally, we add() properties to our Put instance and then call on the table object to execute the put operation we've prepared. The add() method has several forms; in our case, we used the three-argument version: add(column_family, column_qualifier, value).

Why Column Families?

You may be tempted to build your whole structure without column families; why not store all of a row's data in a single column family? That solution would be simpler to implement. But there are downsides to avoiding column families, namely, missing out on fine-grained performance tuning. Each column family's performance options are configured independently. These settings affect things such as read and write speed and disk space consumption.

All operations in HBase are atomic at the *row level*. No matter how many columns are affected, the operation will have a consistent view of the particular row being accessed or modified. This design decision helps clients reason intelligently about the data.

Our put operation affects several columns and doesn't specify a timestamp, so all column values will have the same timestamp (the current time in milliseconds). Let's verify by invoking get.

```
hbase> get 'wiki', 'Home'
COLUMN                CELL
 revision:author      timestamp=1296462042029, value=jimbo
 revision:comment     timestamp=1296462042029, value=my first edit
 text:                timestamp=1296462042029, value=Hello world
3 row(s) in 0.0300 seconds
```

As you can see, each column value listed previously has the same timestamp.

Day 1 Wrap-Up

Today, we got a firsthand look at a running HBase server. We learned how to configure it and monitor log files for troubleshooting. Using the HBase shell, we performed basic administration and data manipulation tasks.

In modeling a wiki system, we explored schema design in HBase. We learned how to create tables and manipulate column families. Designing an HBase schema means making choices about column family options and, just as important, our semantic interpretation of features like timestamps and row keys.

We also started poking around in the HBase Java API by executing JRuby code in the shell. In Day 2, we'll take this a step further, using the shell to run custom scripts for big jobs like data import.

Ideally you've begun to shrug off some of the relational concepts that burden terms such as *table*, *row*, and *column*. The difference between how HBase uses these terms and what they mean in other systems will become even starker as we explore deeper into HBase's features.

Day 1 Homework

HBase documentation online generally comes in two flavors: extremely technical and nonexistent. This is slowly changing as "getting started" guides start to appear, but be prepared to spend some time trolling through Javadoc or source code to find answers.

Find

1. Figure out how to use the shell to do the following:

   - Delete individual column values in a row
   - Delete an entire row

2. Bookmark the HBase API documentation for the version of HBase you're using.

Do

1. Create a function called put_many() that creates a Put instance, adds any number of column-value pairs to it, and commits it to a table. The signature should look like this:

```
def put_many( table_name, row, column_values )
  # your code here
end
```

2. Define your put_many() function by pasting it in the HBase shell, and then call it like so:

```
hbase> put_many 'wiki', 'Some title', {
hbase*    "text:" => "Some article text",
hbase*    "revision:author" => "jschmoe",
hbase*    "revision:comment" => "no comment" }
```

4.3 Day 2: Working with Big Data

With Day 1's table creation and manipulation under our belts, it's time to start adding some serious data to our wiki table. Today, we'll script against the HBase APIs, ultimately streaming Wikipedia content right into our wiki! Along the way, we'll pick up some performance tricks for making faster import jobs. Finally, we'll poke around in HBase's internals to see how it partitions data into regions, achieving both performance and disaster recovery goals.

Importing Data, Invoking Scripts

One common problem people face when trying a new database system is how to migrate data into it. Handcrafting Put operations with static strings, like we did in Day 1, is all well and good, but we can do better.

Fortunately, pasting commands into the shell is not the only way to execute them. When you start the HBase shell from the command line, you can specify the name of a JRuby script to run. HBase will execute that script as though it were entered directly into the shell. The syntax looks like this:

```
${HBASE_HOME}/bin/hbase shell <your_script> [<optional_arguments> ...]
```

Since we're interested specifically in "Big Data," let's create a script for importing Wikipedia articles into our wiki table. The WikiMedia Foundation—which oversees Wikipedia, Wictionary, and other projects—periodically publishes data dumps we can use. These dumps are in the form of enormous XML files. Here's an example record from the English Wikipedia:

```
<page>
  <title>Anarchism</title>
  <id>12</id>
  <revision>
    <id>408067712</id>
    <timestamp>2011-01-15T19:28:25Z</timestamp>
    <contributor>
      <username>RepublicanJacobite</username>
      <id>5223685</id>
    </contributor>
    <comment>Undid revision 408057615 by [[Special:Contributions...</comment>
    <text xml:space="preserve">{{Redirect|Anarchist|the fictional character|
...
[[bat-smg:Anarkėzmos]]
    </text>
  </revision>
</page>
```

Because we were so smart, this contains all the information we've already accounted for in our schema: title (row key), text, timestamp, and author. So, we ought to be able to write a script to import revisions without too much trouble.

Streaming XML

First things first. We'll need to parse the huge XML files in a streaming (SAX) fashion, so let's start with that. The basic outline for parsing an XML file in JRuby, record by record, looks like this:

```
hbase/basic_xml_parsing.rb
import 'javax.xml.stream.XMLStreamConstants'

factory = javax.xml.stream.XMLInputFactory.newInstance
reader = factory.createXMLStreamReader(java.lang.System.in)

while reader.has_next

  type = reader.next

  if type == XMLStreamConstants::START_ELEMENT
    tag = reader.local_name
    # do something with tag
  elsif type == XMLStreamConstants::CHARACTERS
    text = reader.text
    # do something with text
  elsif type == XMLStreamConstants::END_ELEMENT
    # same as START_ELEMENT
  end

end
```

Breaking this down, there are a few parts worth mentioning. First, we produce an XMLStreamReader and wire it up to java.lang.System.in, which means it'll be reading from standard input.

Next, we set up a while loop, which will continuously pull out tokens from the XML stream until there are none left. Inside the while loop, we process the current token. What to do depends on whether the token is the start of an XML tag, the end of a tag, or the text in between.

Streaming Wikipedia

Now we can combine this basic XML processing framework with our previous exploration of the HTable and Put interfaces. Here's the resultant script. Most of it should look familiar, and we'll discuss a few novel parts.

hbase/import_from_wikipedia.rb

```ruby
require 'time'

import 'org.apache.hadoop.hbase.client.HTable'
import 'org.apache.hadoop.hbase.client.Put'
import 'javax.xml.stream.XMLStreamConstants'

def jbytes( *args )
  args.map { |arg| arg.to_s.to_java_bytes }
end

factory = javax.xml.stream.XMLInputFactory.newInstance
reader = factory.createXMLStreamReader(java.lang.System.in)

① document = nil
  buffer = nil
  count = 0

  table = HTable.new( @hbase.configuration, 'wiki' )
② table.setAutoFlush( false )

  while reader.has_next
    type = reader.next

③   if type == XMLStreamConstants::START_ELEMENT

      case reader.local_name
      when 'page' then document = {}
      when /title|timestamp|username|comment|text/ then buffer = []
      end

④   elsif type == XMLStreamConstants::CHARACTERS

      buffer << reader.text unless buffer.nil?

⑤   elsif type == XMLStreamConstants::END_ELEMENT

      case reader.local_name
      when /title|timestamp|username|comment|text/
        document[reader.local_name] = buffer.join
      when 'revision'
        key = document['title'].to_java_bytes
        ts = ( Time.parse document['timestamp'] ).to_i

        p = Put.new( key, ts )
        p.add( *jbytes( "text", "", document['text'] ) )
        p.add( *jbytes( "revision", "author", document['username'] ) )
        p.add( *jbytes( "revision", "comment", document['comment'] ) )
        table.put( p )
```

```
      count += 1
      table.flushCommits() if count % 10 == 0
      if count % 500 == 0
        puts "#{count} records inserted (#{document['title']})"
      end
    end
  end
end

table.flushCommits()
exit
```

① The first difference of note is the introduction of a few variables:

- document: Holds the current article and revision data

- buffer: Holds character data for the current field within the document (text, title, author, and so on)

- count: Keeps track of how many articles we've imported so far

② Pay special attention to the use of table.setAutoFlush(false). In HBase, data is *automatically flushed* to disk periodically. This is preferred in most applications. By disabling autoflush in our script, any put operations we execute will be buffered until we call table.flushCommits(). This allows us to batch up writes and execute them when it's convenient for us.

③ Next, let's look at what happens in parsing. If the start tag is a <page>, then reset document to an empty hash. Otherwise, if it's another tag we care about, reset buffer for storing its text.

④ We handle character data by appending it to the buffer.

⑤ For most closing tags, we just stash the buffered contents into the document. If the closing tag is a </revision>, however, we create a new Put instance, fill it with the document's fields, and submit it to the table. After that, we use flushCommits() if we haven't done so in a while and report progress to standard out (puts).

Compression and Bloom Filters

We're almost ready to run the script; we just have one more bit of housecleaning to do first. The text column family is going to contain big blobs of text content; it would benefit from some compression. Let's enable compression and fast lookups:

```
hbase> alter 'wiki', {NAME=>'text', COMPRESSION=>'GZ', BLOOMFILTER=>'ROW'}
0 row(s) in 0.0510 seconds
```

HBase supports two compression algorithms: Gzip (GZ) and Lempel-Ziv-Oberhumer (LZO). The HBase community highly recommends using LZO over Gzip, pretty much unilaterally, but here we're using GZ.

The problem with LZO is the implementation's license. While open source, it's not compatible with Apache's licensing philosophy, so LZO can't be bundled with HBase. Detailed instructions are available online for installing and configuring LZO support. If you want high-performance compression, get LZO.

A Bloom filter is a really cool data structure that efficiently answers the question, "Have I ever seen this thing before?" Originally developed by Burton Howard Bloom in 1970 for use in spell-checking applications, Bloom filters have become popular in data storage applications for determining quickly whether a key exists. If you're unfamiliar with Bloom filters, they're explained briefly in *How Do Bloom Filters Work?*, on page 111.

HBase supports using Bloom filters to determine whether a particular column exists for a given row key (BLOOMFILTER=>'ROWCOL') or just whether a given row key exists at all (BLOOMFILTER=>'ROW'). The number of columns within a column family and the number of rows are both potentially unbounded. Bloom filters offer a fast way of determining whether data exists before incurring an expensive disk read.

Engage!

Now we're ready to kick off the script. Remember that these files are enormous, so downloading and unzipping them is pretty much out of the question. So, what are we going to do?

Fortunately, through the magic of *nix pipes, we can download, extract, and feed the XML into the script all at once. The command looks like this:

```
curl <dump_url> | bzcat | \
${HBASE_HOME}/bin/hbase shell import_from_wikipedia.rb
```

Note that you should replace <dump_url> with the URL of a WikiMedia Foundation dump file of some kind.[2] You should use [project]-latest-pages-articles.xml.bz2 for either the English Wikipedia (~6GB)[3] or the English Wiktionary (~185MB).[4] These files contain all the most recent revisions of pages in the Main namespace. That is, they omit user pages, discussion pages, and so on.

Plug in the URL and run it! You should see output like this (eventually):

---

2.   http://dumps.wikimedia.org

3.   http://dumps.wikimedia.org/enwiki/latest/enwiki-latest-pages-articles.xml.bz2

4.   http://dumps.wikimedia.org/enwiktionary/latest/enwiktionary-latest-pages-articles.xml.bz2

How Do Bloom Filters Work?

Without going too deep into implementation details, a Bloom filter manages a statically sized array of bits initially set to 0. Each time a new blob of data is presented to the filter, some of the bits are flipped to 1. Determining which bits to flip depends on generating a hash from the data and turning that hash into a set of bit positions.

Later, to test whether the filter has been presented with a particular blob in the past, the filter figures out which bits would have to be 1 and checks them. If any are 0, then the filter can unequivocally say "no." If all of the bits are 1, then it reports "yes"; chances are it has been presented with that blob before, but false positives are increasingly likely as more blobs are entered.

This is the trade-off of using a Bloom filter as opposed to a simple hash. A hash will never produce a false positive, but the space needed to store that data is unbounded. Bloom filters use a constant amount of space but will occasionally produce false positives at a predictable rate based on saturation.

```
500 records inserted (Ashmore and Cartier Islands)
1000 records inserted (Annealing)
1500 records inserted (Ajanta Caves)
```

It'll happily chug along as long as you let it or until it encounters an error, but you'll probably want to shut it off after a while. When you're ready to kill the script, press CTRL+C. For now, though, let's leave it running so we can take a peek under the hood and learn about how HBase achieves its horizontal scalability.

Introduction to Regions and Monitoring Disk Usage

In HBase, rows are kept in order, sorted by the row key. A region is a chunk of rows, identified by the starting key (inclusive) and ending key (exclusive). Regions never overlap, and each is assigned to a specific region server in the cluster. In our simplistic stand-alone server, there is only one region server, which will always be responsible for all regions. A fully distributed cluster would consist of many region servers.

So, let's take a look at your HBase server's disk usage, which will give us insight into how the data is laid out. You can inspect HBase's disk usage by opening a command prompt to the hbase.rootdir location you specified earlier and executing the du command. du is a standard *nix command-line utility that tells you how much space is used by a directory and its children, recursively. The -h option tells du to report numbers in human-readable form.

Here's what ours looked like after about 12,000 pages had been inserted and the import was still running:

```
$ du -h
231M    ./.logs/localhost.localdomain,38556,1300092965081
231M    ./.logs
4.0K    ./.META./1028785192/info
12K     ./.META./1028785192/.oldlogs
28K     ./.META./1028785192
32K     ./.META.
12K     ./-ROOT-/70236052/info
12K     ./-ROOT-/70236052/.oldlogs
36K     ./-ROOT-/70236052
40K     ./-ROOT-
72M     ./wiki/517496fecabb7d16af7573fc37257905/text
1.7M    ./wiki/517496fecabb7d16af7573fc37257905/revision
61M     ./wiki/517496fecabb7d16af7573fc37257905/.tmp
12K     ./wiki/517496fecabb7d16af7573fc37257905/.oldlogs
134M    ./wiki/517496fecabb7d16af7573fc37257905
134M    ./wiki
4.0K    ./.oldlogs
365M    .
```

This output tells us a lot about how much space HBase is using and how it's allocated. The lines starting with /wiki describe the space usage for the wiki table. The long-named subdirectory 517496fecabb7d16af7573fc37257905 represents an individual region (the only region so far). Under that, the directories /text and /revision correspond to the text and revision column families, respectively. Finally, the last line sums up all these values, telling us that HBase is using 365MB of disk space.

One more thing. The first two lines at the top of output, starting with /.logs, show us the space used by the write-ahead log (WAL) files. HBase uses write-ahead logging to provide protection against node failures. This is a fairly typical disaster recovery technique. For instance, write-ahead logging in file systems is called *journaling*. In HBase, logs are appended to the WAL before any edit operations (put and increment) are persisted to disk.

For performance reasons, edits are not necessarily written to disk immediately. The system does much better when I/O is buffered and written to disk in chunks. If the *region server* responsible for the affected region were to crash during this limbo period, HBase would use the WAL to determine which operations were successful and take corrective action.

Writing to the WAL is optional and enabled by default. Edit classes like Put and Increment have a setter method called setWriteToWAL() that can be used to exclude the operation from being written to the WAL. Generally you'll want to keep the default option, but in some instances it might make sense to change it. For example, if you're running an import job that you can rerun any time, like our Wikipedia import script, you might want to take the performance benefit of disabling WAL writes over the disaster recovery protection.

Regional Interrogation

If you let the script run long enough, you'll see HBase split the table into multiple regions. Here's our du output again, after about 150,000 pages have been added:

```
$ du -h
40K     ./.logs/localhost.localdomain,55922,1300094776865
44K     ./.logs
24K     ./.META./1028785192/info
4.0K    ./.META./1028785192/recovered.edits
4.0K    ./.META./1028785192/.tmp
12K     ./.META./1028785192/.oldlogs
56K     ./.META./1028785192
60K     ./.META.
4.0K    ./.corrupt
12K     ./-ROOT-/70236052/info
4.0K    ./-ROOT-/70236052/recovered.edits
4.0K    ./-ROOT-/70236052/.tmp
12K     ./-ROOT-/70236052/.oldlogs
44K     ./-ROOT-/70236052
48K     ./-ROOT-
138M    ./wiki/0a25ac7e5d0be211b9e890e83e24e458/text
5.8M    ./wiki/0a25ac7e5d0be211b9e890e83e24e458/revision
4.0K    ./wiki/0a25ac7e5d0be211b9e890e83e24e458/.tmp
144M    ./wiki/0a25ac7e5d0be211b9e890e83e24e458
149M    ./wiki/15be59b7dfd6e71af9b828fed280ce8a/text
6.5M    ./wiki/15be59b7dfd6e71af9b828fed280ce8a/revision
4.0K    ./wiki/15be59b7dfd6e71af9b828fed280ce8a/.tmp
155M    ./wiki/15be59b7dfd6e71af9b828fed280ce8a
145M    ./wiki/0ef3903982fd9478e09d8f17b7a5f987/text
6.3M    ./wiki/0ef3903982fd9478e09d8f17b7a5f987/revision
4.0K    ./wiki/0ef3903982fd9478e09d8f17b7a5f987/.tmp
151M    ./wiki/0ef3903982fd9478e09d8f17b7a5f987
135M    ./wiki/a79c0f6896c005711cf6a4448775a33b/text
6.0M    ./wiki/a79c0f6896c005711cf6a4448775a33b/revision
4.0K    ./wiki/a79c0f6896c005711cf6a4448775a33b/.tmp
141M    ./wiki/a79c0f6896c005711cf6a4448775a33b
591M    ./wiki
4.0K    ./.oldlogs
591M    .
```

The biggest change is that the old region (517496fecabb7d16af7573fc37257905) is now gone, replaced by four new ones. In our stand-alone server, all the regions are served by our singular server, but in a distributed environment, these would be parceled out to the various region servers.

This raises a few questions, such as "How do the region servers know which regions they're responsible for serving?" and "How can you find which region (and, by extension, which region server) is serving a given row?"

If we drop back into the HBase shell, we can query the .META. table to find out more about the current regions. .META. is a special table whose sole purpose is to keep track of all the user tables and which region servers are responsible for serving the regions of those tables.

```
hbase> scan '.META.', { COLUMNS => [ 'info:server', 'info:regioninfo' ] }
```

Even for a small number of regions, you should get a lot of output. Here's a fragment of ours, formatted and truncated for readability:

```
ROW
 wiki,,1300099733696.a79c0f6896c005711cf6a4448775a33b.

COLUMN+CELL
   column=info:server, timestamp=1300333136393, value=localhost.localdomain:3555
   column=info:regioninfo, timestamp=1300099734090, value=REGION => {
     NAME => 'wiki,,1300099733696.a79c0f6896c005711cf6a4448775a33b.',
     STARTKEY => '',
     ENDKEY => 'Demographics of Macedonia',
     ENCODED => a79c0f6896c005711cf6a4448775a33b,
     TABLE => {{...}}

ROW
   wiki,Demographics of Macedonia,1300099733696.0a25ac7e5d0be211b9e890e83e24e458.

COLUMN+CELL
   column=info:server, timestamp=1300333136402, value=localhost.localdomain:35552
   column=info:regioninfo, timestamp=1300099734011, value=REGION => {
     NAME => 'wiki,Demographics of Macedonia,1300099733696.0a25...e458.',
     STARTKEY => 'Demographics of Macedonia',
     ENDKEY => 'June 30',
     ENCODED => 0a25ac7e5d0be211b9e890e83e24e458,
     TABLE => {{...}}
```

Both of the regions listed previously are served by the same server, localhost.local-domain:35552. The first region starts at the empty string row (") and ends with 'Demographics of Macedonia'. The second region starts at 'Demographics of Macedonia' and goes to 'June 30'.

STARTKEY is inclusive, while ENDKEY is exclusive. So, if we were looking for the 'Demographics of Macedonia' row, we'd find it in the second region.

Since rows are kept in sorted order, we can use the information stored in .META. to look up the region and server where any given row should be found. But where is the .META. table stored?

It turns out that the .META. table is split into regions and served by region servers just like any other table would be. To find out which servers have which parts of the .META. table, we have to scan -ROOT-.

```
hbase> scan '-ROOT-', { COLUMNS => [ 'info:server', 'info:regioninfo' ] }
ROW
  .META.,,1
COLUMN+CELL
  column=info:server, timestamp=1300333135782, value=localhost.localdomain:35552
  column=info:regioninfo, timestamp=1300092965825, value=REGION => {
    NAME => '.META.,,1',
    STARTKEY => '',
    ENDKEY => '',
    ENCODED => 1028785192,
    TABLE => {{...}}
```

The assignment of regions to region servers, including .META. regions, is handled by the *master* node, often referred to as HBaseMaster. The master server can also be a region server, performing both duties simultaneously.

When a region server fails, the master server steps in and reassigns responsibility for regions previously assigned to the failed node. The new stewards of those regions would look to the WAL to see what, if any, recovery steps are needed. If the master server fails, responsibility defers to any of the other region servers that step up to become the master.

Scanning One Table to Build Another

Providing you've stopped the import script from running, we can move on to the next task: extracting information from the imported wiki contents.

Wiki syntax is filled with links, some of which link internally to other articles and some of which link to external resources. This interlinking contains a wealth of topological data. Let's capture it!

Our goal is to capture the relationships between articles as directional links, pointing one article *to* another or receiving a link *from* another. An internal article link in wikitext looks like this: *[[<target name>|<alt text>]]*, where *<target name>* is the article to link to, and *<alt text>* is the alternative text to display (optional).

For example, if the text of the article on *Star Wars* contains the string *"[[Yoda|jedi master]]"*, we want to store that relationship twice—once as an outgoing link from *Star Wars* and once as an incoming link to Yoda. Storing the relationship twice means that it's fast to look up both a page's outgoing links and its incoming links.

Where's My TABLE Schema?

The TABLE schema has been removed from the example output of regioninfo scans. This reduces clutter, and we'll be talking about performance-tuning options later. If you're dying to see the schema definition for a table, use the describe command. Here's an example:

```
hbase> describe 'wiki'
hbase> describe '.META.'
hbase> describe '-ROOT-'
```

To store this additional link data, we'll create a new table. Head over to the shell and enter this:

```
hbase> create 'links', {
  NAME => 'to', VERSIONS => 1, BLOOMFILTER => 'ROWCOL'
},{
  NAME => 'from', VERSIONS => 1, BLOOMFILTER => 'ROWCOL'
}
```

In principle, we could have chosen to shove the link data into an existing column family or merely added one or more additional column families to the wiki table, rather than create a new one. Creating a separate table has the advantage that the tables have separate regions. This means that the cluster can more effectively split regions as necessary.

The general guidance for column families in the HBase community is to try to keep the number of families per table down. You can do this either by combining more columns into the same families or by putting families in different tables entirely. The choice is largely decided by whether and how often clients will need to get an entire row of data (as opposed to needing just a few column values).

In our wiki case, we need the text and revision column families to be on the same table so that when we put new revisions in, the metadata and the text share the same timestamp. The links content, by contrast, will never have the same timestamp as the article from which the data came. Further, most client actions will be interested either in the article text or in the extracted information about article links but probably not in both at the same time. So, splitting out the to and from column families into a separate table makes sense.

Constructing the Scanner

With the links table created, we're ready to implement a script that will scan all the rows of the wiki table. Then, for each row, retrieve the wikitext and parse out the links. Finally, for each link found, create incoming and outgoing link table records. The bulk of this script should be pretty familiar to you by now. Most of the pieces are recycled, and we'll discuss the few novel bits.

hbase/generate_wiki_links.rb
```ruby
import 'org.apache.hadoop.hbase.client.HTable'
import 'org.apache.hadoop.hbase.client.Put'
import 'org.apache.hadoop.hbase.client.Scan'
import 'org.apache.hadoop.hbase.util.Bytes'

def jbytes( *args )
  return args.map { |arg| arg.to_s.to_java_bytes }
end

wiki_table = HTable.new( @hbase.configuration, 'wiki' )
links_table = HTable.new( @hbase.configuration, 'links' )
links_table.setAutoFlush( false )
```

① `scanner = wiki_table.getScanner( Scan.new )`

```ruby
linkpattern = /\[\[([^\[\]\|\:\#][^\[\]\|:]*)(?:\|([^\[\]\|]+))?\]\]/
count = 0
```

while `(result = scanner.next())`

② `title = Bytes.toString( result.getRow() )`
`text = Bytes.toString( result.getValue( *jbytes( 'text', '' ) ) )`
`if text`

`put_to = nil`
③ `text.scan(linkpattern) do |target, label|`
`unless put_to`
`put_to = Put.new( *jbytes( title ) )`
`put_to.setWriteToWAL( false )`
`end`

`target.strip!`
`target.capitalize!`

`label = '' unless label`
`label.strip!`

`put_to.add( *jbytes( "to", target, label ) )`
`put_from = Put.new( *jbytes( target ) )`
`put_from.add( *jbytes( "from", title, label ) )`
`put_from.setWriteToWAL( false )`
④ `links_table.put( put_from )`
`end`
⑤ `links_table.put( put_to ) if put_to`
`links_table.flushCommits()`

```
    end
    count += 1
    puts "#{count} pages processed (#{title})" if count % 500 == 0
end
links_table.flushCommits()
exit
```

① First, we grab a Scan object, which we'll use to scan through the wiki table.

② Extracting row and column data requires some byte wrangling but generally isn't too bad either.

③ Each time the linkpattern appears in the page text, we extract the target article and text of the link and then use those values to add to our Put instances.

④ Finally, we tell the table to execute our accumulated Put operations. It's
⑤ possible (though unlikely) for an article to contain no links at all, which is the reason for the if put_to clause.

Using setWriteToWAL(false) for these puts is a judgment call. Since this exercise is for educational purposes and since we could simply rerun the script if anything went wrong, we'll take the speed bonus and accept our fate should the node fail.

Running the Script

If you're ready to throw caution to the wind with reckless abandon, kick off the script.

```
${HBASE_HOME}/bin/hbase shell generate_wiki_links.rb
```

It should produce output like this:

```
500 pages processed (10 petametres)
1000 pages processed (1259)
1500 pages processed (1471 BC)
2000 pages processed (1683)
...
```

As with the previous script, you can let it run as long as you like, even to completion. If you want to stop it, press CTRL+C.

You can monitor the disk usage of the script using du as we've done before. You'll see new entries for the links table we just created, and the size counts will increase as the script runs.

Joe asks:

Couldn't We Have Done This with Mapreduce?

In the introduction, we explained that our examples would be in (J)Ruby and Java-Script. JRuby does not play nice with Hadoop, but if you wanted to use mapreduce using Java, you'd have written this scanner code as a mapreduce job and sent it off to Hadoop.

Generally speaking, tasks like this are ideally suited for a mapreduce implementation. There's a bulk of input in a regular format to be handled by a mapper (scanning an HBase table) and a bulk of output operations to be executed in batches by a reducer (writing rows out to an HBase table).

The Hadoop architecture expects Job instances to be written in Java and wholly encapsulated (including all dependencies) into a jar file that can be sent out to all the nodes of the cluster. Newer versions of JRuby can extend Java classes, but the version that ships with HBase can't.

There are a few open source projects that provide a bridge for running JRuby on Hadoop but nothing yet that specifically works well with HBase. There are rumors that in the future the HBase infrastructure will contain abstractions to make JRuby MR (mapreduce) jobs possible. So, there's hope for the future.

Examining the Output

We just created a scanner programmatically to perform a sophisticated task. Now we'll use the shell's scan command to simply dump part of a table's contents to the console. For each link the script finds in a text: blob, it will indiscriminately create both to and from entries in the links table. To see the kinds of links being created, head over to the shell and scan the table.

```
hbase> scan 'links', STARTROW => "Admiral Ackbar", ENDROW => "It's a Trap!"
```

You should get a whole bunch of output. Of course, you can use the get command to see the links for just a single article.

```
hbase> get 'links', 'Star Wars'
COLUMN CELL
 ...
 links:from:Admiral Ackbar          timestamp=1300415922636, value=
 links:from:Adventure               timestamp=1300415927098, value=
 links:from:Alamogordo, New Mexico  timestamp=1300415953549, value=
 links:to:"weird al" yankovic       timestamp=1300419602350, value=
 links:to:20th century fox          timestamp=1300419602350, value=

 links:to:3-d film                  timestamp=1300419602350, value=
 links:to:Aayla secura              timestamp=1300419602350, value=
 ...
```

In the wiki table, the rows are very regular with respect to columns. As you recall, each row has text:, revision:author, and revision:comment columns. The links table has no such regularity. Each row may have one column or hundreds. And the variety of column names is as diverse as the row keys themselves (titles of Wikipedia articles). That's OK! HBase is a so-called sparse data store for exactly this reason.

To find out just how many rows are now in your table, you can use the count command.

```
hbase> count 'wiki', INTERVAL => 100000, CACHE => 10000
Current count: 100000, row: Alexander wilson (vauxhall)
Current count: 200000, row: Bachelor of liberal studies
Current count: 300000, row: Brian donlevy
...
Current count: 2000000, row: Thomas Hobbes
Current count: 2100000, row: Vardousia
Current count: 2200000, row: Wörrstadt (verbandsgemeinde)
2256081 row(s) in 173.8120 seconds
```

Because of its distributed architecture, HBase doesn't immediately know how many rows are in each table. To find out, it has to count them (by performing a table scan). Fortunately, HBase's region-based storage architecture lends itself to fast distributed scanning. So, even if the operation at hand requires a table scan, we don't have to worry quite as much as we would with other databases.

Day 2 Wrap-Up

Whew, that was a pretty big day! We learned how to write an import script for HBase that parses data out of a stream of XML. Then we used those techniques to stream Wikipedia dumps directly into our wiki table.

We learned more of the HBase API, including some client-controllable performance levers such as setAutoFlush(), flushCommits(), and setWriteToWAL(). Along those lines, we discussed some HBase architectural features such as disaster recovery, provided via the write-ahead log.

Speaking of architecture, we discovered table regions and how HBase divvies up responsibility for them among the region servers in the cluster. We scanned the .META. and -ROOT- tables to get a feel for HBase internals.

Finally, we discussed some of the performance implications of HBase's sparse design. In so doing, we touched on some community best practices regarding the use of columns, families, and tables.

Day 2 Homework

Find

1. Find a discussion or article describing the pros and cons of compression in HBase.

2. Find an article explaining how Bloom filters work in general and how they benefit HBase.

3. Aside from which algorithm to use, what other column family options relate to compression?

4. How does the type of data and expected usage patterns inform column family compression options?

Do

Expanding on the idea of data import, let's build a database containing nutrition facts.

Download the MyPyramid Raw Food Data set from Data.gov.[5] Extract the zipped contents to find Food_Display_Table.xml.

This data consists of many pairs of <Food_Display_Row> tags. Inside these, each row has a <Food_Code> (integer value), <Display_Name> (string), and other facts about the food in appropriately named tags.

1. Create a new table called foods with a single column family to store the facts. What should you use for the row key? What column family options make sense for this data?

2. Create a new JRuby script for importing the food data. Use the SAX parsing style we used earlier for the Wikipedia import script and tailor it for the food data.

3. Pipe the food data into your import script on the command line to populate the table.

4. Finally, using the HBase shell, query the foods table for information about your favorite foods.

---

5.   http://explore.data.gov/Health-and-Nutrition/MyPyramid-Food-Raw-Data/b978-7txq

4.4 Day 3: Taking It to the Cloud

In Days 1 and 2, we got a lot of hands-on experience using HBase in stand-alone mode. Our experimentation so far has focused on accessing a single local server. In reality, if you choose to use HBase, you'll want to have a good sized cluster in order to realize the performance benefits of its distributed architecture.

Here in Day 3, we'll turn our attention toward operating and interacting with a remote HBase cluster. First we'll develop a client application in Ruby and connect to our local server using a binary protocol called Thrift. Then we'll bring up a multinode cluster with a cloud service provider—Amazon EC2—using a cluster management technology called Apache Whirr.

Developing a Thrifty HBase Application

So far, we've been using the HBase shell, but HBase supports a number of protocols for client connectivity. The following is a full list:

Name	Connection Method	Production Ready?
Shell	Direct	Yes
Java API	Direct	Yes
Thrift	Binary protocol	Yes
REST	HTTP	Yes
Avro	Binary protocol	No (still experimental)

In the previous table, the connection method describes whether the protocol makes Java calls directly, shuttles data over HTTP, or moves data using a compact binary format. All of them are production-grade, except for Avro, which is relatively new and should be treated as experimental.

Of all these options, Thrift is probably the most popular for developing client applications. A mature binary protocol with little overhead, Thrift was originally developed and open sourced by Facebook, later to become an Apache Incubator project. Let's get your machine ready to connect with Thrift.

Installing Thrift

Like many things in the database realm, working with Thrift requires a little setup. To connect to our HBase server via Thrift, we'll need to do the following:

1. Have HBase run the Thrift service.
2. Install the Thrift command-line tool.
3. Install libraries for your chosen client language.

4. Generate HBase model files for your language.

5. Create and run a client application.

We'll start by running the Thrift service, which is pretty easy. Start the daemon from the command line like this:

```
${HBASE_HOME}/bin/hbase-daemon.sh start thrift -b 127.0.0.1
```

Next, you'll need to install the thrift command-line tool. The steps for this depend greatly on your particular environment and generally require compiling binaries. To test whether you have this installed correctly, call it on the command line with the -version flag. You should see something like this:

```
$ thrift -version
Thrift version 0.6.0
```

For the client language, we'll use Ruby, although the steps are similar for other languages. Install the Thrift Ruby gem on the command line like so:

```
$ gem install thrift
```

To check whether the gem is installed correctly, we can run this Ruby one-liner:

```
$ ruby -e "require 'thrift'"
```

If you see no output on the command line, that's good! An error message stating "no such file to load" means you should stop here and troubleshoot before moving on.

Generate the Models

Next, we'll generate the language-specific HBase model files. These model files will be the glue that connects our specific HBase version with the particular Thrift version you have installed, so they have to be generated (rather than coming premade).

First, locate the Hbase.thrift file under the ${HBASE_HOME}/src directory. The path should be something like this:

```
${HBASE_HOME}/src/main/resources/org/apache/hadoop/hbase/thrift/Hbase.thrift
```

With the path identified, generate the model files with the following command, replacing your path as indicated:

```
$ thrift --gen rb <path_to_Hbase.thrift>
```

This will create a new folder called gen-rb, which contains the following model files:

- hbase_constants.rb
- hbase.rb
- hbase_types.rb

We'll be using these files next as we build a simple client application.

Building a Client Application

Our program will connect to HBase over Thrift and then list any tables it finds along with their column families. These would be the first steps toward building an administrative interface for HBase. Unlike our previous examples, this script is meant to be run by good old normal Ruby, not JRuby. It could be suitable for inclusion in a Ruby-based web application, for example.

Key this into a new text file (we called ours thrift_example.rb):

hbase/thrift_example.rb
```
$:.push('./gen-rb')
require 'thrift'
require 'hbase'

socket = Thrift::Socket.new( 'localhost', 9090 )
transport = Thrift::BufferedTransport.new( socket )
protocol = Thrift::BinaryProtocol.new( transport )
client = Apache::Hadoop::Hbase::Thrift::Hbase::Client.new( protocol )

transport.open()

client.getTableNames().sort.each do |table|
  puts "#{table}"
  client.getColumnDescriptors( table ).each do |col, desc|
    puts "  #{desc.name}"
    puts "    maxVersions: #{desc.maxVersions}"
    puts "    compression: #{desc.compression}"
    puts "    bloomFilterType: #{desc.bloomFilterType}"
  end
end

transport.close()
```

In the previous code, the first thing we do is make sure Ruby can find the model files by adding gen-rb to the path and including thrift and hbase. After that, we create a connection to the Thrift server and wire it up to an HBase client instance. The client object will be our means for communicating with HBase.

After opening the transport, we iterate over the tables brought back by getTable-Names(). For each table, we iterate over the list of column families returned by getColumnDescriptors() and output some properties to standard output.

Now, let's run the program on the command line. Your output should look similar since we're connecting to the local HBase server we started with earlier.

```
$> ruby thrift_example.rb
links
  from:
    maxVersions: 1
    compression: NONE
    bloomFilterType: ROWCOL
  to:
    maxVersions: 1
    compression: NONE
    bloomFilterType: ROWCOL
wiki
  revision:
    maxVersions: 2147483647
    compression: NONE
    bloomFilterType: NONE
  text:
    maxVersions: 2147483647
    compression: GZ
    bloomFilterType: ROW
```

You'll find that the Thrift API for HBase has most of the same functionality as the Java API we used previously, but many of the concepts are expressed differently. For example, instead of creating a Put instance, in Thrift you create a Mutation to update a single column or a BatchMutation to update several columns in one transaction.

The Hbase.thrift file we used earlier to generate the model files—see *Generate the Models*, on page 123—has a lot of good inline documentation to describe the structures and methods available to you. Check it out!

Introducing Whirr

Setting up a functioning cluster using a cloud service used to be *a lot* of work. Fortunately, Whirr is changing all that. Currently in the Apache Incubator program, Whirr provides tools for launching, connecting to, and destroying clusters of virtual machines. It supports popular services like Amazon's Elastic Compute Cloud (EC2) and RackSpace's Cloud Servers. Whirr currently supports setting up Hadoop, HBase, Cassandra, Voldemort, and ZooKeeper clusters, with support for more technologies like MongoDB and ElasticSearch on the way.

Though service providers like Amazon often supply some means of persisting data after virtual machines have been terminated, we won't be using them. For our purposes, it will suffice to have temporary clusters that lose all data upon termination. If you decide to use HBase in a production capacity later, you may want to set up persistent storage. If so, it's worth considering whether dedicated hardware would better suit your needs. Dynamic services like EC2 are great for horsepower on-the-fly, but you'll generally get more bang for the buck out of a cluster of dedicated physical or virtual machines.

Getting Set Up with EC2

Before you use Whirr to power up a cluster, you'll need to have an account with a supported cloud service provider. In this chapter, we'll describe how to use Amazon's EC2, but you're welcome to use another provider of your choice.

If you don't have an Amazon account already, head over to Amazon's Web Services (AWS) portal and make one.[6] Log in, and then enable EC2 for your account if it isn't activated already.[7] Finally, open the EC2 AWS console page under Accounts Amazon EC2.[8] It should look something like Figure 17, *Amazon EC2 console showing no instances*, on page 127.

You'll need your AWS credentials in order to start up EC2 nodes. Head back to the AWS main page and then choose Account→Security Credentials. Scroll down to the section called Access Credentials, and make a note of your Access Key ID. Under Secret Access Key, click Show, and make a note of this value as well. Respectively, we'll refer to these keys as AWS_ACCESS_KEY_ID and AWS_SECRET_ACCESS_KEY later when we configure Whirr.

Preparing Whirr

With your EC2 credentials in hand, let's get Whirr. Go to the Apache Whirr site[9] and download the latest version. Unzip the downloaded file, and then open a command prompt in this directory. We can test that Whirr is ready to roll by executing the version command.

```
$ bin/whirr version
Apache Whirr 0.6.0-incubating
```

Next, we'll create some passwordless SSH keys for Whirr to use when launching instances (virtual machines).

```
$ mkdir keys
$ ssh-keygen -t rsa -P '' -f keys/id_rsa
```

---

6. http://aws.amazon.com/
7. http://aws.amazon.com/ec2/
8. https://console.aws.amazon.com/ec2/#s=Instances
9. http://incubator.apache.org/whirr/

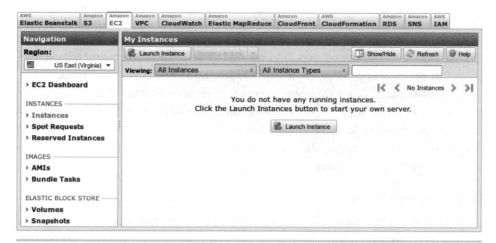

Figure 17—Amazon EC2 console showing no instances

This will create a directory called keys and add to it an id_rsa file and an id_rsa.pub file. With these details out of the way, it's time to start configuring our cluster.

Configuring the Cluster

To specify details about a cluster, we'll supply Whirr with a .properties file containing the relevant settings. Create a file in the Whirr directory called hbase.properties with the following contents (inserting your AWS_ACCESS_KEY_ID and AWS_SECRET_ACCESS_KEY as indicated):

hbase/hbase.properties
```
# service provider
whirr.provider=aws-ec2
whirr.identity=your AWS_ACCESS_KEY_ID here
whirr.credential=your AWS_SECRET_ACCESS_KEY here

# ssh credentials
whirr.private-key-file=keys/id_rsa
whirr.public-key-file=keys/id_rsa.pub

# cluster configuration
whirr.cluster-name=myhbasecluster
whirr.instance-templates=\
  1 zookeeper+hadoop-namenode+hadoop-jobtracker+hbase-master,\
  5 hadoop-datanode+hadoop-tasktracker+hbase-regionserver

# HBase and Hadoop version configuration
whirr.hbase.tarball.url=\
  http://apache.cu.be/hbase/hbase-0.90.3/hbase-0.90.3.tar.gz
whirr.hadoop.tarball.url=\
  http://archive.cloudera.com/cdh/3/hadoop-0.20.2-cdh3u1.tar.gz
```

The first two sections identify the service provider and all relevant credentials —largely boilerplate—while the latter two sections are specific to the HBase cluster that we're going to create. The whirr.cluster-name is unimportant unless you plan on running more than one cluster simultaneously, in which case they should each have different names. The whirr.instance-templates property contains a comma-separated list describing which roles the nodes will play and how many of each there should be. In our case, we want one master and five region servers. Finally, the whirr.hbase.tarball.url forces Whirr to use the same version of HBase we've been using so far.

Launching the Cluster

With all the configuration details saved to hbase.properties, it's time to launch the cluster. On the command line, in the Whirr directory, execute the launch-cluster command, providing it with the properties file we just made.

```
$ bin/whirr launch-cluster --config hbase.properties
```

This will produce a lot of output and may take a while. You can monitor the progress of the launch by returning to the AWS EC2 console. It should look something like Figure 18, *Amazon EC2 console showing HBase instances starting up*, on page 129.

More information about the launch status is available in the whirr.log file in the Whirr directory.

Connecting to the Cluster

Only secure traffic is allowed to the cluster by default, so to connect to HBase, we'll need to open an SSH session. First, we'll need to know the name of a server in the cluster to connect to. In your user's home directory, Whirr created a directory called .whirr/myhbasecluster. In here, you'll find a tab-delimited file called instances that lists all of the cluster's running Amazon instances. The third column contains the publicly addressable domain names of the servers. Take the first one and plug it into this command:

```
$ ssh -i keys/id_rsa ${USER}@<SERVER_NAME>
```

Once connected, start up the HBase shell:

```
$ /usr/local/hbase-0.90.3/bin/hbase shell
```

Once the shell has started up, you can check on the health of the cluster with the status command.

```
hbase> status
6 servers, 0 dead, 2.0000 average load
```

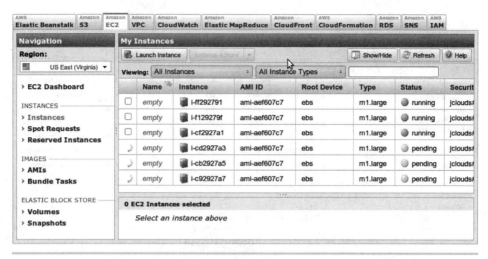

Figure 18—Amazon EC2 console showing HBase instances starting up

From here, you can perform all the same operations we did on Days 1 and 2 such as creating tables and inserting data. Connecting the sample Thrift-based client application to the cluster is left as an exercise in the homework.

Of course, one more thing is worth talking about before we finish out the day: destroying a cluster.

Destroying the Cluster

When you're done with your remote HBase EC2 cluster, use Whirr's destroy-cluster command to shut it down. Note that you will lose any and all data that had been inserted into the cluster when you do so, since we have not configured the instances to use persistent storage.

At the command prompt, in the Whirr directory, run the following:

```
$ bin/whirr destroy-cluster --config hbase.properties
Destroying myhbasecluster cluster
Cluster myhbasecluster destroyed
```

This should take only a little while. Confirm that the instances are shutting down in the AWS console, which should resemble Figure 19, *Amazon EC2 console showing HBase instances shutting down*, on page 130.

If anything goes wrong when shutting these things down, remember that you can still terminate them directly using the AWS console.

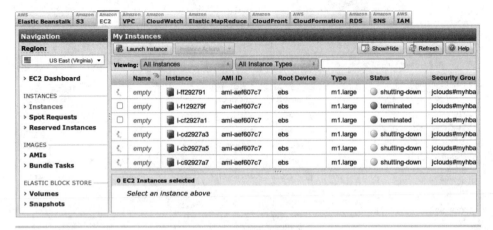

Figure 19—Amazon EC2 console showing HBase instances shutting down

Day 3 Wrap-Up

Today we stepped outside the HBase shell to look at other connection options, including a binary protocol called Thrift. We developed a Thrifty client application, and then we created and administrated a remote cluster in Amazon EC2 using Apache Whirr. Coming up in the homework, you'll string these two things together, querying your remote EC2 cluster from your locally running Thrift app.

Day 3 Homework

In today's homework, you'll connect your local Thrift application to a remotely running HBase cluster. To do this, you'll need to open your cluster to insecure incoming TCP connections. If this were a production environment, a better first step would be to create a secure channel for Thrift—for example by setting up a virtual private network (VPN) with endpoints inside EC2 and our principal network. Such a setup is outside the scope of this book; suffice it to say that we strongly recommend securing your traffic when it matters to do so.

Do

1. With your EC2 cluster running, open an SSH session to a node, start the hbase shell, and then create a table with at least one column family.

2. In the same SSH session, start the Thrift service.

```
$ sudo /usr/local/hbase-0.90.3/bin/hbase-daemon.sh start thrift -b 0.0.0.0
```

3. Use the Amazon EC2 web interface console to open TCP port 9090 in the security group for your cluster (Network & Security > Security Groups > Inbound > Create a new rule).

4. Modify the simple Thrift-based Ruby client app you developed to hit the EC2 node running Thrift instead of localhost. Run the program and confirm that it displays the correct information about your newly created table.

4.5 Wrap-Up

HBase is a juxtaposition of simplicity and complexity. The data storage model is pretty straightforward, with a few built-in schema constraints. It doesn't help, though, that many terms are overloaded with baggage from the relational world (for example, words like *table* and *column*). Most of HBase schema design is deciding on the performance characteristics of your tables and columns.

HBase's Strengths

Noteworthy features of HBase include a robust scale-out architecture and built-in versioning and compression capabilities. HBase's built-in versioning capability can be a compelling feature for certain use cases. Keeping the version history of wiki pages is a crucial feature for policing and maintenance, for instance. By choosing HBase, we don't have to take any special steps to implement page history—we get it for free.

On the performance front, HBase is meant to scale out. If you have huge amounts of data, measured in many gigabytes or terabytes, HBase may be for you. HBase is rack-aware, replicating data within and between datacenter racks so that node failures can be handled gracefully and quickly.

The HBase community is pretty awesome. There's almost always somebody on the IRC channel[10] or mailing lists[11] ready to help with questions and get you pointed in the right direction. Although a number of high-profile companies use HBase for their projects, there is no corporate HBase service provider. This means the people of the HBase community do it for the love of the project and the common good.

---

10. irc://irc.freenode.net/#hbase
11. http://hbase.apache.org/mail-lists.html

HBase's Weaknesses

Although HBase is designed to scale out, it doesn't scale down. The HBase community seems to agree that five nodes is the minimum number you'll want to use. Because it's designed to be big, it can also be harder to administrate. Solving small problems isn't what HBase is about, and nonexpert documentation is tough to come by, which steepens the learning curve.

Additionally, HBase is almost never deployed alone. Rather, it's part of an ecosystem of scale-ready pieces. These include Hadoop (an implementation of Google's MapReduce), the Hadoop distributed file system (HDFS), and Zookeeper (a headless service that aids internode coordination). This ecosystem is both a strength and a weakness; it simultaneously affords a great deal of architectural sturdiness but also encumbers the administrator with the burden of maintaining it.

One noteworthy characteristic of HBase is that it doesn't offer any sorting or indexing capabilities aside from the row keys. Rows are kept in sorted order by their row keys, but no such sorting is done on any other field, such as column names and values. So, if you want to find rows by something other than their key, you need to scan the table or maintain your own index.

Another missing concept is datatypes. All field values in HBase are treated as uninterpreted arrays of bytes. There is no distinction between, say, an integer value, a string, and a date. They're all bytes to HBase, so it's up to your application to interpret the bytes.

HBase on CAP

With respect to CAP, HBase is decidedly CP. HBase makes strong consistency guarantees. If a client succeeds in writing a value, other clients will receive the updated value on the next request. Some databases, like Riak, allow you to tweak the CAP equation on a per-operation basis. Not so with HBase. In the face of reasonable amounts of partitioning—for example, a node failing— HBase will remain available, shunting the responsibility off to other nodes in the cluster. However, in the pathological example, where only one node is left alive, HBase has no choice but to refuse requests.

The CAP discussion gets a little more complex when you introduce cluster-to-cluster replication, an advanced feature we didn't cover in this chapter. A typical multicluster setup could have clusters separated geographically by some distance. In this case, for a given column family, one cluster is the system of record, while the other clusters merely provide access to the replicated data. This system is *eventually consistent* since the replication clusters will serve up the most recent values they're aware of, which may not be the most recent values in the master cluster.

Parting Thoughts

As one of the first nonrelational databases we had ever encountered, HBase was quite a challenge for us. The terminology can be deceptively reassuring, and the installation and configuration are not for the faint of heart. On the plus side, some of the features HBase offers, such as versioning and compression, are quite unique. These aspects can make HBase quite appealing for solving certain problems. And of course, it scales out to many nodes of commodity hardware quite well. All in all, HBase—like a nail gun—is a pretty big tool, so watch your thumbs.

## CHAPTER 5

MongoDB

MongoDB is in many ways like a power drill. Your ability to complete a task is framed largely by the components you choose to use (from drill bits of varying size to sander adapters). MongoDB's strength lies in versatility, power, ease of use, and ability to handle jobs both large and small. Although it's a much newer invention than the hammer, it is increasingly a tool builders reach for quite often.

First publicly released in 2009, MongoDB is a rising star in the NoSQL world. It was designed as a scalable database—the name Mongo comes from "hu*mongo*us"—with performance and easy data access as core design goals. It is a document database, which allows data to persist in a nested state, and importantly, it can query that nested data in an ad hoc fashion. It enforces no schema (similar to Riak but unlike Postgres), so documents can optionally contain fields or types that no other document in the collection contains.

But don't think that MongoDB's flexibility makes it a toy. There are some huge production MongoDB (often just called *Mongo*) deployments out there, like Foursquare, bit.ly, and CERN, for collecting Large Hadron Collider data.

5.1 Hu(mongo)us

Mongo hits a sweet spot between the powerful queryability of a relational database and the distributed nature of other datastores like Riak or HBase. Project founder Dwight Merriman has said that MongoDB is the database he wishes he'd had at DoubleClick, where as the CTO he had to house large-scale data while still being able to satisfy ad hoc queries.

Mongo is a JSON document database (though technically data is stored in a binary form of JSON known as BSON). A Mongo document can be likened to a relational table row without a schema, whose values can nest to an arbitrary

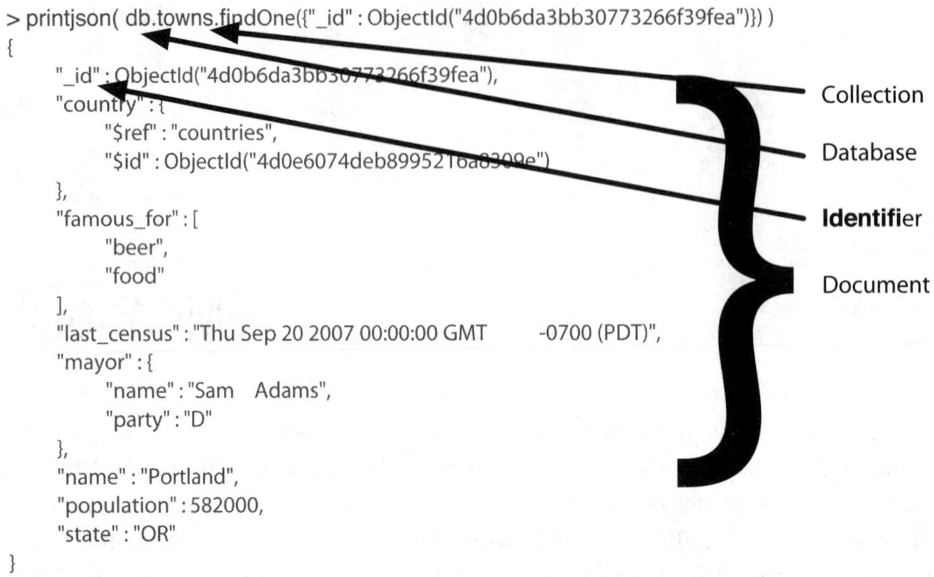

```
> printjson( db.towns.findOne({"_id" : ObjectId("4d0b6da3bb30773266f39fea")}) )
{
    "_id" : ObjectId("4d0b6da3bb30773266f39fea"),
    "country" : {
        "$ref" : "countries",
        "$id" : ObjectId("4d0e6074deb8995216a8309e")
    },
    "famous_for" : [
        "beer",
        "food"
    ],
    "last_census" : "Thu Sep 20 2007 00:00:00 GMT     -0700 (PDT)",
    "mayor" : {
        "name" : "Sam   Adams",
        "party" : "D"
    },
    "name" : "Portland",
    "population" : 582000,
    "state" : "OR"
}
```

Collection

Database

Identifier

Document

Figure 20—A Mongo document printed as JSON

depth. To get an idea of what a JSON document is, check out Figure 20, *A Mongo document printed as JSON*, on page 136.

Mongo is an excellent choice for an ever-growing class of web projects with large-scale data storage requirements but very little budget to buy big-iron hardware. Thanks to its lack of structured schema, Mongo can grow and change along with your data model. If you're in a web startup with dreams of enormity or are already large with the need to scale servers horizontally, consider MongoDB.

5.2   Day 1: CRUD and Nesting

We'll spend today working on some CRUD operations and finish up with performing nested queries in MongoDB. As usual, we won't walk you through the installation steps, but if you visit the Mongo website,[1] you can download a build for your OS or find instructions on how to build from source. If you have OS X, we recommend installing via Homebrew (brew install mongodb). If you use some Debian/Ubuntu variant, try Mongodb.org's own apt-get package.

---

1.   http://www.mongodb.org/downloads

Eric says:
On the Fence

I was on the fence about using a document datastore before making the switch in my own production code. Coming from the relational database world, I found Mongo to be an easy move with its ad hoc queries. And its ability to scale out mirrored my own web-scale dreams. But beyond the structure, I trusted the development team. They readily admitted that Mongo wasn't perfect, but their clear plans (and general adherence to those plans) were based on general web infrastructure use cases, rather than idyllic debates on scalability and replication. This pragmatic focus on usability should shine as you use MongoDB. A trade-off of this evolutionary behavior is that there are several paths to performing any given function in Mongo.

To prevent typos, Mongo requires you to first create the directory where mongod will store its data. A common location is /data/db. Ensure the user you run the server under has permission to read and write to this directory. If it's not already running, you can fire up the Mongo service by running mongod.

Command-Line Fun

To create a new database named book, first run this command in your terminal. It will connect to the MySQL-inspired command-line interface.

```
$ mongo book
```

Typing help in the console is a good start. We're currently in the book database, but you can view others via show dbs and switch databases with the use command.

Creating a collection (similar to a *bucket* in Riak nomenclature) in Mongo is as easy as adding an initial record to the collection. Since Mongo is schema-less, there is no need to define anything up front; merely using it is enough. What's more, our book database doesn't really exist until we first add values into it. The following code creates/inserts a towns collection:

```
> db.towns.insert({
  name: "New York",
  population: 22200000,
  last_census: ISODate("2009-07-31"),
  famous_for: [ "statue of liberty", "food" ],
  mayor : {
    name : "Michael Bloomberg",
    party : "I"
  }
})
```

In the previous section, we said documents were JSON (well, really BSON), so we add new documents in JSON format, where brackets like {...} denote an object (aka a hashtable or Map) with keyed values and where brackets like [...] denote an array. You can nest these values to any depth.

With the show collections command, you can verify the collection now exists.

```
> show collections

system.indexes
towns
```

We just created towns, whereas system.indexes always exists. We can list the contents of a collection via find(). We formatted the output here for readability, but yours may just output as a single wrapped line.

```
> db.towns.find()

{
  "_id" : ObjectId("4d0ad975bb30773266f39fe3"),
  "name" : "New York",
  "population": 22200000,
  "last_census": "Fri Jul 31 2009 00:00:00 GMT-0700 (PDT)",
  "famous_for" : [ "statue of liberty", "food" ],
  "mayor" : { "name" : "Michael Bloomberg", "party" : "I" }
}
```

Unlike a relational database, Mongo does not support server-side joins. A single JavaScript call will retrieve a document *and* all of its nested content, free of charge.

You may have noticed that the JSON output of your newly inserted town contains an _id field of ObjectId. This is akin to SERIAL incrementing a numeric primary key in PostgreSQL. The ObjectId is always 12 bytes, composed of a timestamp, client machine ID, client process ID, and a 3-byte incremented counter. Bytes are laid out as depicted in Figure 21, *An ObjectId layout example*, on page 139.

What's great about this autonumbering scheme is that each process on every machine can handle its own ID generation without colliding with other mongod instances. This design choice gives a hint of Mongo's distributed nature.

JavaScript

Mongo's native tongue is JavaScript, be it as complex as mapreduce queries or as simple as asking for help.

```
> db.help()
> db.towns.help()
```

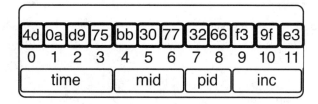

Figure 21—An ObjectId layout example

These commands will list available functions related to the given object. db is a JavaScript object that contains information about the current database. db.x is a JavaScript object representing a collection (named x). Commands are just JavaScript functions.

```
> typeof db
object
> typeof db.towns
object
> typeof db.towns.insert
function
```

If you want to inspect the source code for a function, call it without parameters or parentheses (think more Python than Ruby).

```
db.towns.insert
function (obj, _allow_dot) {
    if (!obj) {
        throw "no object passed to insert!";
    }
    if (!_allow_dot) {
        this._validateForStorage(obj);
    }
    if (typeof obj._id == "undefined") {
        var tmp = obj;
        obj = {_id:new ObjectId};
        for (var key in tmp) {
            obj[key] = tmp[key];
        }
    }
    this._mongo.insert(this._fullName, obj);
    this._lastID = obj._id;
}
```

Let's populate a few more documents into our towns collection by creating our own JavaScript function.

```
mongo/insert_city.js
function insertCity(
  name, population, last_census,
  famous_for, mayor_info
) {
  db.towns.insert({
    name:name,
    population:population,
    last_census: ISODate(last_census),
    famous_for:famous_for,
    mayor : mayor_info
  });
}
```

You can just paste the code into the shell. Then we can call it.

```
insertCity("Punxsutawney", 6200, '2008-31-01',
  ["phil the groundhog"], { name : "Jim Wehrle" }
)

insertCity("Portland", 582000, '2007-20-09',
  ["beer", "food"], { name : "Sam Adams", party : "D" }
)
```

We should now have three towns in our collection, which you can confirm by calling db.towns.find() as before.

Reading: More Fun in Mongo

Earlier we called the find() function without params to get all documents. To access a specific one, you only need to set an _id property. _id is of type ObjectId, and so to query, you must convert a string by wrapping it in an ObjectId(str) function.

```
db.towns.find({ "_id" : ObjectId("4d0ada1fbb30773266f39fe4") })

{
  "_id" : ObjectId("4d0ada1fbb30773266f39fe4"),
  "name" : "Punxsutawney",
  "population" : 6200,
  "last_census" : "Thu Jan 31 2008 00:00:00 GMT-0800 (PST)",
  "famous_for" : [ "phil the groundhog" ],
  "mayor" : { "name" : "Jim Wehrle" }
}
```

The find() function also accepts an optional second parameter: a fields object we can use to filter which fields are retrieved. If we want only the town name (along with _id), pass in name with a value resolving to 1 (or true).

```
db.towns.find({ _id : ObjectId("4d0ada1fbb30773266f39fe4") }, { name : 1 })

{
  "_id" : ObjectId("4d0ada1fbb30773266f39fe4"),
  "name" : "Punxsutawney"
}
```

To retrieve all fields *except* name, set name to 0 (or false or null).

```
db.towns.find({ _id : ObjectId("4d0ada1fbb30773266f39fe4") }, { name : 0 })

{
  "_id" : ObjectId("4d0ada1fbb30773266f39fe4"),
  "population" : 6200,
  "last_census" : "Thu Jan 31 2008 00:00:00 GMT-0800 (PST)",
  "famous_for" : [ "phil the groundhog" ]
}
```

Like PostgreSQL, in Mongo you can construct ad hoc queries by field values, ranges, or a combination of criteria. To find all towns that begin with the letter *P* and have a population less than 10,000, you can use a Perl-compatible regular expression (PCRE)[2] and a range operator.

```
db.towns.find(
  { name : /^P/, population : { $lt : 10000 } },
  { name : 1, population : 1 }
)
{ "name" : "Punxsutawney", "population" : 6200 }
```

Conditional operators in Mongo follow the format of field : { $op : value }, where $op is an operation like $ne (not equal to). You may want a terser syntax, like field < value. But this is JavaScript code, not a domain-specific query language, so queries must comply with JavaScript syntax rules (later today we'll see how to use the shorter syntax in a certain case, but we'll skip that for now).

The good news about the query language being JavaScript is you can construct operations as you would objects. Here, we build criteria where the population must be between 10,000 and 1 million people.

```
var population_range = {}
population_range['$lt'] = 1000000
population_range['$gt'] = 10000
db.towns.find(
  { name : /^P/, population : population_range },
  { name: 1 }
)

{ "_id" : ObjectId("4d0ada87bb30773266f39fe5"), "name" : "Portland" }
```

---

2. http://www.pcre.org/

We are not limited to number ranges but can also retrieve date ranges. We can find all names with a *last_census* less than or equal to January 31, 2008, like this:

```
db.towns.find(
  { last_census : { $lte : ISODate('2008-31-01') } },
  { _id : 0, name: 1 }
)

{ "name" : "Punxsutawney" }
{ "name" : "Portland" }
```

Notice how we suppressed the _id field in the output explicitly by setting it to 0.

Digging Deep

Mongo loves nested array data. You can query by matching exact values...

```
db.towns.find(
  { famous_for : 'food' },
  { _id : 0, name : 1, famous_for : 1 }
)

{ "name" : "New York", "famous_for" : [ "statue of liberty", "food" ] }
{ "name" : "Portland", "famous_for" : [ "beer", "food" ] }
```

...as well as matching partial values...

```
db.towns.find(
  { famous_for : /statue/ },
  { _id : 0, name : 1, famous_for : 1 }
)

{ "name" : "New York", "famous_for" : [ "statue of liberty", "food" ] }
```

...or query by all matching values...

```
db.towns.find(
  { famous_for : { $all : ['food', 'beer'] } },
  { _id : 0, name:1, famous_for:1 }
)

{ "name" : "Portland", "famous_for" : [ "beer", "food" ] }
```

...or the lack of matching values:

```
db.towns.find(
  { famous_for : { $nin : ['food', 'beer'] } },
  { _id : 0, name : 1, famous_for : 1 }
)

{ "name" : "Punxsutawney", "famous_for" : [ "phil the groundhog" ] }
```

But the true power of Mongo stems from its ability to dig down into a document and return the results of deeply nested subdocuments. To query a subdocument, your field name is a string separating nested layers with a dot. For instance, you can find towns with independent mayors...

```
db.towns.find(
  { 'mayor.party' : 'I' },
  { _id : 0, name : 1, mayor : 1 }
)

{
  "name" : "New York",
  "mayor" : {
    "name" : "Michael Bloomberg",
    "party" : "I"
  }
}
```

...or those with mayors who don't have a party:

```
db.towns.find(
  { 'mayor.party' : { $exists : false } },
  { _id : 0, name : 1, mayor : 1 }
)

{ "name" : "Punxsutawney", "mayor" : { "name" : "Jim Wehrle" } }
```

The previous queries are great if you want to find documents with a single matching field, but what if we need to match several fields of a subdocument?

elemMatch

We'll round out our dig with the $elemMatch directive. Let's create another collection that stores countries. This time we'll override each _id to be a string of our choosing.

```
db.countries.insert({
  _id : "us",
  name : "United States",
  exports : {
    foods : [
      { name : "bacon", tasty : true },
      { name : "burgers" }
    ]
  }
})
db.countries.insert({
  _id : "ca",
  name : "Canada",
  exports : {
    foods : [
```

```
      { name : "bacon", tasty : false },
      { name : "syrup", tasty : true }
    ]
  }
})
db.countries.insert({
  _id : "mx",
  name : "Mexico",
  exports : {
    foods : [{
      name : "salsa",
      tasty : true,
      condiment : true
    }]
  }
})
```

To validate the countries were added, we can execute the count function, expecting the number 3.

```
> print( db.countries.count() )
3
```

Let's find a country that not only exports bacon but exports *tasty* bacon.

```
db.countries.find(
  { 'exports.foods.name' : 'bacon',  'exports.foods.tasty' : true },
  { _id : 0, name : 1 }
)

{ "name" : "United States" }
{ "name" : "Canada" }
```

But this isn't what we wanted. Mongo returned *Canada* because it exports bacon and exports tasty syrup. $elemMatch helps us here. It specifies that if a document (or nested document) matches *all* of our criteria, the document counts as a match.

```
db.countries.find(
    {
      'exports.foods' : {
        $elemMatch : {
          name : 'bacon',
          tasty : true
        }
      }
    },
    { _id : 0, name : 1 }
)

{ "name" : "United States" }
```

$elemMatch criteria can utilize advanced operators, too. You can find any country that exports a tasty food that also has a condiment label:

```
db.countries.find(
  {
    'exports.foods' : {
      $elemMatch : {
        tasty : true,
        condiment : { $exists : true }
      }
    }
  },
  { _id : 0, name : 1 }
)

{ "name" : "Mexico" }
```

Mexico is just what we wanted.

Boolean Ops

So far, all of our criteria are implicitly *and* operations. If you try to find a country with the name *United States* and an _id of *mx*, Mongo will yield no results.

```
db.countries.find(
  { _id : "mx", name : "United States" },
  { _id : 1 }
)
```

However, searching for one *or* the other with $or will return two results. Think of this layout like *prefix notation*: OR A B.

```
db.countries.find(
  {
    $or : [
      { _id : "mx" },
      { name : "United States" }
    ]
  },
  { _id:1 }
)

{ "_id" : "us" }
{ "_id" : "mx" }
```

There are so many operators we can't cover them all here, but we hope this has given you a taste of MongoDB's powerful query ability. The following is is not a complete list of the commands but a good chunk of them.

Command	Description
$regex	Match by any PCRE-compliant regular expression string (or just use the // delimiters as shown earlier)
$ne	Not equal to
$lt	Less than
$lte	Less than or equal to
$gt	Greater than
$gte	Greater than or equal to
$exists	Check for the existence of a field
$all	Match all elements in an array
$in	Match any elements in an array
$nin	Does not match any elements in an array
$elemMatch	Match all fields in an array of nested documents
$or	or
$nor	Not or
$size	Match array of given size
$mod	Modulus
$type	Match if field is a given datatype
$not	Negate the given operator check

You can find all the commands on the MongoDB online documentation or grab a cheat sheet from the Mongo website. We will revisit querying in the days to come.

Updating

We have a problem. New York and Punxsutawney are unique enough, but did we add Portland, Oregon, or Portland, Maine (or Texas or the others)? Let's update our towns collection to add some U.S. states.

The update(criteria,operation) function requires two parameters. The first is a criteria query—the same sort of object you would pass to find(). The second parameter is either an object whose fields will replace the matched document(s) or a modifier operation. In this case, the modifier is to $set the field state with the string *OR*.

```
db.towns.update(
  { _id : ObjectId("4d0ada87bb30773266f39fe5") },
  { $set : { "state" : "OR" } }
);
```

You may wonder why the $set operation is even required. Mongo doesn't think in terms of attributes; it has only an internal, implicit understanding of attributes for optimization reasons. But nothing about the interface is *attribute*-oriented. Mongo is *document*-oriented. You will rarely want something like this (notice the lack of $set operation):

```
db.towns.update(
  { _id : ObjectId("4d0ada87bb30773266f39fe5") },
  { state : "OR" }
);
```

This would replace the *entire* matching document with the document you gave it ({ state : "OR" }). Since you didn't give it a command like $set, Mongo assumes you just want to switch them up, so be careful.

We can verify our update was successful by finding it (note our use of findOne() to retrieve only one matching object).

```
db.towns.findOne({ _id : ObjectId("4d0ada87bb30773266f39fe5") })
{
  "_id" : ObjectId("4d0ada87bb30773266f39fe5"),
  "famous_for" : [
    "beer",
    "food"
  ],
  "last_census" : "Thu Sep 20 2007 00:00:00 GMT-0700 (PDT)",
  "mayor" : {
    "name" : "Sam Adams",
    "party" : "D"
  },
  "name" : "Portland",
  "population" : 582000,
  "state" : "OR"
}
```

You can do more than $set a value. $inc (increment a number) is a pretty useful one. Let's increment Portland's population by 1,000.

```
db.towns.update(
  { _id : ObjectId("4d0ada87bb30773266f39fe5") },
  { $inc : { population : 1000} }
)
```

There are more directives than this, such as the $ positional operator for arrays. New operations are added frequently and are updated in the online documentation. Here are the major directives:

Command	Description
$set	Sets the given field with the given value
$unset	Removes the field
$inc	Adds the given field by the given number
$pop	Removes the last (or first) element from an array
$push	Adds the value to an array
$pushAll	Adds all values to an array
$addToSet	Similar to push, but won't duplicate values
$pull	Removes matching value from an array
$pullAll	Removes all matching values from an array

References

As we mentioned previously, Mongo isn't built to perform joins. Because of its distributed nature, joins are pretty inefficient operations. Still, it's sometimes useful for documents to reference each other. In these cases, the Mongo development team suggests you use a construct like { $ref : "collection_name", $id : "reference_id" }. For example, we can update the towns collection to contain a reference to a document in countries.

```
db.towns.update(
  { _id : ObjectId("4d0ada87bb30773266f39fe5") },
  { $set : { country: { $ref: "countries", $id: "us" } } }
)
```

Now you can retrieve Portland from your towns collection.

```
var portland = db.towns.findOne({ _id : ObjectId("4d0ada87bb30773266f39fe5") })
```

Then, to retrieve the town's country, you can query the countries collection using the stored $id.

```
db.countries.findOne({ _id: portland.country.$id })
```

Better yet, in JavaScript, you can ask the town document the name of the collection stored in the fields reference.

```
db[ portland.country.$ref ].findOne({ _id: portland.country.$id })
```

The last two queries are equivalent; the second is just a bit more data-driven.

Deleting

Removing documents from a collection is simple. Merely replace the find function with a call to remove(), and all matched criteria will be removed. It's

Spelling Bee Warning

Mongo is not very friendly when it comes to misspellings. If you haven't run across this problem yet, you probably will at some point, so be warned. You can draw parallels between static and dynamic programming languages. You define static up front, while dynamic will accept values you may not have intended, even nonsensical types like person_name = 5.

Documents are schemaless, so Mongo has no way of knowing if you intended on inserting pipulation into your city or meant to querying on lust_census; it will happily insert those fields or return no matching values.

Flexibility has its price. *Caveat emptor.*

important to note that the entire matching document will be removed, not simply a matching element or a matching subdocument.

We recommend running find() to verify your criteria before running remove(). Mongo won't think twice before running your operation. Let's remove all countries that export bacon that isn't tasty.

```
var bad_bacon = {
  'exports.foods' : {
    $elemMatch : {
      name : 'bacon',
      tasty : false
    }
  }
}
db.countries.find( bad_bacon )

{
  "_id" : ObjectId("4d0b7b84bb30773266f39fef"),
  "name" : "Canada",
  "exports" : {
    "foods" : [
      {
        "name" : "bacon",
        "tasty" : false
      },
      {
        "name" : "syrup",
        "tasty" : true
      }
    ]
  }
}
```

Everything looks good. Let's remove it.

```
db.countries.remove( bad_bacon )
db.countries.count()
```

```
2
```

Now when you run count(), verify we are left with only two countries. If so, our delete was successful!

Reading with Code

Let's close out this day with one more interesting query option: code. You can request that MongoDB run a decision function across your documents. We placed this last because it should always be a last resort. These queries run quite slowly, you can't index them, and Mongo can't optimize them. But sometimes it's hard to beat the power of custom code.

Say we're looking for a population between 6,000 and 600,000 people.

```
db.towns.find( function() {
  return this.population > 6000 && this.population < 600000;
} )
```

Mongo even has a shortcut for simple decision functions.

```
db.towns.find("this.population > 6000 && this.population < 600000")
```

You can run custom code with other criteria using the $where clause. In this example, the query also filters for towns famous for groundhogs.

```
db.towns.find( {
  $where : "this.population > 6000 && this.population < 600000",
  famous_for : /groundhog/
} )
```

A word of warning: Mongo will brutishly run this function against each document, and there is no guarantee that the given field exists. For example, if you assume a *population* field exists and *population* is missing in even a single document, the entire query will fail, since the JavaScript cannot properly execute. Be careful when you write custom JavaScript functions, and be comfortable using JavaScript before attempting custom code.

Day 1 Wrap-Up

Today we took a peek at our first document database, MongoDB. We saw how we can store nested structured data as JSON objects and query that data at any depth. You learned that a *document* can be envisioned as a schemaless row in the relational model, keyed by a generated _id. A set of documents is called a *collection* in Mongo, similar to a *table* in PostgreSQL.

Unlike the previous styles we've encountered, with collections of sets of simple datatypes, Mongo stores complex, denormalized documents, stored and retrieved as collections of arbitrary JSON structures. Mongo tops off this flexible storage strategy with a powerful query mechanism not constrained by any predefined schema.

Its denormalized nature makes a document datastore a superb choice for storing data with unknown qualities, while other styles (such as relational or columnar) prefer you know in advance and require schema migrations to add or edit fields.

Day 1 Homework

Find

1. Bookmark the online MongoDB documentation.
2. Look up how to construct regular expressions in Mongo.
3. Acquaint yourself with command-line db.help() and db.collections.help() output.
4. Find a Mongo driver in your programming language of choice (Ruby, Java, PHP, and so on).

Do

1. Print a JSON document containing { "hello" : "world" }.

2. Select a town via a case-insensitive regular expression containing the word *new*.

3. Find all cities whose names contain an *e* and are famous for food or beer.

4. Create a new database named *blogger* with a collection named *articles*— insert a new article with an author name and email, creation date, and text.

5. Update the article with an array of comments, containing a comment with an author and text.

6. Run a query from an external JavaScript file.

5.3 Day 2: Indexing, Grouping, Mapreduce

Increasing MongoDB's query performance is the first item on today's docket, followed by some more powerful and complex grouped queries. Finally, we'll round out the day with some data analysis using mapreduce, similar to what we did with Riak.

Indexing: When Fast Isn't Fast Enough

One of Mongo's useful built-in features is indexing to increase query performance—something, as we've seen, that's not available on all NoSQL databases. MongoDB provides several of the best data structures for indexing, such as the classic B-tree, and other additions such as two-dimensional and spherical GeoSpatial indexes.

For now we're going to do a little experiment to see the power of MongoDB's B-tree index by populating a series of phone numbers with a random country prefix (feel free to replace this code with your own country code). Enter the following code into your console. This will generate 100,000 phone numbers (it may take a while), between *1-800-555-0000* and *1-800-565-9999*.

```
mongo/populate_phones.js
populatePhones = function(area,start,stop) {
  for(var i=start; i < stop; i++) {
    var country = 1 + ((Math.random() * 8) << 0);
    var num = (country * 1e10) + (area * 1e7) + i;
    db.phones.insert({
      _id: num,
      components: {
        country: country,
        area: area,
        prefix: (i * 1e-4) << 0,
        number: i
      },
      display: "+" + country + " " + area + "-" + i
    });
  }
}
```

Run the function with a three-digit area code (like 800) and a range of seven-digit numbers (5,550,000 to 5,650,000—please verify your zeros when typing).

```
populatePhones( 800, 5550000, 5650000 )
db.phones.find().limit(2)
```

```
{ "_id" : 18005550000, "components" : { "country" : 1, "area" : 800,
  "prefix" : 555, "number" : 5550000 }, "display" : "+1 800-5550000" }
{ "_id" : 88005550001, "components" : { "country" : 8, "area" : 800,
  "prefix" : 555, "number" : 5550001 }, "display" : "+8 800-5550001" }
```

Whenever a new collection is created, Mongo automatically creates an index by the _id. These indexes can be found in the system.indexes collection. The following query shows all indexes in the database:

```
db.system.indexes.find()
```

```
{ "name" : "_id_", "ns" : "book.phones", "key" : { "_id" : 1 } }
```

Most queries will include more fields than just the _id, so we need to make indexes on those fields.

We're going to create a B-tree index on the display field. But first, let's verify that the index will improve speed. To do this, we'll first check a query without an index. The explain() method is used to output details of a given operation.

```
db.phones.find({display: "+1 800-5650001"}).explain()
```

```
{
  "cursor" : "BasicCursor",
  "nscanned" : 109999,
  "nscannedObjects" : 109999,
  "n" : 1,
  "millis" : 52,
  "indexBounds" : {
  }
}
```

Your output will not equal ours, but note the millis field—milliseconds to complete the query—will likely be double digits.

We create an index by calling ensureIndex(fields,options) on the collection. The fields parameter is an object containing the fields to be indexed against. The options parameter describes the type of index to make. In this case, we're building a unique index on display that should just drop duplicate entries.

```
db.phones.ensureIndex(
  { display : 1 },
  { unique : true, dropDups : true }
)
```

Now try find() again, and check explain() to see whether the situation improves.

```
db.phones.find({ display: "+1 800-5650001" }).explain()
```

```
{
  "cursor" : "BtreeCursor display_1",
  "nscanned" : 1,
  "nscannedObjects" : 1,
  "n" : 1,
  "millis" : 0,
  "indexBounds" : {
    "display" : [
      [
        "+1 800-5650001",
        "+1 800-5650001"
      ]
    ]
  }
}
```

The millis value changed from 52 to 0—an infinity improvement (52 / 0)! Just kidding, but it is an orders of magnitude speedup. Also notice the cursor changed from a Basic to a B-tree cursor (it's called a cursor because it points to where values are stored; it doesn't contain them). Mongo is no longer doing a full collection scan but instead walking the tree to retrieve the value. Importantly, scanned objects dropped from 109999 to 1—since it has become just a unique lookup.

explain() is a useful function, but you'll use it only when testing specific query calls. If you need to profile in a normal test or production environment, you'll need the *system profiler*.

Let's set the profiling level to 2 (level 2 stores all queries; profiling level 1 stores only slower queries greater than 100 milliseconds) and then run find() as normal.

```
db.setProfilingLevel(2)
db.phones.find({ display : "+1 800-5650001" })
```

This will create a new object in the system.profile collection, which you can read as any other table. *ts* is the timestamp of when the query was performed, *info* is a string description of the operation, and *millis* is the length of time it took.

```
db.system.profile.find()

{
  "ts" : ISODate("2011-12-05T19:26:40.310Z"),
  "op" : "query",
  "ns" : "book.phones",
  "query" : { "display" : "+1 800-5650001" },
  "responseLength" : 146,
  "millis" : 0,
  "client" : "127.0.0.1",
  "user" : ""
}
```

Like yesterday's nested queries, Mongo can build your index on nested values. If you wanted to index on all area codes, use the dot-notated field representation: components.area. In production, you should always build indexes in the background using the { background : 1 } option.

```
db.phones.ensureIndex({ "components.area": 1 }, { background : 1 })
```

If we find() all of the system indexes for our phones collection, the new one should appear last. The first index is always automatically created to quickly look up by _id, and the second is the unique index we made previously.

```
db.system.indexes.find({ "ns" : "book.phones" })

{
  "name" : "_id_",
  "ns" : "book.phones",
  "key" : { "_id" : 1 }
}
{
  "_id" : ObjectId("4d2c96d1df18c2494fa3061c"),
  "ns" : "book.phones",
  "key" : { "display" : 1 },
  "name" : "display_1",
  "unique" : true,
  "dropDups" : true
}
{
  "_id" : ObjectId("4d2c982bdf18c2494fa3061d"),
  "ns" : "book.phones",
  "key" : { "components.area" : 1 },
  "name" : "components.area_1"
}
```

Our *book.phones* indexes have rounded out quite nicely.

We should close this section by noting that creating an index on a large collection can be slow and resource-intensive. You should always consider these impacts when building an index by creating indexes off-peak times, running index creation in the background, and running them manually rather than using automated index creation. There are plenty more indexing tricks and tips online, but these are the basics that are good to know.

Aggregated Queries

The queries we investigated yesterday are useful for basic extraction of data, but any post-processing would be up to you to handle. For example, say we wanted to count the phone numbers greater than 559–9999; we would prefer the database perform such a count on the back end. Like in PostgreSQL, count() is the most basic aggregator. It takes a query and returns a number (of matches).

```
db.phones.count({'components.number': { $gt : 5599999 } })
```

```
50000
```

To see the power of the next few aggregating queries, let's add another 100,000 phone numbers to our phones collection, this time with a different area code.

```
populatePhones( 855, 5550000, 5650000 )
```

> ## Change Is Good
>
> Aggregated queries return a structure other than the individual documents we're used to. count() aggregates the result into a count of documents, distinct() aggregates the results into an array of results, and group() returns documents of its own design. Even mapreduce generally takes a bit of effort to retrieve objects that resemble your internal stored documents.

The distinct() command returns each matching value (not a full document) where one or more exists. We can get the distinct component numbers that are less than 5,550,005 in this way:

```
db.phones.distinct('components.number', {'components.number': { $lt : 5550005 } })
```

```
[ 5550000, 5550001, 5550002, 5550003, 5550004 ]
```

Although we have two 5,550,000 numbers (one with an 800 area code and one with 855), it appears in the list only once.

The group() aggregate query is akin to GROUP BY in SQL. It's also the most complex basic query in Mongo. We can count all phone numbers greater than 5,599,999 and group the results into different buckets keyed by area code. key is the field we want to group by, cond (condition) is the range of values we're interested in, and reduce takes a function that manages how the values are to be output.

Remember mapreduce from the Riak chapter? Our data is already *mapped* into our existing collection of documents. No more mapping is necessary; simply reduce the documents.

```
db.phones.group({
  initial: { count:0 },
  reduce:  function(phone, output) { output.count++; },
  cond:    { 'components.number': { $gt : 5599999 } },
  key:     { 'components.area' : true }
})
```

```
[ { "800" : 50000, "855" : 50000 } ]
```

The following two examples are, admittedly, odd use cases. They serve only to show the flexibility of group().

You can easily replicate the count() function with the following group() call. Here we leave off the aggregating key:

```
db.phones.group({
  initial: { count:0 },
  reduce:  function(phone, output) { output.count++; },
```

```
  cond:     { 'components.number': { $gt : 5599999 } }
})
```

```
[ { "count" : 100000 } ]
```

The first thing we did here was set an initial object with a field named count set to 0—fields created here will appear in the output. Next we describe what to do with this field by declaring a reduce function that adds one for every document we encounter. Finally, we gave group a condition restricting which documents to reduce over. Our result was the same as count() because our condition was the same. We left off a key, since we want every document encountered added to our list.

We can also replicate the distinct() function. For performance sake, we'll start by creating an object to store the numbers as fields (we're effectively creating an ad hoc *set*). In the reduce function (which is run for each matching document), we just set the value to 1 as a placeholder (it's the field we want).

Technically this is all we need. However, if we want to really replicate distinct(), we should return an array of integers. So, we add a finalize(out) method that is run one last time before returning a value to convert the object into an array of field values. The function then converts those number strings into integers (if you really want to see the sausage being made, run the following without the finalize function set).

```
db.phones.group({
  initial: { prefixes : {} },
  reduce:  function(phone, output) {
    output.prefixes[phone.components.prefix] = 1;
  },
  finalize: function(out) {
    var ary = [];
    for(var p in out.prefixes) { ary.push( parseInt( p ) ); }
    out.prefixes = ary;
  }
})[0].prefixes
```

```
[ 555, 556, 557, 558, 559, 560, 561, 562, 563, 564 ]
```

The group() function is powerful—like SQL's GROUP BY—but Mongo's implementation has a downside, too. First, you are limited to a result of 10,000 documents. Moreover, if you shard your Mongo collection (which we will tomorrow) group() won't work. There are also much more flexible ways of crafting queries. For these and other reasons, we'll dive into MongoDB's version of mapreduce in just a bit. But first, we'll touch on the boundary between client-side and server-side commands, which is a distinction that has important consequences for your applications.

Server-Side Commands

If you were to run the following function through a command line (or through a driver), the client will pull each phone locally, all 100,000 of them, and save each phone document one by one to the server.

```
mongo/update_area.js
update_area = function() {
  db.phones.find().forEach(
    function(phone) {
      phone.components.area++;
      phone.display = "+"+
        phone.components.country+" "+
        phone.components.area+"-"+
        phone.components.number;
      db.phone.update({ _id : phone._id }, phone, false);
    }
  )
}
```

However, the Mongo db object provides a command named eval(), which passes the given function to the server. This dramatically reduces chatter between the client and server since the code is executed remotely.

```
> db.eval(update_area)
```

In addition to evaluating JavaScript functions, there are several other prebuilt commands in Mongo, most of which are executed on the server, although some require executing only under the admin database (which you can access by entering use admin).

```
> use admin
> db.runCommand("top")
```

The top command will output access details about all collections on the server.

```
> use book
> db.listCommands()
```

On running listCommands(), you may notice a lot of commands we've used. In fact, you can execute many common commands through the runCommand() method, such as counting the number of phones. However, you may notice a slightly different output.

```
> db.runCommand({ "count" : "phones" })
{ "n" : 100000, "ok" : 1 }
```

The number (n) returned is correct (100,000), but the format is an object with an *ok* field. That's because db.phones.count() is a wrapper function created for our convenience by the shell's JavaScript interface, whereas runCommand() is a count executed on the server. Remember that we can play detective on how a function like count() works by leaving off the calling parentheses.

```
> db.phones.count
function (x) {
    return this.find(x).count();
}
```

Interesting! collection.count() is just a convenience wrapper for calling count() on the results of find() (which itself is just a wrapper for a native query object that returns a cursor pointing to results). If you run *that* query…

```
> db.phones.find().count
```

you will get a much larger function (too much to print here). But look in the code, and after a bunch of setup, you'll find lines like this:

```
var res = this._db.runCommand(cmd);
if (res && res.n != null) {
    return res.n;
}
```

Double interesting! count() executes runCommand() and returns the value from the n field.

runCommand

And while we're digging into how methods work, let's take a look at the runCommand() function.

```
> db.runCommand
function (obj) {
    if (typeof obj == "string") {
        var n = {};
        n[obj] = 1;
        obj = n;
    }
    return this.getCollection("$cmd").findOne(obj);
}
```

It turns out that runCommand() is also a helper function that wraps a call to a collection named $cmd. You can execute any command using a call directly to this collection.

```
> db.$cmd.findOne({'count' : 'phones'})
{ "n" : 100000, "ok" : 1 }
```

This is bare-metal and how drivers generally communicate to the Mongo server.

Diversion

We took this diversion for two reasons:

- To drive home the idea that most of the magic you execute on the mongo console is executed on the server, not the client, which just provides convenient wrapper functions.

- We can leverage the concept of executing server-side code for our own gain to create something in MongoDB that's similar to the *stored procedures* we saw in PostgreSQL.

Any JavaScript function can be stored in a special collection named system.js. This is a normal collection; you just save the function by setting the name as the _id, and value is the function object.

```
> db.system.js.save({
    _id:'getLast',
    value:function(collection){
      return collection.find({}).sort({'_id':1}).limit(1)[0]
    }
})
```

What we normally would do next is execute it on the server directly. The eval() function passes the string to the server, evaluates it as JavaScript code, and returns the results.

```
> db.eval('getLast(db.phones)')
```

It should return the same values as calling getLast(collection) locally.

```
> db.system.js.findOne({'_id': 'getLast'}).value(db.phones)
```

It's worth mentioning that eval() blocks the mongod as it runs, so it's mainly useful for quick one-offs and tests, not common production procedures. You can use this function inside $where and mapreduce, too. We have the last weapon in our arsenal to begin executing mapreduce in MongoDB.

Mapreduce (and Finalize)

The Mongo mapreduce pattern is similar to Riak's, with a few small differences. Rather than the map() function returning a converted value, Mongo requires your mapper to call an emit() function with a key. The benefit here is that you can emit more than once per document. The reduce() function accepts a single key and a list of values that were emitted to that key. Finally, Mongo provides an optional third step called finalize(), which is executed only once per mapped value after the reducers are run. This allows you to perform any final calculations or cleanup you may need.

Since we already know the basics of mapreduce, we'll skip the intro wading-pool example and go right to the high-dive. Let's generate a report that counts all phone numbers that contain the same digits for each country. First we'll store a helper function that extracts an array of all distinct numbers (understanding how this helper works is not imperative to understanding the overall mapreduce).

mongo/distinct_digits.js
```
distinctDigits = function(phone){
  var
    number = phone.components.number + '',
    seen = [],
    result = [],
    i = number.length;
  while(i--) {
    seen[+number[i]] = 1;
  }
  for (i=0; i<10; i++) {
    if (seen[i]) {
      result[result.length] = i;
    }
  }
  return result;
}
db.system.js.save({_id: 'distinctDigits', value: distinctDigits})
```

Load the file in the `mongo` command line. If the file exists in the same directory you launched `mongo` from, you need only the filename; otherwise, a full path is required.

```
> load('distinct_digits.js')
```

With all that in, we can do a quick test (if you have some trouble, don't feel shy about adding a smattering of print() functions).

```
db.eval("distinctDigits(db.phones.findOne({ 'components.number' : 5551213 }))")
```

```
[ 1, 2, 3, 5 ]
```

Now we can get to work on the mapper. As with any mapreduce function, deciding what fields to map by is a crucial decision, since it dictates the aggregated values that you return. Since our report is finding distinct numbers, the array of distinct values is one field. But since we also need to query by country, that is another field. We add both values as a compound key: {digits : X, country : Y}.

Our goal is to simply count these values, so we emit the value 1 (each document represents one item to count). The reducer's job is to sum all those 1s together.

```
mongo/map_1.js
map = function() {
  var digits = distinctDigits(this);
  emit({digits : digits, country : this.components.country}, {count : 1});
}
```

```
mongo/reduce_1.js
reduce = function(key, values) {
  var total = 0;
  for(var i=0; i<values.length; i++) {
    total += values[i].count;
  }
  return { count : total };
}

results = db.runCommand({
  mapReduce: 'phones',
  map:       map,
  reduce:    reduce,
  out:       'phones.report'
})
```

Since we set the collection name via the out parameter (out : 'phones.report'), you can query the results like any other. It's a materialized view that you can see in the show tables list.

```
> db.phones.report.find({'_id.country' : 8})
{
  "_id" : { "digits" : [ 0, 1, 2, 3, 4, 5, 6 ], "country" : 8 },
  "value" : { "count" : 19 }
}
{
  "_id" : { "digits" : [ 0, 1, 2, 3, 5 ], "country" : 8 },
  "value" : { "count" : 3 }
}
{
  "_id" : { "digits" : [ 0, 1, 2, 3, 5, 6 ], "country" : 8 },
  "value" : { "count" : 48 }
}
{
  "_id" : { "digits" : [ 0, 1, 2, 3, 5, 6, 7 ], "country" : 8 },
  "value" : { "count" : 12 }
}
has more
```

Type it to continue iterating through the results. Note the unique emitted keys are under the field _ids, and all of the data returned from the reducers are under the field value.

If you prefer that the mapreducer just output the results, rather than outputting to a collection, you can set the out value to { inline : 1 }, but bear in mind there is a limit to the size of a result you can output. As of Mongo 2.0, that limit is 16MB.

Recall from the Riak chapter that reducers can have either mapped (emitted) results or other reducer results as inputs. Why would the output of one reducer feed into the input of another if they are mapped to the same key? Think of how this would look if run on separate servers, as shown in Figure 22, *A Mongo map reduce call over two servers*, on page 164.

Each server must run its own map() and reduce() functions and then push those results to be merged with the service that initiated the call, gathering them up. Classic divide and conquer. If we had renamed the output of the reducer to total instead of count, we would have needed to handle both cases in the loop, as shown here:

```
mongo/reduce_2.js
reduce = function(key, values) {
  var total = 0;
  for(var i=0; i<values.length; i++) {
    var data = values[i];
    if('total' in data) {
      total += data.total;
    } else {
      total += data.count;
    }
  }
  return { total : total };
}
```

However, Mongo predicted that you might need to perform some final changes, such as rename a field or some other calculations. If we really need the output field to be total, we can implement a finalize() function, which works the same way as the finalize function under group().

Day 2 Wrap-Up

On Day 2 we've expanded our query power by including several aggregate queries: count(), distinct(), and topped off by group(). To speed up the response time of these queries, we used MongoDB's indexing options. When more power is required, the ever-present mapReduce() is available.

db.runCommand({'mapReduce'...})

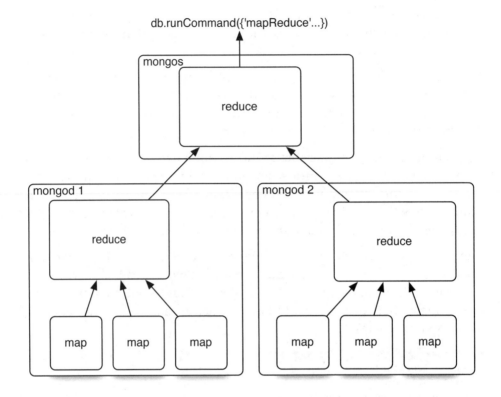

Figure 22—A Mongo map reduce call over two servers

Day 2 Homework

Find

1. A shortcut for admin commands.
2. The online documentation for queries and cursors.
3. The MongoDB documentation for mapreduce.
4. Through the JavaScript interface, investigate the code for three collections functions: help(), findOne(), and stats().

Do

1. Implement a finalize method to output the count as the total.

2. Install a Mongo driver for a language of your choice, and connect to the database. Populate a collection through it, and index one of the fields.

5.4   Day 3: Replica Sets, Sharding, GeoSpatial, and GridFS

Mongo has a powerful ability to store and query data in a variety of ways. But then again, so can other databases. What makes document databases unique is their ability to efficiently handle arbitrarily nested, schemaless data documents. What makes Mongo special in the realm of document stores is its ability to scale across several servers, by replicating (copying data to other servers) or sharding collections (splitting a collection into pieces) and performing queries in parallel. Both promote availability.

Replica Sets

Mongo was built to scale out, not to run stand-alone. It was built for data consistency and partition tolerance, but sharding data has a cost: if one part of a collection is lost, the whole thing is compromised. What good is querying against a collection of countries that contains only the western hemisphere? Mongo deals with this implicit sharding weakness in a simple manner: duplication. You should rarely run a single Mongo instance in production but rather replicate the stored data across multiple services.

Rather than muck with our existing database, today we'll start from scratch and spawn a few new servers. Mongo's default port is 27017, so we'll start up each server on other ports. Recall you must create the data directories first, so create three of them:

```
$ mkdir  ./mongo1 ./mongo2 ./mongo3
```

Next we'll fire up the Mongo servers. This time we'll add the replSet flag with the name *book* and specify the ports. While we're at it, let's turn on the REST flag so we can use the web interface.

```
$ mongod --replSet book --dbpath ./mongo1 --port 27011 --rest
```

Open another terminal window, and run the next command, which launches another server, pointing to a different directory, available on another port. Then open a third terminal to start the third server.

```
$ mongod --replSet book --dbpath ./mongo2 --port 27012 --rest
$ mongod --replSet book --dbpath ./mongo3 --port 27013 --rest
```

Notice that you get a lot of this noise on the output.

```
[startReplSets] replSet can't get local.system.replset config from self \
  or any seed (EMPTYCONFIG)
```

That's a good thing; we've yet to initialize our replica set, and Mongo is letting us know that. Fire up a mongo shell to one of the servers, and execute the rs.initiate() function.

```
$ mongo localhost:27011
> rs.initiate({
  _id: 'book',
  members: [
    {_id: 1, host: 'localhost:27011'},
    {_id: 2, host: 'localhost:27012'},
    {_id: 3, host: 'localhost:27013'}
  ]
})
> rs.status()
```

Notice we're using a new object called rs (replica set). Like other objects, it has a help() method you can call. Running the status() command will let us know when our replica set is running, so just keep checking the status for completion before continuing. If you watch the three server outputs, you should see that one server outputs this line:

```
[rs Manager] replSet PRIMARY
```

And two servers will have the following output:

```
[rs_sync] replSet SECONDARY
```

PRIMARY will be the master server. Chances are, this will be the server on port 27011 (since it started first); however, if it's not, go ahead and fire up a console to the primary. Just insert any old thing on the command line, and we'll try an experiment.

```
> db.echo.insert({ say : 'HELLO!' })
```

After the insert, exit the console, and then let's test that our change has been replicated by shutting down the master node; pressing CTRL+C is sufficient. If you watch the logs of the remaining two servers, you should see that one of the two has now been promoted to master (it will output the replSet PRIMARY line). Open a console into that machine (for us it was *localhost:27012*), and db.echo.find() should contain your value.

We'll play one more round of our console-shuffle game. Open a console into the remaining SECONDARY server. Just to be sure, run the isMaster() function. Ours looked like this:

```
$ mongo localhost:27013
MongoDB shell version: 1.6.2
connecting to: localhost:27013/test
> db.isMaster()
{
  "setName" : "book",
  "ismaster" : false,
  "secondary" : true,
  "hosts" : [
    "localhost:27013",
    "localhost:27012",
    "localhost:27011"
  ],
  "primary" : "localhost:27012",
  "ok" : 1
}
```

In this shell, let's attempt to insert another value.

```
> db.echo.insert({ say : 'is this thing on?' })
not master
```

The message *not master* is letting us know that we cannot write to a secondary node. Nor can you directly read from it. There is only one master per replica set, and you must interact with it. It is the gatekeeper to the set.

Replicating data has its own issues not found in single-source databases. In the Mongo setup, one problem is deciding who gets promoted when a master node goes down. Mongo deals with this by giving each mongod service a vote, and the one with the freshest data is elected the new master. Right now you should still have two mongod services running. Go ahead and shut down the current master. Remember, when we did this with three nodes, one of the others just got promoted to be the new master. But this time something different happened. The output of the last remaining server will be something like this:

```
[ReplSetHealthPollTask] replSet info localhost:27012 is now down (or...
[rs Manager] replSet can't see a majority, will not try to elect self
```

This comes down to the Mongo philosophy of server setups and the reason we should always have an odd number of servers (three, five, and so on).

Go ahead and relaunch the other servers and watch the logs. When the nodes are brought back up, they go into a recovery state and attempt to resync their data with the new master node. "What a minute!?" (we hear you cry). "So, what if the original master had data that did not yet propagate?" Those operations are dropped. A write in a Mongo replica set isn't considered successful until most nodes have a copy of the data.

The Problem with Even Nodes

The concept of replication is easy enough to grasp: you write to one MongoDB server, and that data is duplicated across others within the replica set. If one server is unavailable, then one of the others can be promoted and serve requests. But there are more ways a server can be unavailable than a server crash. Sometimes, the network connection between nodes is down. In that case, Mongo dictates that *a majority of nodes that can still communicate make up the network.*

MongoDB expects an odd number of total nodes in the replica set. Consider a five-node network, for example. If connection issues split it into a three-node fragment and a two-node fragment, the larger fragment has a clear majority and can elect a master and continue servicing requests. With no clear majority, a quorum couldn't be reached.

To see why an odd number of nodes is preferred, consider what might happen to a four-node replica set. Say a network partition causes two of the servers to lose connectivity from the other two. One set will have the original master, but since it can't see a *clear majority* of the network, the master steps down. The other set will similarly be unable to elect a master because it too can't communicate with a clear majority of nodes. Both sets are now unable to process requests and the system is effectively down. Having an odd number of total nodes would have made this particular scenario—a fragmented network where each fragment has less than a clear majority—less likely to occur.

Some databases (e.g., CouchDB) are built to allow multiple masters, but Mongo is not, and so it isn't prepared to resolve data updates between them. MongoDB deals with conflicts between multiple masters by simply not allowing them.

Unlike, say, Riak, Mongo always knows the most recent value; the client needn't decide. Mongo's concern is strong consistency on writes, and preventing a multimaster scenario is not a bad method for achieving it.

Voting and Arbiters

You may not always want to have an odd number of servers replicating data. In that case, you can either launch an arbiter (generally recommended) or increase voting rights on your servers (generally not recommended). In Mongo, an arbiter is a voting but nonreplicating server in the replica set. You launch it just like any other server, but on configuration set a flag, like this: { _id: 3, host: 'localhost:27013', arbiterOnly : true}. Arbiters are useful for breaking ties, like the U.S. vice president in the Senate. By default each mongod instance has a single vote.

Sharding

One of the central reasons for Mongo to exist is to safely and quickly handle very large datasets. The clearest method of achieving this is through horizontal sharding by value ranges—or just *sharding* for brevity. Rather than a single server hosting all values in a collection, some range of values are split (or in other words, sharded) onto other servers. For example, in our phone numbers collection, we may put all phone numbers less than 1-500-000-0000 onto Mongo server A and put numbers greater than or equal to 1-500-000-0001 onto a server B. Mongo makes this easier by autosharding, managing this division for you.

Let's launch a couple of (nonreplicating) mongod servers. Like replica sets, there's a special parameter necessary to be considered a shard server (which just means this server is capable of sharding).

```
$ mkdir ./mongo4 ./mongo5
$ mongod --shardsvr --dbpath ./mongo4 --port 27014
$ mongod --shardsvr --dbpath ./mongo5 --port 27015
```

Now we need a server to actually keep track of our keys. Imagine we created a table to store city names alphabetically. We need some way to know that (for example) cities starting with A–N go to server mongo4 and O–Z go to server mongo5. In Mongo you create a *config server* (which is just a regular mongod) that keeps track of which server (mongo4 or mongo5) owns what values.

```
$ mkdir ./mongoconfig
$ mongod --configsvr --dbpath ./mongoconfig --port 27016
```

Finally, we need to run a fourth server called mongos, which is the single point of entry for our clients. The mongos server will connect to the mongoconfig config server to keep track of the sharding information stored there. We'll set it on port 27020 with a chunkSize of 1. (Our chunkSize is 1MB, which is the smallest value allowed. This is just for our small dataset, so we can watch sharding

mongos vs. mongoconfig

You may wonder why Mongo separates configuration and the mongos *point of entry* into two different servers. This is because in production environments they will generally live on different physical servers. The config server (itself replicated) manages the sharded information for other sharded servers, while mongos will likely live on your local application server where clients can easily connect (without needing to manage which shards to connect to).

take place. In production you'd use the default or a much bigger number.) We point mongos to the config server:port with the --configdb flag.

```
$ mongos --configdb localhost:27016 --chunkSize 1 --port 27020
```

A neat thing about mongos is that it is a lightweight clone of a full mongod server. Nearly any command you can throw at a mongod, you can throw at a mongos, which makes it the perfect go-between for clients to connect to multiple sharded servers. A picture of our server setup may help (Figure 23, *Our little baby sharded cluster*, on page 171).

Now let's jump into the mongos server console on the admin database. We're going to configure some sharding.

```
$ mongo localhost:27020/admin
> db.runCommand( { addshard : "localhost:27014" } )
{ "shardAdded" : "shard0000", "ok" : 1 }
> db.runCommand( { addshard : "localhost:27015" } )
{ "shardAdded" : "shard0001", "ok" : 1 }
```

With that set up, now we have to give it the database and collection to shard and the field to shard by (in our case, the city name).

```
> db.runCommand( { enablesharding : "test" } )
{ "ok" : 1 }
> db.runCommand( { shardcollection : "test.cities", key : {name : 1} } )
{ "collectionsharded" : "test.cities", "ok" : 1 }
```

With all that setup out of the way, let's load some data. If you download the book code, you'll find a 12MB data file named mongo_cities1000.json that contains data for every city in the world with a population of more than 1,000 people. Download that file, and run the following import script that imports the data into our mongos server:

```
$ mongoimport -h localhost:27020 -db test --collection cities \
  --type json mongo_cities1000.json
```

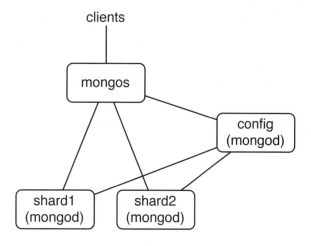

Figure 23—Our little baby sharded cluster

From the mongos console, type use test to go back to the test environment from the admin environment.

GeoSpatial Queries

Mongo has a neat trick built into it. Although we've focused on server setups today, no day would be complete without a little bit of razzle-dazzle, and that's Mongo's ability to quickly perform geospatial queries. First connect to the mongos sharded server.

```
$ mongo localhost:27020
```

The core of the geospatial secret lies in indexing. It's a special form of indexing geographic data called *geohash* that not only finds values of a specific value or range quickly but finds nearby values quickly in ad hoc queries. Conveniently, at the end of our previous section, we installed a lot of geographic data. So to query it, step 1 is to index the data on the location field. The *2d* index must be set on any two value fields, in our case a hash (for example, { longitude:1.48453, latitude:42.57205 }), but it could easily have been an array (for example, [1.48453, 42.57205]).

```
> db.cities.ensureIndex({ location : "2d" })
```

If we were not dealing with a sharded collection, we could easily query for cities at or near a location. However, the following will work only with non-sharded collections in our current version of Mongo.

```
> db.cities.find({ location : { $near : [45.52, -122.67] } }).limit(5)
```

This should be patched in future versions for sharded collections. But in the meantime, to query a sharded cities collection for other cities near a location, use the geoNear() command. Here is a sample of what it can return:

```
> db.runCommand({geoNear : 'cities', near : [45.52, -122.67],
  num : 5, maxDistance : 1})
{
  "ns" : "test.cities",
  "near" : "1000110001000000011100101011100011001001110001111110",
  "results" : [
    {
      "dis" : 0.007105400003747849,
      "obj" : {
        "_id" : ObjectId("4d81c216a5d037634ca98df6"),
        "name" : "Portland",
        ...
      }
    },
    ...
  ],
  "stats" : {
    "time" : 0,
    "btreelocs" : 53,
    "nscanned" : 49,
    "objectsLoaded" : 6,
    "avgDistance" : 0.02166813996454613,
    "maxDistance" : 0.07991909980773926
  },
  "ok" : 1
}
```

geoNear() also helps with troubleshooting geospatial commands. It returns a gold mine of useful information such as distance from the queried point, average and max distance of the returned set, and index information.

GridFS

One downside of a distributed system can be the lack of a single coherent filesystem. Say you operate a website where users can upload images of themselves. If you run several web servers on several different nodes, you must manually replicate the uploaded image to each web server's disk or create some alternative central system. Mongo handles this scenario by its own distributed filesystem called GridFS.

Mongo comes bundled with a command-line tool for interacting with the GridFS. The great thing is we don't have to set up anything special to use it. If we list the files in the mongos managed shards using the command mongofiles, we get an empty list.

```
$ mongofiles -h localhost:27020 list
```

```
connected to: localhost:27020
```

But upload any file.

```
$ mongofiles -h localhost:27020 put my_file.txt
```

```
connected to: localhost:27020
added file: { _id: ObjectId('4d81cc96939936015f974859'), filename: "my_file.txt", \
  chunkSize: 262144, uploadDate: new Date(1300352150507), \
  md5: "844ab0d45e3bded0d48c2e77ed4f3b0e", length: 3067 }
done!
```

And *voila*! If we list the contents of mongofiles, we'll find the uploaded name name.

```
$ mongofiles -h localhost:27020 list
```

```
connected to: localhost:27020
my_file.txt      3067
```

Back in our mongo console, we can see the collections Mongo stores the data in.

```
> show collections
```

```
cities
fs.chunks
fs.files
system.indexes
```

Since they're just plain old collections, they can be replicated or queried like any other.

Day 3 Wrap-Up

This wraps up our investigation of MongoDB. Today we focused on how Mongo enhances data durability with replica sets and supports horizontal scaling with sharding. We looked at good server configurations and how Mongo provides the mongos server to act as a relay for handling autosharding between multiple nodes. Finally, we toyed with some of Mongo's built-in tools, such as geospatial queries and GridFS.

Day 3 Homework

Find

1. Read the full replica set configuration options in the online docs.
2. Find out how to create a spherical geo index.

Do

1. Mongo has support for bounding shapes (namely, squares and circles). Find all cities within a 50-mile box around the center of London.[3]

2. Run six servers: three servers in a replica set, and each replica set is one of two shards. Run a config server and mongos. Run GridFS across them (this is the final exam).

5.5 Wrap-Up

We hope this taste of MongoDB has piqued your fancy and showed you how it earns the moniker of the "humongous" database. We covered a lot in a single chapter, but as usual, we only clawed at the surface.

Mongo's Strengths

Mongo's primary strength lies in its ability to handle huge amounts of data (and huge amounts of requests) by replication and horizontal scaling. But it also has an added benefit of a very flexible data model, since you needn't ever conform to a schema and can simply nest any values you would generally join using SQL in an RDBMS anyway.

Finally, MongoDB was built to be easy to use. You may have noticed the similarity between Mongo commands and SQL database concepts (minus the server-side joins). This is not by accident and is one reason Mongo is gaining so much mind share from former object-relational model (ORM) users. It's different enough to scratch a lot of developer itches but not so different it becomes a wholly different and scary monster.

Mongo's Weaknesses

How Mongo encourages denormalization of schemas (by not having any) might be a bit too much for some to swallow. Some developers find the cold, hard constraints of a relational database reassuring. It can be dangerous to insert any old value of any type into any collection. A single typo can cause hours of headache if you don't think to look at field names and collection names as a possible culprit. Mongo's flexibility is generally not important if your data model is already fairly mature and locked down.

Because Mongo is focused on large datasets, it works best in large clusters, which can require some effort to design and manage. Unlike Riak, where

---

3. http://www.mongodb.org/display/DOCS/Geospatial+Indexing

adding new nodes is transparent and relatively painless for operations, setting up a Mongo cluster requires a little more forethought.

Parting Thoughts

Mongo is an excellent choice if you are currently using a relational database to store your data through an ORM out of habit. We often recommend it to Rails, Django, and Model-View-Controller (MVC) developers, since they can then perform validations and field management through the models at the application layer and because schema migrations become a thing of the past (for the most part). Adding new fields to a document is as easy as adding a new field to your data model, and Mongo will happily accept the new terms. We find Mongo to be a much more natural answer to many common problem scopes for application-driven datasets than relational databases.

## CHAPTER 6

CouchDB

Ratchet wrenches are light and convenient tools you carry around for a range of big and small jobs. Like power drills, you can swap out variously sized bits like sockets or screws. Unlike a power drill that needs to be plugged into 120 volts of AC power, however, a wrench is happy to rest in your pocket and run on elbow grease. Apache CouchDB is like that. Able to scale down as well as up, CouchDB fits problem spaces of varying size and complexity with ease.

CouchDB is the quintessential JSON- and REST-based document-oriented database. First released in 2005, CouchDB was designed with the Web in mind and all the innumerable flaws, faults, failures, and glitches that come with it. Consequently, CouchDB offers a robustness unmatched by most other databases. Whereas other systems tolerate occasional network drops, CouchDB thrives even when connectivity is only rarely available.

Somewhat like MongoDB, CouchDB stores *documents*—JSON objects consisting of key-value pairs where values may be any of several types, including other objects nested to any depth. There is no ad hoc querying, though; indexed views produced by incremental mapreduce are the principal way you find documents.

6.1 Relaxing on the Couch

CouchDB lives up to its tag line: relax. Instead of focusing only on big-iron cluster installations, CouchDB aims to support a variety of deployment scenarios from the datacenter down to the smartphone. You can run CouchDB on your Android phone, on your MacBook, and in your datacenter. Written in Erlang, CouchDB is heartily built—the only way to shut it down is to kill the process! With its append-only storage model, your data is virtually incorruptible and easy to replicate, back up, and restore.

CouchDB is document-oriented, using JSON as its storage and communication language. Like Riak, all calls to CouchDB happen over its REST interface. Replication can be one-way or bidirectional and ad hoc or continuous. CouchDB gives you a lot of flexibility to decide how to structure, protect, and distribute your data.

Comparing CouchDB and MongoDB

One of the big questions we wanted to address in this book is "What's the difference between CouchDB and MongoDB?" On the surface, CouchDB and MongoDB—which we covered in Chapter 5, *MongoDB*, on page 135—can seem quite similar. They're both document-oriented datastores with an affinity for JavaScript that use JSON for data transport. There are many differences, though, ranging from project philosophy to implementation to scalability characteristics. We'll cover many of these as we explore the beautiful simplicity of CouchDB.

During our three-day tour we'll explore many of CouchDB's compelling features and design choices. We'll start, as always, with individual CRUD commands and then move on to indexing through mapreduce views. As we've done with other databases, we'll import some structured data and then use it to explore some advanced concepts. Finally, we'll develop some simple event-driven client-side applications using Node.js and learn how CouchDB's master-master replication strategy deals with conflicting updates. Let's get to it!

6.2 Day 1: CRUD, Futon, and cURL Redux

Today we're going to kick-start our CouchDB exploration by using CouchDB's friendly Futon web interface to perform basic CRUD operations. After that, we'll revisit cURL—which we used to communicate with Riak in Chapter 3, *Riak*, on page 51—to make REST calls. All libraries and drivers for CouchDB end up sending REST requests under the hood, so it makes sense to start by understanding how they work.

Getting Comfortable with Futon

CouchDB comes with a useful web interface called Futon. Once you have CouchDB installed and running, open a web browser to http://localhost:5984/_utils/. This will open the Overview page pictured in Figure 24, *CouchDB Futon: Overview page*, on page 179.

Before we can start working with documents, we need to create a database to house them. We're going to create a database to store musicians along with

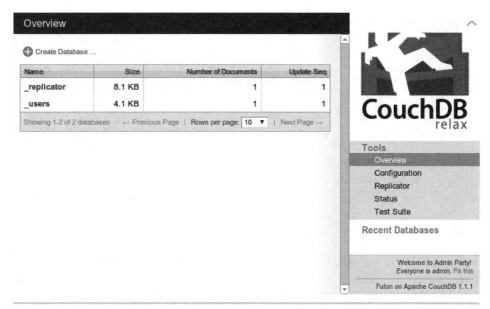

Figure 24—CouchDB Futon: Overview page

Figure 25—CouchDB Futon: creating a document

their album and track data. Click the Create Database... button. In the pop-up, enter *music* and click Create. This will redirect you automatically to the database's page. From here, we can create new documents or open existing ones.

On the music database's page, click the New Document button. This will take you to a new page that looks like Figure 25, *CouchDB Futon: creating a document*, on page 179.

Welcome to Admin Party!

In Futon, you may notice the warning at the bottom of the right column explaining that everyone is an admin. Were this destined to become a production server, your next step would be to click the "Fix this" link and create an admin user to restrict who can do what. In our case, leaving it open is fine for now and will make our other tasks easier.

Just as in MongoDB, a document consists of a JSON object containing key-value pairs called *fields*. All documents in CouchDB have an _id field, which must be unique and can never be changed. You can specify an _id explicitly, but if you don't, CouchDB will generate one for you. In our case, the default is fine, so click Save Document to finish.

Immediately after saving the document, CouchDB will assign it an additional field called _rev. The _rev field will get a new value every time the document changes. The format for the revision string consists of an integer followed by a dash and then a pseudorandom unique string. The integer at the beginning denotes the numerical revision—in this case 1.

Field names that begin with an underscore have special meaning to CouchDB, and _id and _rev are particularly important. To update or delete an existing document, you must provide *both* an _id and the matching _rev. If either of these do not match, CouchDB will reject the operation. This is how it prevents conflicts—by ensuring only the most recent document revisions are modified.

There are no transactions or locking in CouchDB. To modify an existing record, you first read it out, taking note of the _id and _rev. Then, you request an update by providing the full document, including the _id and _rev. All operations are first come, first served. By requiring a matching _rev, CouchDB ensures that the document you think you're modifying hasn't been altered behind your back while you weren't looking.

With the document page still open, click the Add Field button. In the Field column, enter *name*, and in the Value column, enter *The Beatles*. Click the green check mark next to the value to ensure it sticks, and then click the Save Document button. Notice how the _rev field now begins with 2.

CouchDB is not limited to storing string values. It can handle any JSON structure nested to any depth. Click the Add Field button again. This time, set Field to *albums*, and for Value enter the following (this is not an exhaustive list):

Figure 26—CouchDB Futon: document with an array value

```
[
  "Help!",
  "Sgt. Pepper's Lonely Hearts Club Band",
  "Abbey Road"
]
```

After you click Save Document, it should look like Figure 26, *CouchDB Futon: document with an array value*, on page 181.

There's more relevant information about an album than just its name, so let's add some. Modify the albums field and replace the value you just set with this:

```
[{
  "title": "Help!",
  "year": 1965
},{
  "title": "Sgt. Pepper's Lonely Hearts Club Band",
  "year": 1967
},{
  "title": "Abbey Road",
  "year": 1969
}]
```

After you save the document, this time you should be able to expand the albums value to expose the nested documents underneath. It should resemble Figure 27, *CouchDB Futon: document with deep nested values*, on page 182.

Clicking the Delete Document button would do what you might expect; it would remove the document from the music database. But don't do it just yet. Instead, let's drop down to the command line and take a look at how to communicate with CouchDB over REST.

Figure 27—CouchDB Futon: document with deep nested values

Performing RESTful CRUD Operations with cURL

All communication with CouchDB is REST-based, and this means issuing commands over HTTP. CouchDB isn't the first database we've talked about with this quality. Riak—covered in Chapter 3, *Riak*, on page 51—also relies on REST for all client communication. And like we did with Riak, we can communicate with CouchDB using the command-line tool cURL.

Here we'll perform some basic CRUD operations before moving on to the topic of views. To start, open a command prompt and run the following:

```
$ curl http://localhost:5984/
{"couchdb":"Welcome","version":"1.1.1"}
```

Issuing GET requests (cURL's default) retrieves information about the thing indicated in the URL. Accessing the root as you just did merely informs you that CouchDB is up and running and what version is installed. Next let's get some information about the music database we created earlier (output formatted here for readability):

```
$ curl http://localhost:5984/music/
{
  "db_name":"music",
  "doc_count":1,
  "doc_del_count":0,
  "update_seq":4,
```

```
  "purge_seq":0,
  "compact_running":false,
  "disk_size":16473,
  "instance_start_time":"1326845777510067",
  "disk_format_version":5,
  "committed_update_seq":4
}
```

This returns some information about how many documents are in the database, how long the server has been up, and how many operations have been performed.

Reading a Document with GET

To retrieve a specific document, append its _id to the database URL like so:

```
$ curl http://localhost:5984/music/74c7a8d2a8548c8b97da748f43000ac4
{
  "_id":"74c7a8d2a8548c8b97da748f43000ac4",
  "_rev":"4-93a101178ba65f61ed39e60d70c9fd97",
  "name":"The Beatles",
  "albums": [
    {
      "title":"Help!",
      "year":1965
    },{
      "title":"Sgt. Pepper's Lonely Hearts Club Band",
      "year":1967
    },{
      "title":"Abbey Road",
      "year":1969
    }
  ]
}
```

In CouchDB, issuing GET requests is always safe. CouchDB won't make any changes to documents as the result of a GET. To make changes, you have to use other HTTP commands like PUT, POST, and DELETE.

Creating a Document with POST

To create a new document, use POST. Make sure to specify a Content-Type header with the value *application/json*; otherwise, CouchDB will refuse the request.

```
$ curl -i -X POST "http://localhost:5984/music/" \
 -H "Content-Type: application/json" \
 -d '{ "name": "Wings" }'
HTTP/1.1 201 Created
Server: CouchDB/1.1.1 (Erlang OTP/R14B03)
```

```
Location: http://localhost:5984/music/74c7a8d2a8548c8b97da748f43000f1b
Date: Wed, 18 Jan 2012 00:37:51 GMT
Content-Type: text/plain;charset=utf-8
Content-Length: 95
Cache-Control: must-revalidate

{
  "ok":true,
  "id":"74c7a8d2a8548c8b97da748f43000f1b",
  "rev":"1-2fe1dd1911153eb9df8460747dfe75a0"
}
```

The HTTP response code 201 Created tells us that our creation request was successful. The body of the response contains a JSON object with useful information such as the _id and _rev values.

Updating a Document with PUT

The PUT command is used to update an existing document or create a new one with a specific _id. Just like GET, the URL for a PUT URL consists of the database URL followed by the document's _id.

```
$ curl -i -X PUT \
  "http://localhost:5984/music/74c7a8d2a8548c8b97da748f43000f1b" \
  -H "Content-Type: application/json" \
  -d '{
    "_id": "74c7a8d2a8548c8b97da748f43000f1b",
    "_rev": "1-2fe1dd1911153eb9df8460747dfe75a0",
    "name": "Wings",
    "albums": ["Wild Life", "Band on the Run", "London Town"]
  }'
HTTP/1.1 201 Created
Server: CouchDB/1.1.1 (Erlang OTP/R14B03)
Location: http://localhost:5984/music/74c7a8d2a8548c8b97da748f43000f1b
Etag: "2-17e4ce41cd33d6a38f04a8452d5a860b"
Date: Wed, 18 Jan 2012 00:43:39 GMT
Content-Type: text/plain;charset=utf-8
Content-Length: 95
Cache-Control: must-revalidate

{
  "ok":true,
  "id":"74c7a8d2a8548c8b97da748f43000f1b",
  "rev":"2-17e4ce41cd33d6a38f04a8452d5a860b"
}
```

Unlike MongoDB, in which you modify documents *in place*, with CouchDB you always overwrite the entire document to make any change. The Futon web interface we saw earlier may have made it look like you could modify a single field in isolation, but behind the scenes it was rerecording the whole document when you hit Save.

As we mentioned earlier, both the _id and _rev fields must exactly match the document being updated, or the operation will fail. To see how, try executing the same PUT operation again.

```
HTTP/1.1 409 Conflict
Server: CouchDB/1.1.1 (Erlang OTP/R14B03)
Date: Wed, 18 Jan 2012 00:44:12 GMT
Content-Type: text/plain;charset=utf-8
Content-Length: 58
Cache-Control: must-revalidate

{"error":"conflict","reason":"Document update conflict."}
```

You'll get an HTTP 409 Conflict response with a JSON object describing the problem. This is how CouchDB enforces consistency.

Removing a Document with DELETE

Finally, we can use the DELETE operation to remove a document from the database.

```
$ curl -i -X DELETE \
  "http://localhost:5984/music/74c7a8d2a8548c8b97da748f43000f1b" \
  -H "If-Match: 2-17e4ce41cd33d6a38f04a8452d5a860b"
HTTP/1.1 200 OK
Server: CouchDB/1.1.1 (Erlang OTP/R14B03)
Etag: "3-42aafb7411c092614ce7c9f4ab79dc8b"
Date: Wed, 18 Jan 2012 00:45:36 GMT
Content-Type: text/plain;charset=utf-8
Content-Length: 95
Cache-Control: must-revalidate

{
  "ok":true,
  "id":"74c7a8d2a8548c8b97da748f43000f1b",
  "rev":"3-42aafb7411c092614ce7c9f4ab79dc8b"
}
```

The DELETE operation will supply a new revision number, even though the document is gone. It's worth noting that the document wasn't really removed from disk, but rather a new empty document was appended, flagging the document as deleted. Just like with an update, CouchDB does not modify documents in place. But for all intents and purposes, it's deleted.

Day 1 Wrap-Up

Now that we've learned how to do basic CRUD operations in Futon and cURL, we're about ready to move onto more advanced topics. In Day 2 we'll dig into creating indexed *views*, which will provide other avenues for retrieving documents than just specifying them by their _id values.

Day 1 Homework

Find

1. Find the CouchDB HTTP Document API documentation online.

2. We've already used GET, POST, PUT, and DELETE. What other HTTP commands are supported?

Do

1. Use cURL to PUT a new document into the music database with a specific _id of your choice.

2. Use curl to create a new database with a name of your choice, and then delete that database also via cURL.

3. Again using cURL, create a new document that contains a text document as an attachment. Lastly, craft and execute a cURL request that will return just that document's attachment.

6.3 Day 2: Creating and Querying Views

In CouchDB, a *view* is a window into the documents contained in a database. Views are the principal way that documents are accessed in all but trivial cases—like those individual CRUD operations we saw in Day 1. Today, we'll discover how to create the functions that make up a view. We'll also learn how to perform ad hoc queries against views using cURL. Finally, we'll import music data, which will make the views more salient and demonstrate how to use couchrest, a popular Ruby library for working with CouchDB.

Accessing Documents Through Views

A view consists of mapper and reducer functions that are used to generate an ordered list of key-value pairs. Both keys and values can be any valid JSON. The simplest view is called _all_docs. It is provided out of the box for all databases and contains an entry for each document in the database, keyed by its string _id.

To retrieve all the things in the database, issue a GET request for the _all_docs view.

```
$ curl http://localhost:5984/music/_all_docs
{
  "total_rows":1,
  "offset":0,
  "rows":[{
    "id":"74c7a8d2a8548c8b97da748f43000ac4",
    "key":"74c7a8d2a8548c8b97da748f43000ac4",
    "value":{
      "rev":"4-93a101178ba65f61ed39e60d70c9fd97"
    }
  }]
}
```

You can see in the previous output the one document we've created so far. The response is a JSON object that contains an array of rows. Each row is an object with three fields:

- id is the document's _id.
- key is the JSON key produced by the mapreduce functions.
- value is the associated JSON value, also produced through mapreduce.

In the case of _all_docs, the id and key fields match, but for custom views this will almost never be the case.

By default, views won't include all of each document's content in the value returned. To retrieve all of the document's fields, add the include_docs=true URL parameter.

```
$ curl http://localhost:5984/music/_all_docs?include_docs=true
{
  "total_rows":1,
  "offset":0,
  "rows":[{
    "id":"74c7a8d2a8548c8b97da748f43000ac4",
    "key":"74c7a8d2a8548c8b97da748f43000ac4",
    "value":{
      "rev":"4-93a101178ba65f61ed39e60d70c9fd97"
    },
    "doc":{
      "_id":"74c7a8d2a8548c8b97da748f43000ac4",
      "_rev":"4-93a101178ba65f61ed39e60d70c9fd97",
      "name":"The Beatles",
      "albums":[{
        "title":"Help!",
        "year":1965
      },{
        "title":"Sgt. Pepper's Lonely Hearts Club Band",
```

188 • Chapter 6. CouchDB

```
      "year":1967
    },{
      "title":"Abbey Road",
      "year":1969
    }]
  }
}]
}
```

Here you can see that the other properties name and albums have been added to the value object in the output. With this basic structure in mind, let's make our own views.

Writing Your First View

Now that we've gotten a rough overview of how views work, let's try creating our own views. To start, we'll reproduce the behavior of the _all_docs view, and after that, we'll make increasingly complex views to extract deeper information from our documents for indexing.

To execute a temporary view, open a browser to Futon[1] as we did in Day 1. Next open the music database by clicking the link. In the upper-right corner of the music database's page, choose "Temporary view..." from the View drop-down. It should bring you to a page that resembles Figure 28, *CouchDB Futon: temporary view*, on page 189.

The code in the left Map Function box should look like this:

```
function(doc) {
  emit(null, doc);
}
```

If you click the Run button underneath the map function, CouchDB will execute this function once for each document in the database, passing in that document as the doc parameter each time. This will generate a table with a single row of results resembling the following:

Key	Value
null	{_id: "74c7a8d2a8548c8b97da748f43000ac4", _rev: "4-93a101178ba65f61ed39e60d70c9fd97", name: "The Beatles", albums: [{title: "Help!", year: 1965}, {title: "Sgt. Pepper's Lonely Hearts Club Band", year: 1967}, {title: "Abbey Road", year: 1969}]}

The secret to this output, and all views, is the emit() function (this works just like the MongoDB function of the same name). emit takes two arguments: the key and the value. A given map function may call emit one time, many times,

---

1.   http://localhost:5984/_utils/

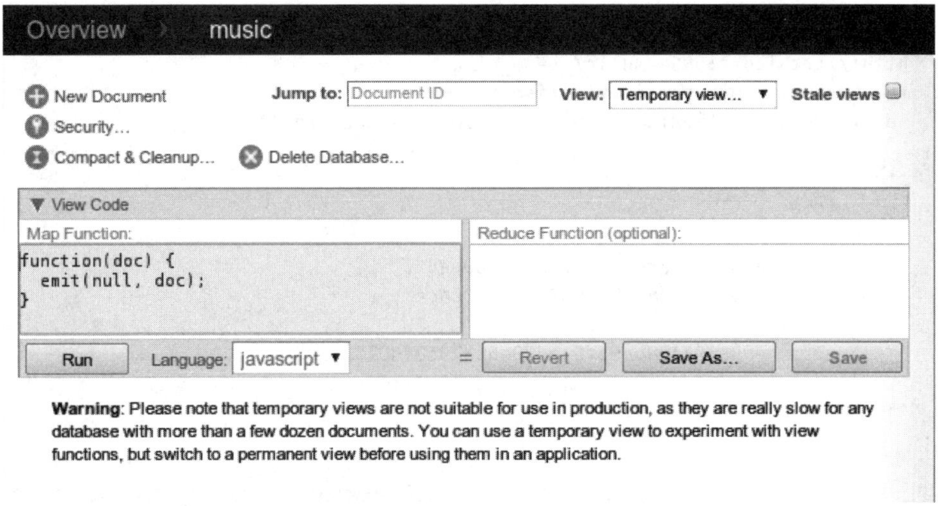

Figure 28—CouchDB Futon: temporary view

or no times for a given document. In the previous case, the map function emits the key-value pair null/doc. As we see in the output table, the key is indeed null, and the value is the same object we saw in Day 1 when we requested it directly from cURL.

To make a mapper that achieves the same thing as _all_docs, we need to emit something a little different. Recall that _all_docs emits the document's _id field for the key and a simple object containing only the _rev field for the value. With that in mind, change the Map Function code to the following, and then click Run.

```
function(doc) {
  emit(doc._id, { rev: doc._rev });
}
```

The output table should now resemble the following table, echoing the same key-value pair we saw earlier when enumerating records via _all_docs:

Key	Value
"74c7a8d2a8548c8b97da748f43000ac4"	{rev: "4-93a101178ba65f61ed39e60d70c9fd97"}

Note that you don't have to use Futon to execute temporary views. You may also send a POST request to the _temp_view handler. In this case, you pass in your map function as a JSON object in the request body.

```
$ curl -X POST \
  http://localhost:5984/music/_temp_view \
  -H "Content-Type: application/json" \
  -d '{"map":"function(doc){emit(doc._id,{rev:doc._rev});}"}'
{
  "total_rows":1,
  "offset":0,
  "rows":[{
    "id":"74c7a8d2a8548c8b97da748f43000ac4",
    "key":"74c7a8d2a8548c8b97da748f43000ac4",
    "value":{
      "rev":"4-93a101178ba65f61ed39e60d70c9fd97"
    }
  }]
}
```

The response is now identical to what we'd expect from _all_docs. But what
happens when we add the include_docs=true parameter? Let's find out!

```
$ curl -X POST \
  http://localhost:5984/music/_temp_view?include_docs=true \
  -H "Content-Type: application/json" \
  -d '{"map":"function(doc){emit(doc._id,{rev:doc._rev});}"}'
{
  "total_rows":1,
  "offset":0,
  "rows":[{
    "id":"74c7a8d2a8548c8b97da748f43000ac4",
    "key":"74c7a8d2a8548c8b97da748f43000ac4",
    "value":{
      "rev":"4-93a101178ba65f61ed39e60d70c9fd97"
    },
    "doc":{
      "_id":"74c7a8d2a8548c8b97da748f43000ac4",
      "_rev":"4-93a101178ba65f61ed39e60d70c9fd97",
      "name":"The Beatles",
      "albums":[...]
    }
  }]
}
```

This time, instead of integrating additional fields into the value object, a separate property called doc is added to the row result containing the full document.

A custom view may emit any value, even null. Providing a separate doc property
prevents problems that might otherwise arise with combining the row value
with the document. Next, let's see how to save a view so that CouchDB can
index the results.

Saving a View as a Design Document

When CouchDB executes a temporary view, it must execute the provided map function for *each and every document* in the database. This is extremely resource-intensive, chewing up a lot of processing power, and it's slow. You should use temporary views only for development purposes. For production, you should store your views in *design documents*.

A design document is a real document in the database, just like the Beatles document we created earlier. As such, it can show up in views and be replicated to other CouchDB servers in the usual fashion. To save a temporary view as a design document in Futon, click the Save As... button, and then fill in the Design Document and View Name fields.

Design documents always have IDs that start with _design/ and contain one or more views. The view name distinguishes this view from others housed in the same design document. Deciding which views belong in which design documents is largely application-specific and subject to taste. As a general rule, you should group views based on what they do relative to your data. We'll see examples of this as we create more interesting views.

Finding Artists by Name

Now that we've covered the basics of view creation, let's develop an application-specific view. Recall that our music database stores artist information, including a name field that contains the band's name. Using the normal GET access pattern or the _all_docs view, we can access documents by their _id values, but we're more interested in looking up bands by name.

In other words, today we can look up the document with _id equal to 74c7a8d2a8548c8b97da748f43000ac4, but how do we find the document with name equal to *The Beatles*? For this, we need a view. In Futon, head back to the Temporary View page, enter the following Map Function code, and click Run.

couchdb/artists_by_name_mapper.js
```javascript
function(doc) {
  if ('name' in doc) {
    emit(doc.name, doc._id);
  }
}
```

This function checks whether the current document has a name field and, if so, emits the name and document _id as the relevant key-value pair. This should produce a table like this:

Key	Value
"The Beatles"	"74c7a8d2a8548c8b97da748f43000ac4"

Click the Save As... button; then for Design Document, enter *artists* and for View Name enter *by_name*. Click Save to persist the change.

Finding Albums by Name

Finding artists by name is pretty useful, but we can do more. This time, let's make a view that lets us find albums. This will be the first example where the map function will emit more than one result per document.

Again return to the Temporary View page; then enter the following mapper:

```
couchdb/albums_by_name_mapper.js
function(doc) {
  if ('name' in doc && 'albums' in doc) {
    doc.albums.forEach(function(album){
      var
        key = album.title || album.name,
        value = { by: doc.name, album: album };
      emit(key, value);
    });
  }
}
```

This function checks whether the current document has a name field and an albums field. If so, it emits a key-value pair for each album where the key is the album's title or name and the value is a compound object containing the artist's name and the original album object. It produces a table like this:

Key	Value
"Abbey Road"	{by: "The Beatles", album: {title: "Abbey Road", year: 1969}}
"Help!"	{by: "The Beatles", album: {title: "Help!", year: 1965}}
"Sgt. Pepper's Lonely Hearts Club Band"	{by: "The Beatles", album: {title: "Sgt. Pepper's Lonely Hearts Club Band", year: 1967}}

Just like we did with the Artists By Name view, click the Save As... button. This time, for Design Document, enter *albums*, and for View Name enter *by_name*. Click Save to persist the change. Now let's see how to query these documents.

Querying Our Custom Artist and Album Views

Now that we have a couple of custom design documents saved, let's jump back to the command line and query them with the curl command. We'll start with the Artists By Name view. On the command line, execute the following:

```
$ curl http://localhost:5984/music/_design/artists/_view/by_name
{
  "total_rows":1,
  "offset":0,
  "rows":[{
    "id":"74c7a8d2a8548c8b97da748f43000ac4",
    "key":"The Beatles",
    "value":"74c7a8d2a8548c8b97da748f43000ac4"
  }]
}
```

To query a view, construct the path /<database_name>/_design/<design_doc>/_view/
<view_name>, replacing the parts as appropriate. In our case, we're querying
the by_name view in the artists design document of the music database. No surprise
here that the output includes our one document, keyed by the band name.

Next, let's try to find Albums By Name:

```
$ curl http://localhost:5984/music/_design/albums/_view/by_name
{
  "total_rows":3,
  "offset":0,
  "rows":[{
    "id":"74c7a8d2a8548c8b97da748f43000ac4",
    "key":"Abbey Road",
    "value":{
      "by":"The Beatles",
      "album":{
        "title":"Abbey Road",
        "year":1969
      }
    }
  },{
    "id":"74c7a8d2a8548c8b97da748f43000ac4",
    "key":"Help!",
    "value":{
      "by":"The Beatles",
      "album":{
        "title":"Help!",
        "year":1965
      }
    }
  },{
    "id":"74c7a8d2a8548c8b97da748f43000ac4",
    "key":"Sgt. Pepper's Lonely Hearts Club Band",
    "value":{
      "by":"The Beatles",
      "album":{
        "title":"Sgt. Pepper's Lonely Hearts Club Band",
        "year":1967
```

```
            }
         }
    }]
}
```

CouchDB will ensure that the records are presented in alphanumerical order by the emitted keys. In effect, this is the indexing that CouchDB offers. When designing your views, it's important to pick emitted keys that will make sense when ordered. Requesting a view in this fashion returns the whole set, but what if we want just a subset? One way to do that is to use the key URL parameter. When you specify a key, only rows with that exact key are returned.

```
$ curl 'http://localhost:5984/music/_design/albums/_view/by_name?key="Help!"'
{
  "total_rows":3,
  "offset":1,
  "rows":[{
    "id":"74c7a8d2a8548c8b97da748f43000ac4",
    "key":"Help!",
    "value":{
      "by":"The Beatles",
      "album":{"title":"Help!","year":1965}
    }
  }]
}
```

Notice the total_rows and offset fields in the response. The total_rows field counts the total number of records in the view, not just the subset returned for this request. The offset field tells us how far into that full set the first record presented appears. Based on these two numbers and the length of the rows, we can calculate how many more records there are in the view on both sides.

Requests for views can be sliced a few other ways beyond the keys parameter, but to really see them in action, we're going to need more data.

Importing Data Into CouchDB Using Ruby

Importing data is a recurring problem that you'll face no matter what database you end up using. CouchDB is no exception here. In this section, we'll use Ruby to import structured data into our music database. Through this you'll see how to perform bulk imports into CouchDB, and it'll also give us a nice pool of data to work with when we create more advanced views.

We'll use music data from Jamendo.com,[2] a site devoted to hosting freely licensed music. Jamendo provides all their artist, album, and track data in

---

2.   http://www.jamendo.com/

a structured XML format, making it ideal for importing into a document-oriented database like CouchDB.

Head over to Jamendo's NewDatabaseDumps page[3] and download dbdump_artistalbumtrack.xml.gz.[4] The zipped file is only about 15MB. To parse Jamendo's XML file, we'll use the libxml-ruby gem.

Rather than writing our own Ruby-CouchDB driver or issuing HTTP requests directly, we'll use a popular Ruby gem called couchrest that wraps these calls into a convenient Ruby API. We'll be using only a few methods from the API, but if you want to continue using this driver for your own projects, the documentation is quite good.[5]

On the command line, install the necessary gems:

```
$ gem install libxml-ruby couchrest
```

Just like we did for Wikipedia data in Chapter 4, *HBase*, on page 93, we'll use a SAX-style parser to process documents sequentially for insert as they're streamed in through standard input. Here's the code:

couchdb/import_from_jamendo.rb
```
① require 'rubygems'
  require 'libxml'
  require 'couchrest'

  include LibXML

② class JamendoCallbacks
    include XML::SaxParser::Callbacks
③   def initialize()
      @db = CouchRest.database!("http://localhost:5984/music")
      @count = 0
      @max = 100 # maximum number to insert
      @stack = []
      @artist = nil
      @album = nil
      @track = nil
      @tag = nil
      @buffer = nil
    end
④   def on_start_element(element, attributes)
      case element
      when 'artist'
        @artist = { :albums => [] }
```

---

3. http://developer.jamendo.com/en/wiki/NewDatabaseDumps
4. http://img.jamendo.com/data/dbdump_artistalbumtrack.xml.gz
5. http://rdoc.info/github/couchrest/couchrest/master/

```
      @stack.push @artist
    when 'album'
      @album = { :tracks => [] }
      @artist[:albums].push @album
      @stack.push @album
    when 'track'
      @track = { :tags => [] }
      @album[:tracks].push @track
      @stack.push @track
    when 'tag'
      @tag = {}
      @track[:tags].push @tag
      @stack.push @tag
    when 'Artists', 'Albums', 'Tracks', 'Tags'
      # ignore
    else
      @buffer = []
    end
  end

⑤ def on_characters(chars)
    @buffer << chars unless @buffer.nil?
  end

⑥ def on_end_element(element)
    case element
    when 'artist'
      @stack.pop
      @artist['_id'] = @artist['id'] # reuse Jamendo's artist id for doc _id
      @artist[:random] = rand
      @db.save_doc(@artist, false, true)
      @count += 1
      if !@max.nil? && @count >= @max
        on_end_document
      end
      if @count % 500 == 0
        puts "  #{@count} records inserted"
      end
    when 'album', 'track', 'tag'
      top = @stack.pop
      top[:random] = rand
    when 'Artists', 'Albums', 'Tracks', 'Tags'
      # ignore
    else
      if @stack[-1] && @buffer
        @stack[-1][element] = @buffer.join.force_encoding('utf-8')
        @buffer = nil
      end
    end
  end
```

```
    def on_end_document()
      puts "TOTAL: #{@count} records inserted"
      exit(1)
    end
  end
```

```
⑦ parser = XML::SaxParser.io(ARGF)
  parser.callbacks = JamendoCallbacks.new
  parser.parse
```

① To kick things off, we bring in the rubygems module and the specific gems that we need.

② The standard way to use LibXML is by defining a callbacks class. Here we define a JamendoCallbacks class to encapsulate our SAX handlers for various events.

③ The first thing our class does during initialization is connect to our local CouchDB server using the CouchRest API and then create the music database (if it doesn't exist already). After that, it sets up some instance variables for storing state information during the parse. Note that if you set the @max parameter to nil, all documents will be imported, not just the first 100.

④ Once parsing has started, the on_start_element() method will handle any opening tags. Here we watch for certain especially interesting tags like <artist>, <album>, <track>, and <tag>. We specifically ignore certain container elements—<Artists>, <Albums>, <Tracks>, and <Tags>—and treat all others as properties to be set on the nearest container items.

⑤ Whenever the parser encounters character data, we buffer it to be added as a property to the current container element (the end of @stack).

⑥ Much of the interesting stuff happens in the on_end_element() method. Here, we close out the current container element by popping it off the stack. If the tag closes an <artist> element, we take the opportunity to save off the document in CouchDB with the @db.save_doc() method. For any container element, we also add a random property containing a freshly generated random number. We'll use this later when selecting a random track, album, or artist.

⑦ Ruby's ARGF stream combines standard input and any files specified on the command line. We feed this into LibXML and specify an instance of our JamendoCallbacks class to handle the tokens—start tags, end tags, and character data—as they're encountered.

To run the script, pipe the unzipped XML content into the import script:

```
$ zcat dbdump_artistalbumtrack.xml.gz | ruby import_from_jamendo.rb
TOTAL: 100 records inserted
```

When the import has finished, drop back down to the command line, and we'll see how our views look. First let's pull up a few artists. The limit URL parameter specifies that we want only that number of documents in the response (or less).

```
$ curl http://localhost:5984/music/_design/artists/_view/by_name?limit=5
{"total_rows":100,"offset":0,"rows":[
{"id":"370255","key":"\"\"ATTIC\"\"","value":"370255"},
{"id":"353262","key":"10centSunday","value":"353262"},
{"id":"367150","key":"abdielyromero","value":"367150"},
{"id":"276","key":"AdHoc","value":"276"},
{"id":"364713","key":"Adversus","value":"364713"}
]}
```

The previous request started at the very beginning of the list of artists. To jump to the middle, we can use the startkey parameter:

```
$ curl http://localhost:5984/music/_design/artists/_view/by_name?\
limit=5\&startkey=%22C%22
{"total_rows":100,"offset":16,"rows":[
{"id":"340296","key":"CalexB","value":"340296"},
{"id":"353888","key":"carsten may","value":"353888"},
{"id":"272","key":"Chroma","value":"272"},
{"id":"351138","key":"Compartir D\u00f3na Gustet","value":"351138"},
{"id":"364714","key":"Daringer","value":"364714"}
]}
```

Previously, we started with artists whose names began with *C*. Specifying an endkey provides another way to limit the returned content. Here we specify that we want artists only between *C* and *D*:

```
$ curl http://localhost:5984/music/_design/artists/_view/by_name?\
startkey=%22C%22\&endkey=%22D%22
{"total_rows":100,"offset":16,"rows":[
{"id":"340296","key":"CalexB","value":"340296"},
{"id":"353888","key":"carsten may","value":"353888"},
{"id":"272","key":"Chroma","value":"272"},
{"id":"351138","key":"Compartir D\u00f3na Gustet","value":"351138"}
]}
```

To get the rows in reverse order, use the descending URL parameter. Be sure to reverse your startkey and endkey as well.

```
$ curl http://localhost:5984/music/_design/artists/_view/by_name?\
startkey=%22D%22\&endkey=%22C%22\&descending=true
{"total_rows":100,"offset":16,"rows":[
```

```
{"id":"351138","key":"Compartir D\u00f3na Gustet","value":"351138"},
{"id":"272","key":"Chroma","value":"272"},
{"id":"353888","key":"carsten may","value":"353888"},
{"id":"340296","key":"CalexB","value":"340296"}
]}
```

A number of other URL parameters are available for modifying view requests, but these are the most common and are the ones you'll reach for most often. Some of the URL parameters have to do with grouping, which comes from the reducer part of CouchDB mapreduce views. We'll explore these tomorrow.

Day 2 Wrap-Up

Today we covered some good ground. We learned how to create basic views in CouchDB and save them into design documents. We explored different ways of querying views to get subsets of the indexed content. Using Ruby and a popular gem called couchrest, we imported structured data and used it to support our views. Leading into tomorrow, we'll expand on these ideas by creating more advanced views by adding reducers and then move on to other APIs that CouchDB supports.

Day 2 Homework

Find

1. We've seen that the emit() method can output keys that are strings. What other types of values does it support? What happens when you emit an array of values as a key?

2. Find a list of available URL parameters (like limit and startkey) that can be appended to view requests and what they do.

Do

1. The import script import_from_jamendo.rb assigned a random number to each artist by adding a property called random. Create a mapper function that will emit key-value pairs where the key is the random number and the value is the band's name. Save this in a new design document named _design/random with the view name artist.

2. Craft a cURL request that will retrieve a random artist.

   Hint: You'll need to use the startkey parameter, and you can produce a random number on the command line via `ruby -e 'puts rand'`.

3. The import script also added a random property for each album, track, and tag. Create three additional views in the _design/random design document with the view names album, track, and tag to match the earlier artist view.

6.4 Day 3: Advanced Views, Changes API, and Replicating Data

In Days 1 and 2 we learned how to perform basic CRUD operations and interact with views for finding data. Building on this experience, today we'll take a closer look at views, dissecting the reduce part of the mapreduce equation. After that, we'll develop some Node.js applications in JavaScript to leverage CouchDB's unique Changes API. Lastly, we'll discuss replication and how CouchDB handles conflicting data.

Creating Advanced Views with Reducers

Mapreduce-based views provide the means by which we can harness CouchDB's indexing and aggregation facilities. In Day 2, all our views consisted of only mappers. Now we're going to add reducers to the mix, developing new capabilities against the Jamendo data we imported in Day 2.

One great thing about the Jamendo data is its depth. Artists have albums, which have tracks. Tracks, in turn, have attributes including tags. We'll now turn our attention to tags to see whether we can write a deep inspecting view to collect and count them.

First, return to the Temporary View page, and then enter the following map function:

```
couchdb/tags_by_name_mapper.js
function(doc) {
  (doc.albums || []).forEach(function(album){
    (album.tracks || []).forEach(function(track){
      (track.tags || []).forEach(function(tag){
        emit(tag.idstr, 1);
      });
    });
  });
}
```

This function digs into the artist document and then down into each album, each track, and finally each tag. For each tag, it emits a key-value pair consisting of the tag's idstr property (a string representation of the tag, like "rock") and the number 1.

With the map function in place, enter the following under Reduce Function:

couchdb/simple_count_reducer.js

```
function(key, values, rereduce) {
  return sum(values);
}
```

This code merely sums the numbers in the values list—which we'll talk about momentarily once we've run the view. Finally, click the Run button. The output should resemble the following table:

Key	Value
"17sonsrecords"	1
"17sonsrecords"	1
"17sonsrecords"	1
"17sonsrecords"	1
"17sonsrecords"	1
"acid"	1
"acousticguitar"	1
"acousticguitar"	1
"action"	1
"action"	1

This shouldn't be too surprising. The value is always 1 as we indicated in the mapper, and the Key fields exhibit as much repetition as there is in the tracks themselves. Notice, however, the Reduce checkbox in the top-right corner of the output table. Check that box, and then look at the table again. It should now look something like this:

Key	Value
"17sonsrecords"	5
"acid"	1
"acousticguitar"	2
"action"	2
"adventure"	3
"aksband"	1
"alternativ"	1
"alternativ"	3
"ambient"	28
"autodidacta"	17

What happened? In short, the reducer *reduced* the output by combining like mapper rows in accordance with our Reducer Function. The CouchDB mapreduce engine works conceptually like the other mapreducers we've seen before (Riak's *Introducing Mapreduce*, on page 63, and MongoDB's *Mapreduce (and Finalize)*, on page 160). Specifically, here's a high-level outline of the steps CouchDB takes to build a view:

1. Send documents off to the mapper function.

2. Collect all the emitted values.

3. Sort emitted rows by their keys.

4. Send chunks of rows with the same keys to the reduce function.

5. If there was too much data to handle all reductions in a single call, call the reduce function again but with previously reduced values.

6. Repeat recursive calls to the reduce function as necessary until no duplicate keys remain.

Reduce functions in CouchDB take three arguments: key, values, and rereduce. The first argument, key, is an array of tuples—two element arrays containing the key emitted by the mapper and the _id of the document that produced it. The second argument, values, is an array of values corresponding to the keys.

The third argument, rereduce, is a boolean value that will be true if this invocation is a *rereduction*. That is, rather than being sent keys and values that were emitted from mapper calls, this call is sent the products of previous reducer calls. In this case, the key parameter will be null.

Stepping Through Reducer Calls

Let's work through an example based on the output we just saw.

Consider documents (artists) with tracks that have been tagged as "ambient." The mappers run on the documents and emit key-value pairs of the form "ambient"/1.

At some point, enough of these have been emitted that CouchDB invokes a reducer. That call might look like this:

```
reduce(
  [["ambient", id1], ["ambient", id2], ...],    // keys are the same
  [1, 1, ...],                                    // values are all 1
  false                                           // rereduce is false
)
```

Recall that in our reducer function we take the sum() of values. Since they're all 1, the sum will simply be the length—effectively a count of how many tracks have the "ambient" tag. CouchDB keeps this return value for later processing. For the sake of this example, let's call that number 10.

Some time later, after CouchDB has run these kinds of calls several times, it decides to combine the intermediate reducer results by executing a rereduce:

```
reduce(
  null,                // key array is null
  [10, 10, 8],         // values are outputs from previous reducer calls
  true                 // rereduce is true
)
```

Our reducer function again takes the sum() of values. This time, the values add up to 28. Rereduce calls may be recursive. They go on as long as there is reduction to be done, until all the intermediate values have been combined into one.

Most mapreduce systems, including the ones used by other databases we've covered in this book like Riak and MongoDB, throw away the output of mappers and reducers after the work is done. In those systems, mapreduce is seen as a means to an end—something to be executed whenever the need arises, each time starting from scratch. Not so with CouchDB.

Once a view is codified into a design document, CouchDB will keep the intermediate mapper and reducer values until a change to a document would invalidate the data. At that time, CouchDB will incrementally run mappers and reducers to correct for the updated data. It won't start from scratch, recalculating everything each time. This is the genius of CouchDB views. CouchDB is able to use mapreduce as its primary indexing mechanism by not tossing away intermediate data values.

Watching CouchDB for Changes

CouchDB's incremental approach to mapreduce is an innovative feature, to be sure; it's one of many that set CouchDB apart from other databases. The next feature we'll investigate is the Changes API. This interface provides mechanisms for watching a database for changes and getting updates instantly.

The Changes API makes CouchDB a perfect candidate for a system of record. Imagine a multidatabase system where data is streaming in from several directions and other systems need to be kept up-to-date (we'll actually do this in the next chapter, Section 8.4, *Day 3: Playing with Other Databases*, on page 291). Examples might include a search engine backed by Lucene or ElasticSeach or a caching layer implemented on memcached or Redis. You could have different maintenance scripts kick off in response to changes too —performing tasks such as database compaction and remote backups. In short, this simple API opens up a world of possibilities. Today we'll learn how to harness it.

To make use of the API, we're going to develop some simple client applications using Node.js.[6] Node.js is a server-side JavaScript platform built on the V8 JavaScript engine—the same one used in Google's Chrome browser. Because Node.js is event-driven and code for it is written in JavaScript, it's a natural fit for integrating with CouchDB. If you don't already have Node.js, head over to the Node.js site and install the latest stable version (we use version 0.6).

The three flavors of the Changes API are polling, long-polling, and continuous. We'll talk about each of these in turn. As always, we'll start with cURL to get close to the bare metal and then follow up with a programmatic approach.

cURLing for Changes

The first and simplest way to access the Changes API is through the polling interface. Head to the command line, and try the following (the output was truncated for brevity; yours may differ):

```
$ curl http://localhost:5984/music/_changes
{
  "results":[{
    "seq":1,
    "id":"370255",
    "changes":[{"rev":"1-a7b7cc38d4130f0a5f3eae5d2c963d85"}]
  },{
    "seq":2,
    "id":"370254",
    "changes":[{"rev":"1-2c7e0deec3ffca959ba0169b0e8bfcef"}]
  },{
    ... 97 more records ...
  },{
    "seq":100,
    "id":"357995",
    "changes":[{"rev":"1-aa649aa53f2858cb609684320c235aee"}]
  }],
  "last_seq":100
}
```

---

6.   http://nodejs.org/

When you send a GET request for _changes with no other parameters, CouchDB will respond with everything it has. Just like accessing views, you can specify a limit parameter to request just a subset of the data, and adding include_docs=true will cause full documents to be returned.

Typically you won't want all the changes from the beginning of time. You're more likely to want the changes that have occurred since you last checked. For this, use the since parameter.

```
$ curl http://localhost:5984/music/_changes?since=99
{
  "results":[{
    "seq":100,
    "id":"357995",
    "changes":[{"rev":"1-aa649aa53f2858cb609684320c235aee"}]
  }],
  "last_seq":100
}
```

If you specify a since value that's higher than the last sequence number, you'll get an empty response:

```
$ curl http://localhost:5984/music/_changes?since=9000
{
  "results":[
  ],
  "last_seq":9000
}
```

Using this method, the client application would check back periodically to find out whether any new changes have occurred, taking application-specific actions accordingly.

Polling is a fine solution if your need for up-to-date changes can suffer delays between updates. If updates are relatively rare, this would be the case. For example, if you were pulling blog entries, polling every five minutes might be just fine.

If you want updates quicker, without incurring the overhead of reopening connections, then longpolling is a better option. When you specify the URL parameter feed=longpoll, CouchDB will leave the connection open for some time, waiting for changes to happen before finishing the response. Try this:

```
$ curl 'http://localhost:5984/music/_changes?feed=longpoll&since=9000'
{"results":[
```

You should see the beginning of a JSON response but nothing else. If you leave the terminal open long enough, CouchDB will eventually close the connection by finishing it:

```
],
"last_seq":9000}
```

From a development perspective, writing a driver that watches CouchDB for changes using polling is equivalent to writing one for longpolling. The difference is essentially just how long CouchDB is willing to leave the connection open. Now let's turn our attention to writing a Node.js application that watches and uses the change feed.

Polling for Changes with Node.js

Node.js is a strongly event-driven system, so our CouchDB watcher will adhere to this principle as well. Our driver will watch the changes feed and emit change events whenever CouchDB reports changed documents. To get started, we'll look at a skeletal outline of our driver, talk about the major pieces, and then fill in the feed-specific details.

Without further ado, here's the outline of our watcher program, as well as a brief discussion of what it does:

couchdb/watch_changes_skeleton.js

```
var
  http = require('http'),
  events = require('events');

/**
 * create a CouchDB watcher based on connection criteria;
 * follows node.js EventEmitter pattern, emits 'change' events.
 */
① exports.createWatcher = function(options) {

② var watcher = new events.EventEmitter();

  watcher.host = options.host || 'localhost';
  watcher.port = options.port || 5984;
  watcher.last_seq = options.last_seq || 0;
  watcher.db = options.db || '_users';

③ watcher.start = function() {
    // ... feed-specific implementation ...
  };

  return watcher;

};
```

```
     // start watching CouchDB for changes if running as main script
④ if (!module.parent) {
     exports.createWatcher({
       db: process.argv[2],
       last_seq: process.argv[3]
     })
       .on('change', console.log)
       .on('error', console.error)
       .start();
   }
```

①   exports is a standard object provided by the CommonJS Module API that
Node.js implements. Adding the createWatcher() method to exports makes it
available to other Node.js scripts that might want to use this as a library.
The options argument allows the caller to specify which database to watch
as well as override other connection settings.

②   createWatcher() produces an EventEmitter object that the caller can use to listen
for change events. The relevant capabilities of an EventEmitter is that you
can listen to events by calling its on() method and trigger events by calling
its emit() method.

③   watcher.start() is responsible for issuing HTTP requests to watch CouchDB
for changes. When changes to documents happen, watcher should emit
them as change events. All of the feed-specific implementation details will
be in here.

④   The last chunk of code at the bottom specifies what the script should do
if it's called directly from the command line. In this case, the script will
invoke the createWatcher() method and then set up listeners on the returned
object that dump results to standard output. Which database to connect
to and what sequence ID number to start from can be set via command-
line arguments.

So far, there's nothing specific to CouchDB at all in this code. It's all just
Node.js's way of doing things. This code may look foreign to you, especially
if you haven't developed with an event-driven server technology before, but
it's one we'll be using increasingly in this book going forward.

With the skeleton in place, let's add the code to connect to CouchDB via
longpolling and emit events. The following is just the code that goes inside
the watcher.start() method. Written inside the previous outline (where the comment says *feed-specific implementation*), the new complete file should be called
watch_changes_longpolling.js.

```
couchdb/watch_changes_longpolling_impl.js
   var
①  http_options = {
       host: watcher.host,
       port: watcher.port,
       path:
         '/' + watcher.db + '/_changes' +
         '?feed=longpoll&include_docs=true&since=' + watcher.last_seq
     };

② http.get(http_options, function(res) {
     var buffer = '';
     res.on('data', function (chunk) {
       buffer += chunk;
     });
     res.on('end', function() {
③      var output = JSON.parse(buffer);
        if (output.results) {
          watcher.last_seq = output.last_seq;
          output.results.forEach(function(change){
            watcher.emit('change', change);
          });
          watcher.start();
        } else {
          watcher.emit('error', output);
        }
      })
   })
   .on('error', function(err) {
     watcher.emit('error', err);
   });
```

① The first thing this script does is set up the http_options configuration object
    in preparation for the request. The path points to the same _changes URL
    we've been using, with feed set to longpoll and include_docs=true.

② After that, the script calls http.get(), a Node.js library method that fires off
    a GET request according to our settings. The second parameter to http.get
    is a callback that will receive an HTTPResponse. The response object emits
    data events as the content is streamed back, which we add to the buffer.

③ Finally, when the response object emits an end event, we parse the buffer
    (which should contain JSON). From this we learn the new last_seq value,
    emit a change event, and then reinvoke watcher.start() to wait for the next
    change.

To run this script in command-line mode, execute it like this (output truncated
for brevity):

```
$ node watch_changes_longpolling.js music
{ seq: 1,
  id: '370255',
  changes: [ { rev: '1-a7b7cc38d4130f0a5f3eae5d2c963d85' } ],
  doc:
   { _id: '370255',
     _rev: '1-a7b7cc38d4130f0a5f3eae5d2c963d85',
     albums: [ [Object] ],
     id: '370255',
     name: '"""ATTIC"""',
     url: 'http://www.jamendo.com/artist/ATTIC_(3)',
     mbgid: '',
     random: 0.4121620435325435 } }
{ seq: 2,
  id: '370254',
  changes: [ { rev: '1-2c7e0deec3ffca959ba0169b0e8bfcef' } ],
  doc:
   { _id: '370254',
     _rev: '1-2c7e0deec3ffca959ba0169b0e8bfcef',
... 98 more entries ...
```

Hurrah, our app works! After outputting a record for each document, the process will keep running, polling CouchDB for future changes.

Feel free to modify a document in Futon directly or increase the @max value on import_from_jamendo.rb and run it again. You'll see those changes reflected on the command line. Next we'll see how to go full-steam ahead and use the continuous feed to get even snappier updates.

Watching for Changes Continuously

The polling and longpolling feeds produced by the _changes service both produce proper JSON results. The *continuous* feed does things a little differently. Instead of combining all available changes into a results array and closing the stream afterward, it sends each change separately and keeps the connection open. This way, it's ready to return more JSON serialized change notification objects as changes become available.

To see how this works, try the following (output truncated for readability):

```
$ curl 'http://localhost:5984/music/_changes?since=97&feed=continuous'
{"seq":98,"id":"357999","changes":[{"rev":"1-0329f5c885...87b39beab0"}]}
{"seq":99,"id":"357998","changes":[{"rev":"1-79c3fd2fe6...1e45e4e35f"}]}
{"seq":100,"id":"357995","changes":[{"rev":"1-aa649aa53f...320c235aee"}]}
```

Eventually, if no changes have happened for a while, CouchDB will close the connection after outputting a line like this:

```
{"last_seq":100}
```

The benefit of this method over polling or longpolling is the reduced overhead that accompanies leaving the connection open. There's no time lost reestablishing the HTTP connections. On the other hand, the output isn't straight JSON, which means it's a bit more of a chore to parse. Also, it's not a good fit if your client is a web browser. A browser downloading the feed asynchronously might not receive any of the data until the entire connection finishes (better to use longpolling in this case).

Filtering Changes

As we've just seen, the Changes API provides a unique window into the goings on of a CouchDB database. On the plus side, it provides all the changes in a single stream. However, sometimes you may want just a subset of changes, rather than the fire hose of everything that has ever changed. For example, you may be interested only in document deletions or maybe only in documents that have a particular quality. This is where *filter functions* come in.

A filter is a function that takes in a document (and request information) and makes a decision as to whether that document ought to be allowed through the filter. This is gated by the return value. Let's explore how this works. Considering our music database, most artist documents we've been inserting have a country property that contains a three-letter code. Say we were interested only in bands from Russia (RUS). Our filter function might look like the following:

```
function(doc) {
  return doc.country === "RUS";
}
```

If we added this to a design document under the key filters, we'd be able to specify it when issuing requests for _changes. But before we do, let's expand the example. Rather than always wanting Russian bands, it'd be better if we could parameterize the input so the country could be specified in the URL.

Here's a parameterized country-based filter function:

```
function(doc, req) {
  return doc.country === req.query.country;
}
```

Notice this time how we're comparing the document's country property to a parameter of the same name passed in the request's query string. To see this in action, let's create a new design document just for geography-based filters and add it:

```
$ curl -X PUT \
  http://localhost:5984/music/_design/wherabouts \
  -H "Content-Type: application/json" \
  -d '{"language":"javascript","filters":{"by_country":
    "function(doc,req){return doc.country === req.query.country;}"
  }}'
{
  "ok":true,
  "id":"_design/wherabouts",
  "rev":"1-c08b557d676ab861957eaeb85b628d74"
}
```

Now we can make a country-filtered changes request:

```
$ curl "http://localhost:5984/music/_changes?\
filter=wherabouts/by_country&\
country=RUS"
{"results":[
{"seq":10,"id":"5987","changes":[{"rev":"1-2221be...a3b254"}]},
{"seq":57,"id":"349359","changes":[{"rev":"1-548bde...888a83"}]},
{"seq":73,"id":"364718","changes":[{"rev":"1-158d2e...5a7219"}]},
...
```

Using filters, you have the power to set up a sort of pseudosharding, where only a subset of records are replicated between nodes. It's not quite the same as truly sharded systems like MongoDB or HBase, but it does afford a means of splitting the responsibility of servicing certain kinds of requests. For instance, your main CouchDB server might have separate filters for users, orders, messages, and inventory. Separate CouchDB servers could replicate changes based on these filters, each supporting a different aspect of the business.

Since filter functions may contain arbitrary JavaScript, more sophisticated logic can be put into them. Testing for deeply nested fields would be similar to what we did for creating views. You could also use regular expressions for testing properties or compare them mathematically (for example, filtering by a date range). There's even a user context property on the request object (req.userCtx) you can use to find out more about the credentials provided with the request.

We'll revisit Node.js and the CouchDB Changes API in Chapter 8, *Redis*, on page 261 when we build a multidatabase application. For now, though, it's time to move on to the last distinguishing feature of CouchDB we're going to cover: replication.

CouchDB or BigCouch?

CouchDB's approach makes sense in a lot of use cases. It certainly fills a niche that the other databases we've discussed largely don't address. On the other hand, sometimes it's nice to selectively replicate data between nodes in order to capitalize on available disk space. That is, instead of having all nodes have all the data, keep only a certain number of copies. This is the *N* in NWR—discussed in *Nodes/Writes/Reads*, on page 74.

This isn't a feature that CouchDB offers out of the box, but don't worry! BigCouch has you covered. Developed and maintained by Cloudant, BigCouch offers a CouchDB-compatible interface (with only a few minor differences[a]). Under the surface, though, it implements the sharding and replication strategy of a Dynamo-inspired database like Riak.

Installing BigCouch is quite a chore—much harder than vanilla CouchDB—but may be worth it if your deployment scenario consists of a big-iron datacenter.

---

a.   http://bigcouch.cloudant.com/api

Replicating Data in CouchDB

CouchDB is all about asynchronous environments and data durability. According to CouchDB, the safest place to store your data is everywhere, and it gives you the tools to do it. Some other databases we've looked at maintain a single master node to guarantee consistency. Still others ensure it with a quorum of agreeing nodes. CouchDB does neither of these; instead, it supports something called multi-master or master-master replication.

Each CouchDB server is equally able to receive updates, respond to requests, and delete data, regardless of whether it's able to connect to any other server. In this model, changes are selectively replicated in one direction, and all data is subject to replication in the same way. In other words, there is no sharding. Servers participating in replication will all have all of the data.

Replication is the last major topic in CouchDB that we'll be discussing. First we'll see how to set up ad hoc and continuous replication between databases. Then we'll work through the implications of conflicting data and how to make applications capable of handling these cases gracefully.

To begin, click the Replicator link in the Tools menu on the right side of the page. It should open a page that looks like Figure 29, *CouchDB Futon: Replicator*, on page 213. In the "Replicate changes from" dialog, choose *music* from the left drop-down menu and enter *music-repl* in the right-side slot. Leave the Continuous checkbox unchecked, and then click Replicate. Click OK to create

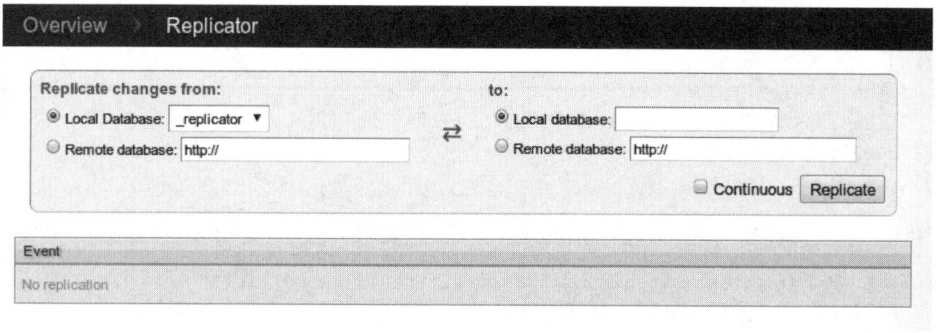

Figure 29—CouchDB Futon: Replicator

the music-repl database when prompted. This should produce an event message in the event log below the form.

To confirm that the replication request worked, go back to the Futon Overview page. There should now be a new database called music-repl with the same number of documents as the music database. If it has fewer, give it some time and refresh the page—CouchDB may be in the process of catching up. Don't be concerned if the Update Seq values don't match. That's because the original music database had deletions and updates to documents, whereas the music-repl database had only insertions to bring it up to speed.

Creating Conflicts

Next we'll create a conflict and then explore how to deal with it. Keep the Replicator page handy because we're going to be triggering ad hoc replication between music and music-repl frequently.

Drop back to the command line, and enter this to create a document in the music database:

```
$ curl -X PUT "http://localhost:5984/music/theconflicts" \
 -H "Content-Type: application/json" \
 -d '{ "name": "The Conflicts" }'
{
  "ok":true,
  "id":"theconflicts",
  "rev":"1-e007498c59e95d23912be35545049174"
}
```

On the Replicator page, click Replicate to trigger another synchronization. We can confirm that the document was successfully replicated by retrieving it from the music-repl database.

```
$ curl "http://localhost:5984/music-repl/theconflicts"
{
  "_id":"theconflicts",
  "_rev":"1-e007498c59e95d23912be35545049174",
  "name":"The Conflicts"
}
```

Next, let's update it in music-repl by adding an album called *Conflicts of Interest*.

```
$ curl -X PUT "http://localhost:5984/music-repl/theconflicts" \
  -H "Content-Type: application/json" \
  -d '{
    "_id": "theconflicts",
    "_rev": "1-e007498c59e95d23912be35545049174",
    "name": "The Conflicts",
    "albums": ["Conflicts of Interest"]
  }'
{
  "ok":true,
  "id":"theconflicts",
  "rev":"2-0c969fbfa76eb7fcdf6412ef219fcac5"
}
```

And create a conflicting update in music proper by adding a different album: *Conflicting Opinions*.

```
$ curl -X PUT "http://localhost:5984/music/theconflicts" \
  -H "Content-Type: application/json" \
  -d '{
    "_id": "theconflicts",
    "_rev": "1-e007498c59e95d23912be35545049174",
    "name": "The Conflicts",
    "albums": ["Conflicting Opinions"]
  }'
{
  "ok":true,
  "id":"theconflicts",
  "rev":"2-cab47bf4444a20d6a2d2204330fdce2a"
}
```

At this point, both the music and music-repl databases have a document with an _id value of theconflicts. Both documents are at version 2 and derived from the same base revision (1-e007498c59e95d23912be35545049174). Now the question is, what happens when we try to replicate between them?

Resolving Conflicts

With our document now in a conflicting state between the two databases, head back to the Replicator page and kick off another replication. If you were expecting this to fail, you may be shocked to learn that the operation succeeds just fine. So, how did CouchDB deal with the discrepancy?

It turns out that CouchDB basically just picks one and calls that one the winner. Using a deterministic algorithm, all CouchDB nodes will pick the same winner when a conflict is detected. However, the story doesn't end there. CouchDB stores the unselected "loser" documents as well so that a client application can review the situation and resolve it at a later date.

To find out which version of our document won during the last replication, we can request it using the normal GET request channel. By adding the con-flicts=true URL parameter, CouchDB will also include information about the conflicting revisions.

```
$ curl http://localhost:5984/music-repl/theconflicts?conflicts=true
{
  "_id":"theconflicts",
  "_rev":"2-cab47bf4444a20d6a2d2204330fdce2a",
  "name":"The Conflicts",
  "albums":["Conflicting Opinions"],
  "_conflicts":[
    "2-0c969fbfa76eb7fcdf6412ef219fcac5"
  ]
}
```

So, we see that the second update won. Notice the _conflicts field in the response. It contains a list of other revisions that conflicted with the chosen one. By adding a rev parameter to a GET request, we can pull down those conflicting revisions and decide what to do about them.

```
$ curl http://localhost:5984/music-repl/theconflicts?rev=2-0c969f...
{
  "_id":"theconflicts",
  "_rev":"2-0c969fbfa76eb7fcdf6412ef219fcac5",
  "name":"The Conflicts",
  "albums":["Conflicts of Interest"]
}
```

The takeaway here is that CouchDB does not try to intelligently merge con-flicting changes. How to merge two documents is highly application-specific, and a general solution isn't practical. In our case, combining the two albums arrays by concatenating them makes sense, but one could easily think of scenarios where the appropriate action is not obvious.

For example, consider you're maintaining a database of calendar events. One copy is on your smartphone; another is on your laptop. You get a text message from a party planner specifying the venue for the party you're hosting, so you update your phone database accordingly. Later, back at the office, you receive another email from the planner specifying a *different* venue. So, you update your laptop database and then replicate between them. CouchDB has no way of knowing which of the two venues is correct. The best it can do is make them consistent, keeping the old value around so you can verify which of the conflicting values should be kept. It would be up to the application to determine the right user interface for presenting this situation and asking for a decision.

Day 3 Wrap-Up

And so ends our tour of CouchDB. Here in Day 3 we started out by learning how to add reducer functions to our mapreduce-generated views. After that, we took a deep dive into the Changes API, including a jaunt into the world of event-driven server-side JavaScript development with Node.js. Lastly, we took a brief look at how CouchDB achieves its master-master replication strategy and how client applications can detect and correct for conflicts.

Day 3 Homework

Find

1. What native reducers are available in CouchDB? What are the benefits of using native reducers over custom JavaScript reducers?

2. How can you filter the changes coming out of the _changes API on the server side?

3. Like everything in CouchDB, the tasks of initializing and canceling replication are controlled by HTTP commands under the hood. What are the REST commands to set up and remove replication relationships between servers?

4. How can you use the _replicator database to persist replication relationships?

Do

1. Create a new module called watch_changes_continuous.js based on the skeletal Node.js module described in the section *Polling for Changes with Node.js*, on page 206.

2. Implement watcher.start() such that it monitors the continuous _changes feed. Confirm that it produces the same output as watch_changes_longpolling.js.

   Hint: If you get stuck, you can find an example implementation in the downloads that accompany this book.

3. Documents with conflicting revisions have a _conflicts property. Create a view that emits conflicting revisions and maps them to the doc _id.

6.5 Wrap-Up

Through this chapter we've seen how to do a pretty wide range of tasks with CouchDB, from performing basic CRUD operations to building views out of mapreduce functions. We saw how to watch for changes, and we explored developing nonblocking event-driven client applications. Finally, we learned how to perform ad hoc replication between databases and how to detect and resolve conflicts. Despite all of this content, there's still a lot we didn't cover, but now it's time to wrap things up before heading off to our next database.

CouchDB's Strengths

CouchDB is a robust and stable member of the NoSQL community. Built on the philosophy that networks are unreliable and hardware failure is imminent, CouchDB offers a heartily decentralized approach to data storage. Small enough to live in your smartphone and big enough to support the enterprise, CouchDB affords a variety of deployment situations.

CouchDB is as much an API as a database. In this chapter, we focused on the canonical Apache CouchDB project, but there are an increasing number of alternative implementations and CouchDB service providers built on hybrid back ends. Because CouchDB is made "of the Web, for the Web," it's fairly straightforward to layer in web technologies—such as load balancers and caching layers—and still end up with something that's true to CouchDB's APIs.

CouchDB's Weaknesses

Of course, CouchDB isn't for everything. CouchDB's mapreduce-based views, while novel, can't perform all the fancy data slicing you'd expect from a relational database. In fact, you shouldn't be running ad hoc queries *at all* in production. Also, CouchDB's replication strategy isn't always the right choice. CouchDB replication is all or nothing, meaning all replicated servers will have the same contents. There is no sharding to distribute content around the datacenter. The principal reason for adding more CouchDB nodes is not to spread the data around so much as to increase throughput for read and write operations.

Parting Thoughts

CouchDB's attention to robustness in the face of uncertainty makes it a great choice if your system must stand up to the harsh realities of the wild Internet. By leveraging standard webisms like HTTP/REST and JSON, CouchDB fits in easily wherever web technologies are prevalent, which is increasingly everywhere. Inside the walled garden of a datacenter, CouchDB can still make sense if you commit to managing conflicts when they arise or if you pursue an alternative implementation like BigCouch, but don't expect to get sharding right out of the box.

There are plenty of other features that make CouchDB unique and special that we didn't have time to cover. A short list would include ease of backups, binary attachments to documents, and CouchApps—a system for developing and deploying web apps directly through CouchDB with no other middleware. Having said that, we hope we've provided enough of an overview to whet your appetite for more. Try CouchDB for your next data-driven web app; you won't be disappointed!

## CHAPTER 7

Neo4J

A bungee cord may not seem a standard carpentry tool, just like Neo4j may not seem like a standard database. Bungee cord is used to tie things together —no matter how awkwardly shaped the objects may be. If your ability to tie a table to a column to a pickup truck in the most organic way is of the utmost importance, this is your go-to tool.

Neo4j is a new type of NoSQL datastore called a *graph database*. As the name implies, it stores data as a graph (in the mathematical sense). It's known for being "whiteboard friendly," meaning if you can draw a design as boxes and lines on a whiteboard, you can store it in Neo4j. Neo4j focuses more on the *relationships between* values than on the commonalities *among sets of* values (such as collections of documents or tables of rows). In this way, it can store highly variable data in a natural and straightforward way.

Neo4j is small enough to be embedded into nearly any application. On the other end of the spectrum, Neo4j can store tens of billions of nodes and as many edges. And with its cluster support with master-slave replication across many servers, it can handle most any sized problem you can throw at it.

7.1 Neo4J Is Whiteboard Friendly

Imagine you must create a wine suggestion engine where wines have different varieties, regions, wineries, vintages, and designations. Perhaps you need to keep track of articles by authors describing wines. Perhaps you want to let users track their favorites.

A relational model may create a category table and a many-to-many relationship between a single winery's wine and some combination of categories and other data. But this isn't quite how humans mentally model data. Compare these two figures: Figure 30, *Wine suggestion schema in relational UML*, on

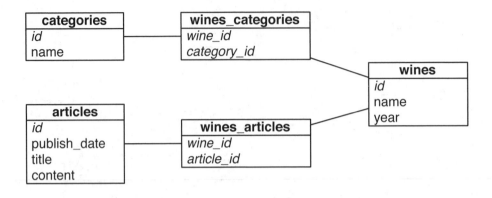

Figure 30—Wine suggestion schema in relational UML

page 220 and Figure 31, *Wine suggestion data on a whiteboard*, on page 221. There's an old saying in the relational database world: *on a long enough timeline, all fields become optional.* Neo4j handles this implicitly by providing values and structure only where necessary. If a wine blend has no vintage, instead add a bottle year and point the vintages to the blend node. There is no schema to adjust.

Over the next three days we'll learn how to interact with Neo4j through a console and then through REST and search indexes. We'll work with some larger graphs with graph algorithms. Finally, on Day 3, we'll take a peek at the enterprise tools Neo4j provides for mission-critical applications, from full ACID-compliant transactions to high-availability clustering and incremental backups.

In this chapter, we'll use the Neo4j 1.7 Enterprise edition. Most of the actions we perform can actually use the GPL Community edition, but we'll require some enterprise functionality for Day 3: high availability.

7.2 Day 1: Graphs, Groovy, and CRUD

Today we're really going to jump in with both feet. In addition to exploring the Neo4j web interface, we'll get deep into graph database terminology and CRUD. Much of today will be learning how to query a graph database through a process called *walking*. The concepts here differ significantly from other databases we've looked at so far, which have largely taken a document- or record-based view of the world. In Neo4j, it's all about relationships.

Figure 31—Wine suggestion data on a whiteboard

But before we get to all that, let's start with the web interface to see how Neo4j represents data in graph form and how to walk around that graph. After you've downloaded and unzipped the Neo4j package, cd into the directory and start up the server with this:

```
$ bin/neo4j start
```

To make sure you're up and running, try curling this URL:

```
$ curl http://localhost:7474/db/data/
```

Like CouchDB, the default Neo4j package comes equipped with a substantial web administration tool and data browser, which is excellent for playing with toy commands. If that weren't enough, it has one of the coolest graph data browsers we've ever seen. This is perfect for getting started, since graph traversal can feel very awkward at first try.

Neo4j's Web Interface

Launch a web browser, and navigate to the administration page.

```
http://localhost:7474/webadmin/
```

You'll be greeted by a colorful yet empty graph like the one pictured in Figure 32, *The web administration page dashboard*, on page 222. Click the Data Browser option at the top. A new Neo4j install will have a preexisting reference node: node 0.

A *node* in a graph database is not entirely unlike the nodes we talked about in prior chapters. Previously, when we spoke of a *node*, we meant a physical server in a network. If you viewed the entire network as a huge interconnected

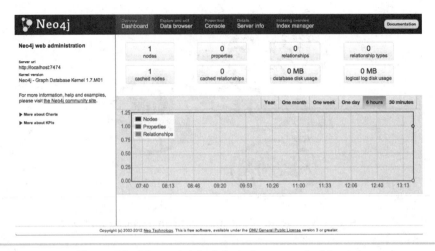

Figure 32—The web administration page dashboard

graph, a server node was a point, or *vertex*, between the server *relationships*, or *edges*.

In Neo4j, a node is conceptually similar; it's a vertex between edges that may hold data, as a set of key-values. Click the + Property button and set the key to *name* and value to *Prancing Wolf Ice Wine 2007* to represent a specific wine and vintage. Next, click the + Node button pictured below:

To the new node, add the property name with a value of *Wine Expert Monthly* (we'll write it in shorthand like this: [name : "Wine Expert Monthly"]). The node number will be automatically incremented.

Now we have two nodes sitting out there but nothing connecting them. Since Wine Expert reported on the Prancing Wolf wine, we need to relate the two by creating an edge. Click the + Relationship button, and set from node 1 to node 0 with type reported_on.

You'll get a URL to this specific relationship...

```
http://localhost:7474/db/data/relationship/0
```

that shows *Node 1 reported_on Node 0*.

Just like nodes, relationships can contain properties. Click the + Add Property button and enter the property [rating : 92] so we can keep track of what score the wine received.

This particular ice wine is created from the *riesling* grape, so let's add that information too. We could add the property directly to the wine node, but riesling is a general category that could apply to other wines, so let's create a new node and set its property to [name : "riesling"]. Next add another relationship from node 0 to 2 as grape_type and give it the property [style : "ice wine"].

But what does our graph look like? If you click the "switch view mode" button (the squiggle-looking one beside + Relationship), you'll see something like Figure 33, *A graph of nodes related to the current one*, on page 224.

The Style button brings up a menu where you can choose which profile is used for rendering the graph visualization. To see more useful information on the diagram, click Style and then New Profile. This will take you to the "Create new visualization profile" page. Enter the name *wines* at the top, and then change the label from {id} to {id}: {prop.name}. Click Save to bring you back to the visualization page. Now you can choose *wines* from the Style menu, which should produce something like Figure 34, *A graph of nodes using a custom profile*, on page 224.

Although the web interface is an easy way to make a few edits, we need a more powerful interface for production work.

Neo4j via Gremlin

There are several languages that interoperate with Neo4j: Java code, REST, Cypher, Ruby console, and others. The one we'll use today is called Gremlin, which is a graph traversal language written in the Groovy programming language. You needn't actually know Groovy to use Gremlin, however, so think of it as just another declarative domain-specific language, like SQL.

Like other consoles we've explored, Gremlin provides access to the underlying language infrastructure on which it's based. This means you can use Groovy constructs and Java libraries in Gremlin. We found it a powerful and more natural way of interacting with graphs than Neo4j's native Java code. And even better, the Gremlin console is available in the Web Admin; just click the Console link at the top, and choose Gremlin.

As a matter of convention, g is a variable that represents the graph object. Graph *actions* are functions called on it.

Since Gremlin is a general-purpose graph traversal language, it uses general mathematic graph terms. Where Neo4j calls a graph data point a *node*, Gremlin prefers *vertex*, and rather than *relationship*, Gremlin calls it an *edge*.

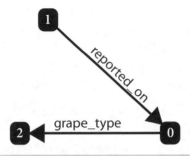

Figure 33—A graph of nodes related to the current one

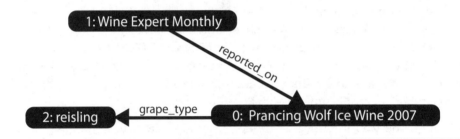

Figure 34—A graph of nodes using a custom profile

To access all of the vertices in this graph, there is a property simply named V for vertices.

```
gremlin> g.V
==>v[0]
==>v[1]
==>v[2]
```

along with a sister property named E, for edges.

```
gremlin> g.E
==> e[0][1-reported_on->0]
==> e[1][0-grape_type->2]
```

You can grab a particular vertex by passing a node number into the v (lower-case) method.

```
gremlin> g.v(0)
==> v[0]
```

To make sure you have the correct vertex, you can list its properties via the map() method. Note that you can chain method calls in Groovy/Gremlin.

```
gremlin> g.v(0).map()
==> name=Prancing Wolf Ice Wine 2007
```

Although using v(0) will retrieve the exact node, you could also filter out all nodes by some value you want. For example, to retrieve *riesling* by name, you can use the {...} filter syntax, which in Groovy code is called a *closure*. All of the code between the curly braces, {...}, define the function that, if it returns true, will walk that vertex. The it keyword inside the closure represents the current object and is automatically populated for your use.

```
gremlin> g.V.filter{it.name=='riesling'}
==> v[2]
```

Once you have a vertex, you can get the outgoing edges by calling outE() on the returned vertex. Incoming edges are retrieved by inE(), and both incoming and outgoing are called by bothE().

```
gremlin> g.V.filter{it.name=='Wine Expert Monthly'}.outE()
==> e[0][1-reported_on->0]
```

Note that in Groovy, like Ruby, method parentheses are optional for methods, so calling outE is fine too.

```
gremlin> g.V.filter{it.name=='Wine Expert Monthly'}.outE
==> e[0][1-reported_on->0]
```

From the out edges, you can walk to incoming vertices with inV—that is, the vertices into which the edges point. The reported_on edge from Wine Expert points into the *Prancing Wolf Ice Wine 2007* vertex, so outE.inV will return it. Then retrieve the name property by calling it on the vertex.

```
gremlin> g.V.filter{it.name=='Wine Expert Monthly'}.outE.inV.name
==> Prancing Wolf Ice Wine 2007
```

The expression outE.inV asks for any vertices to which the input vertices have edges. The reverse operation (asking for all vertices that have edges *into* the input vertices) is achieved with inE.outV. Because these two operations are so common, Gremlin has shorthand versions of both. The expression out is short for outE.inV, and in is short for inE.outV.

```
gremlin> g.V.filter{it.name=='Wine Expert Monthly'}.out.name
==> Prancing Wolf Ice Wine 2007
```

A winery makes more than one wine, so if we plan to add more, we should add the winery as a joining node and add an edge to the Prancing Wolf.

```
gremlin> pwolf = g.addVertex([name : 'Prancing Wolf Winery'])
==> v[3]
gremlin> g.addEdge(pwolf, g.v(0), 'produced')
==> e[2][3-produced->0]
```

From here we'll add a couple more rieslings: Kabinett and Spatlese.

```
gremlin> kabinett = g.addVertex([name : 'Prancing Wolf Kabinett 2002'])
==> v[4]
gremlin> g.addEdge(pwolf, kabinett, 'produced')
==> e[3][3-produced->4]
gremlin> spatlese = g.addVertex([name : 'Prancing Wolf Spatlese 2007'])
==> v[5]
gremlin> g.addEdge(pwolf, spatlese, 'produced')
==> e[4][3-produced->5]
```

Let's wrap up this little graph by adding some edges from the riesling vertex to the newly added vertices. We'll set the riesling variable by filtering the riesling node; next() is necessary to grab the first vertex out of the pipeline— something we will go over in more detail shortly.

```
gremlin> riesling = g.V.filter{it.name=='riesling'}.next()
==> v[2]
gremlin> g.addEdge([style:'kabinett'], kabinett, riesling, 'grape_type')
==> e[5][4-grape_type->2]
```

The Spatlese can be pointed to riesling in a similar way, but with the style set to spatlese. With all this data added, in the visualizer your graph should look like Figure 35, *A graph of nodes after adding data with Gremlin*, on page 227.

The Power of Pipes

You can think of Gremlin operations as a series of pipes. Each pipe takes a collection as input and pushes a collection as output. A collection may have one item, many items, or no items at all. The items may be vertices, edges, or property values.

For example, the outE pipe takes in a collection of vertices and sends out a collection of edges. The series of pipes is called a *pipeline* and expresses *declaratively* what the problem is. Contrast this with a typical *imperative* programming approach, which would require you to describe the steps to solve the problem. Using pipes is one of the most concise ways to query a graph database.

At its heart, Gremlin is a language to build these pipes. Specifically, it is built on top of a Java project named Pipes. To explore the pipe concept, let's return to our wine graph. Suppose we want to find wines that are similar to a given wine—that is, they have the same type. We can follow an ice wine that also shares a grape_type edge with other out nodes (ignoring the initial wine node).

```
ice_wine = g.v(0)
ice_wine.out('grape_type').in('grape_type').filter{ !it.equals(ice_wine) }
```

Figure 35—A graph of nodes after adding data with Gremlin

If you've worked in Smalltalk or Rails with scopes, this style of method chaining will seem familiar to you. But compare the previous to using the standard Neo4j Java API shown next, where a node's relationships must be iterated through in order to access the varietal nodes.

```
enum WineRelationshipType implements RelationshipType {
  grape_type
}

import static WineRelationshipType.grape_type;

public static List<Node> same_variety( Node wine ) {
  List<Node> wine_list = new ArrayList<Node>();
  // walk into all out edges from this vertex
  for( Relationship outE : wine.getRelationships( grape_type ) ) {
    // walk into all in edges from this edge's out vertex
    for( Edge inE : outE.getEndNode().getRelationships( grape_type ) ) {
      // only add vertices that are not the given vertex
      if( !inE.getStartNode().equals( wine ) ) {
        wine_list.add( inE.getStartNode() );
      }
    }
  }

  return wine_list;
}
```

Rather than nesting and iterating as shown earlier, the Pipes project designed a way to declare incoming and outgoing vertices. You create a sequence of in and out pipes, filters, and request values from the pipeline. Then iteratively call the pipeline's hasNext() method, which returns the next matching node. In other words, the pipeline walks the tree for you. Until the pipeline is requested, you're simply declaring how the walk will occur.

To illustrate, here's another implementation of the same_variety() method, which uses Pipes rather than explicitly looping:

Jim says:
jQuery and Gremlin

Users of the popular jQuery JavaScript library may find Gremlin's collection-oriented traversal method to be quite familiar. Consider this HTML snippet:

```
<ul id="navigation">
  <li>
    <a name="section1">section 1</a>
  </li>
  <li>
    <a name="section2">section 2</a>
  </li>
</ul>
```

Now suppose we want to find the text of all tags with the name section1 that are children of list items (<li>) under the navigation element (id=navigation). One way to do that in jQuery is with code like this:

```
$('[id=navigation]').children('li').children('[name=section1]').text()
```

Next, consider what a Gremlin query might look like for a similar data set, imagining that each parent node has an edge pointing to each of its children. Pretty similar, eh?

```
g.V.filter{it.id=='navigation'}.out.filter{it.tag=='li'}.
out.filter{it.name=='section1'}.text
```

```
public static void same_variety( Vertex wine ) {
  List<Vertex> wine_list = new ArrayList<Vertex>();
  Pipe inE       = new InPipe( "grape_type" );
  Pipe outE      = new OutPipe( "grape_type" );
  Pipe not_wine = new ObjectFilterPipe( wine, true );
  Pipe<Vertex,Vertex> pipeline =
    new Pipeline<Vertex,Vertex>( outE, inE, not_wine );
  pipeline.setStarts( Arrays.asList( wine ) );
  while( pipeline.hasNext() ) {
    wine_list.add( pipeline.next() );
  }
  return wine_list;
}
```

Deep down Gremlin is a Pipe-building language. The work of walking the graph is still being done on the Neo4j server, but Gremlin simplifies the effort of building queries that Neo4j can understand.

Pipeline vs. Vertex

To grab a collection containing just one specific vertex, we can filter it from the list of all nodes. This is what we have been doing when we call, for

Eric says:
Cypher Language

Cypher is the other graph query language supported by Neo4j, based on pattern matching and a SQL-like syntax. The clauses feel familiar, making it easy to understand what's going on. Particularly, the MATCH clause is very intuitive, resulting in ASCII art–like expressions.

At first I didn't like Cypher's verbosity, but over time as my eyes adjusted to reading its grammar, I've become a fan.

Look at this Cypher equivalent of our "similar wines" query:

```
START ice_wine=node(0)
MATCH (ice_wine) -[:grape_type]-> () <-[:grape_type]- (similar)
RETURN similar
```

We've started by binding ice_wine to node 0. The MATCH clause uses identifiers within parentheses to indicate nodes and typed "arrows" like -[:grape_type]-> for directional relationships. I actually like this construct, because it's easy to visualize the node walk.

It can quickly get advanced, however. This is a more real-world style example—every bit as powerful and wordy as SQL.

```
START ice_wine=node:wines(name="Prancing Wolf Ice Wine 2007")
MATCH ice_wine -[:grape_type]-> wine_type <-[:grape_type]- similar
WHERE wine_type =~ /(?i)riesl.*/
RETURN wine_type.name, collect(similar) as wines, count(*) as wine_count
ORDER BY wine_count desc
LIMIT 10
```

While I chose to focus on Gremlin in the main chapter, the two languages are natural complements and happily coexist. In day-to-day work, you'll find reasons to use either, depending on how you think about the problem at hand.

example, g.V.filter{it.name=='reisling'}. The V property is the list of all nodes, from which we're culling a sublist. But when we want the vertex itself, we need to call next(). This method retrieves the first vertex from the pipeline. It's akin to the difference between an array of one element and the element itself.

If you look at the class constructed by calling the filter's class property, notice it returns GremlinPipeline.

```
gremlin> g.V.filter{it.name=='Prancing Wolf Winery'}.class
==>class com.tinkerpop.gremlin.pipes.GremlinPipeline
```

Compare that to the class of the next node from the pipeline. It returns something else, the Neo4jVertex.

```
gremlin> g.V.filter{it.name=='Prancing Wolf Winery'}.next().class
==>class com.tinkerpop.blueprints.pgm.impls.neo4j.Neo4jVertex
```

Although the console conveniently lists the nodes retrieved from the pipeline, it remains a pipeline until you retrieve something from it.

Schemaless Social

Creating a social aspect to the graph is as easy as adding more nodes. Suppose we want to add three people—two who know each other and one stranger, each with their own wine preferences.

Alice has a bit of a sweet tooth and so is a big ice wine fan.

```
alice = g.addVertex([name:'Alice'])
ice_wine = g.V.filter{it.name=='Prancing Wolf Ice Wine 2007'}.next()
g.addEdge(alice, ice_wine, 'likes')
```

Tom loves Kabinett and ice wine and trusts anything written by *Wine Expert Monthly*.

```
tom = g.addVertex([name:'Tom'])
kabinett = g.V.filter{it.name=='Prancing Wolf Kabinett 2002'}.next()
g.addEdge(tom, kabinett, 'likes')
g.addEdge(tom, ice_wine, 'likes')
g.addEdge(tom, g.V.filter{it.name=='Wine Expert Monthly'}.next(), 'trusts')
```

Patty is friends with both Tom and Alice but is new to wine and has yet to choose any favorites.

```
patty = g.addVertex([name:'Patty'])
g.addEdge(patty, tom, 'friends')
g.addEdge(patty, alice, 'friends')
```

Without changing any fundamental structure of our existing graph, we were able to superimpose behavior beyond our original intent. The new nodes are related, as visualized in the following:

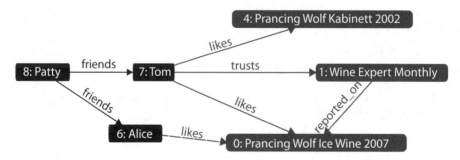

Stepping Stones

We've looked at a few core Gremlin *steps*, or Pipe-processing units. Gremlin provides many more. Let's take a look at more of these building blocks that not only walk the graph but also transform objects, filter steps, and produce side effects like counting nodes grouped by criteria.

We've seen inE, outE, inV, and outV, which are *transform steps* for retrieving the incoming and outgoing edges and vertices. Two other types are bothE and bothV, which just follow an edge, regardless of whether it is directed *in* or *out*.

This retrieves both Alice and all of her friends. We'll tack name to the end to get each vertice's name property. Since we don't care which direction the friend edge goes, we'll use bothE and bothV.

```
alice.bothE('friends').bothV.name

==> Alice
==> Patty
```

If we don't want Alice, the except() filter lets us pass in a list of nodes we don't want, and it walks the rest.

```
alice.bothE('friends').bothV.except([alice]).name

==> Patty
```

The opposite of except() is retain(), which, as you may have guessed, walks only matching nodes.

Another option is to instead filter the last vertex with a code block, where the current step is not equal to the alice vertex.

```
alice.bothE('friends').bothV.filter{!it.equals(alice)}.name
```

What if you wanted to know friends of Alice's friends? You could just repeat the steps like so:

```
alice.bothE('friends').bothV.except([alice]).
bothE('friends').bothV.except([alice])
```

In the same fashion, we could get friends of Alice's friends' friends by adding more bothE/bothV/except calls to the chain. But that's a lot of typing, and it's not possible to write this for a variable number of steps in this manner. The loop() method does just that. It repeats some number of previous steps and continues while the given closure is still true.

The following code will loop the previous three steps by counting periods back from the loop call. So, except is one, bothV is two, and bothE is three.

```
alice.bothE('friends').bothV.except([alice]).loop(3){
  it.loops <= 2
}.name
```

After each time through the looped series of steps, loop() invokes the given in the closure—that is, the code between the {...} brackets. In here, the it.loops property keeps track of how many times the current loop has been executed. In our case, we check and return whether this number is less than or equal to 2, meaning the loop will execute two times and stop. In effect, the closure is very much like the clause for a while loop in a typical programming language.

```
==>Tom
==>Patty
==>Patty
```

The loop worked, correctly finding both Tom and Patty. But now we have two copies of Patty. That's because one matches Patty as a friend of Alice, and the other matches because she is friends with Tom. So, now we need a way to filter out duplicate objects, which the dedup() (de-duplicate) filter provides.

```
alice.bothE('friends').bothV.except([alice]).loop(3){
  it.loops <= 2
}.dedup.name
```

```
==>Tom
==>Patty
```

To get more insight into the path taken to arrive at these values, you can follow the friend->friend path by using the paths() transform.

```
alice.bothE('friends').bothV.except([alice]).loop(3){
  it.loops <= 2
}.dedup.name.paths
```

```
==> [v[7], e[12][9-friends->7], v[9], e[11][9-friends->8], v[8], Tom]
==> [v[7], e[12][9-friends->7], v[9], e[11][9-friends->8], v[9], Patty]
```

All traversals you've done so far have been to walk forward through a graph. Sometimes you need to take two steps forward and two steps back. Starting with the Alice node, we walk out two steps and then back two, which returns us to the Alice node.

```
gremlin> alice.outE.inV.back(2).name
==> Alice
```

The last commonly used step we'll investigate is groupCount(), which walks through the nodes and counts duplicate values, capturing them in a map.

Consider this example that collects all the name properties of all vertices in the graph and counts how many of each there are:

```
gremlin> name_map = [:]
gremlin> g.V.name.groupCount( name_map )
gremlin> name_map
==> Prancing Wolf Ice Wine 2007=1
==> Wine Expert Monthly=1
==> riesling=1
==> Prancing Wolf Winery=1
==> Prancing Wolf Kabinett 2002=1
==> Prancing Wolf Spatlese 2007=1
==> Alice=1
==> Tom=1
==> Patty=1
```

In Groovy/Gremlin, a map is denoted by the nomenclature [:] and is pretty much identical to the Ruby/JavaScript object literal {}. Notice how all of the values are 1. This is exactly what we'd expect, since we haven't repeated any names, and the V collection has exactly one copy of each node in our graph.

Next, let's count up the number of wines liked by each person in our system. We can get all of the liked vertices and count up the numbers per name.

```
gremlin> wines_count = [:]
gremlin> g.V.outE('likes').outV.name.groupCount( wines_count )
gremlin> wines_count
==> Alice=1
==> Tom=2
```

As we should expect, Alice liked one wine, and Tom liked two.

Getting Groovy

Besides the Gremlin steps, we also get the wide array of Groovy language constructs and methods. Groovy has a map function (a la mapreduce) named collect() and a reduce function named inject(). Using these, we can preform mapreduce-like queries.

Consider the case where we want to count how many wines have not yet been rated. We can do this by first mapping out a list of true/false values indicating whether each wine has been rated. Then, we can run that list through a reducer to count up all the trues and falses. The mapping part uses collect and looks like this:

```
rated_list = g.V.in('grape_type').collect{
  !it.inE('reported_on').toList().isEmpty()
}
```

In the previous code, the expression g.V.in('grape_type') returns all the nodes that have an incoming grape_type relationship. Only wines will have this type of edge, so we have our list of all wines in the system. Next, in the collect closure, we determine whether the wine in question has any incoming report-ed_on edges. The toList() call forces the pipeline to become a true list, which we can then test for emptiness. The rated_list produced by this code will be a list of true and false values.

To count how many wines have not been rated, we can run that list through a reducer using the inject() method.

```
rated_list.inject(0){ count, is_rated ->
  if (is_rated) {
    count
  } else {
    count + 1
  }
}
```

In Groovy, the arrow operator (->) separates the input arguments for a closure from the body of the closure. In our reducer, we need to keep track of the accumulated count and process whether the current wine has been rated or not, which is the reason for count and is_rated. The 0 part of inject(0) initialized count to 0 before the first invocation. Then, within the body of the closure function, we either return the current count if the wine has already been rated or return that value plus 1 if it hasn't been rated. The final output will be the number of false values in the list (that is, the count of unrated wines).

```
==> 2
```

So, it turns out that two of our wines are as yet unrated.

With all these tools available, you can craft many powerful combinations of graph traversals and transformations. Suppose we want to find all of the pairs of friends in our graph. To do that, first we need to find all edges with a friends type and then output the names of both people who share that edge by using the transform operation.

```
g.V.outE('friends').transform{[it.outV.name.next(), it.inV.name.next()]}
```

```
==> [Patty, Tom]
==> [Patty, Alice]
```

In the previous code, the return value of the transform closure is an array literal ([...]) with two elements: the output and input vertices to the friend edge.

To find all people and the wines they like, we transform our output of people (identified as vertices with friends) into a list with two elements: the name of the person and a list of wines they like.

```
g.V.both('friends').dedup.transform{
  [ it.name, it.out('likes').name.toList() ]
}

==> [Alice, [Prancing Wolf Ice Wine 2007]]
==> [Patty, []]
==> [Tom, [Prancing Wolf Ice Wine 2007, Prancing Wolf Kabinett 2002]]
```

Gremlin definitely takes a little getting used to, especially if you haven't done much Groovy programming before. Once you get the hang of it, you'll find it's an expressive and powerful way to perform queries against Neo4j.

Domain-Specific Steps

Graph traversal is nice, but businesses and organizations tend to converse in domain-specific languages. For example, we wouldn't normally ask "What is the vertex with the incoming edge of grape_type sharing the outgoing edge of this wine's vertex?" but rather "What varietal is this wine?"

Gremlin is already a language specific to the domain of querying graph databases, but what about making the language even more specific? Gremlin lets us do this by creating new steps that are semantically meaningful to the data stored in the graph.

Let's start by creating a new step named varietal that seeks to answer the question posed before. When varietal() is called on a vertex, it will look for outgoing edges of type grape_type and step to those related vertices.

We're getting into a bit of Groovy-foo here, so we'll first look at our code to create the step and then describe it line by line.

neo4j/varietal.groovy
```
Gremlin.defineStep( 'varietal',
  [Vertex, Pipe],
  {_().out('grape_type').dedup}
)
```

First we tell the Gremlin engine we're adding a new step called varietal. The second line tells Gremlin that this new step should attach to both Vertex and Pipe classes (when in double, just use both). The last line is where the magic happens. Effectively, this creates a closure that contains the code this step should execute. The underscore and parentheses represent the current pipeline object. From this object, we walk to any neighbor nodes related by a grape_type edge—that is, the varietal node. We end with dedup to remove any possible duplicates.

Calling our new step is just like any other step. For example, the following gets the name of the ice wine's varietal:

```
g.V.filter{it.name=='Prancing Wolf Ice Wine 2007'}.varietal.name
```

```
==> riesling
```

Let's try another one. This time we're making a step for a commonly requested action: get all friends' favorite wines.

```
neo4j/friendsuggest.groovy
Gremlin.defineStep( 'friendsuggest',
  [Vertex, Pipe],
  {
    _().sideEffect{start = it}.both('friends').
    except([start]).out('likes').dedup
  }
)
```

Just like last time, we give Gremlin our new friendsuggest step name and bind it to Vertex and Pipe. This time, our code will filter out the current person. We do that by setting the current vertex/pipe to a variable (start) by using the sideEffect{start = it} function. Then we get all friends nodes, except for the current person (we don't want to list Alice as her own friend).

Now we're cooking with pipes! We can call this new step as we normally would.

```
g.V.filter{it.name=='Patty'}.friendsuggest.name
```

```
==> Prancing Wolf Ice Wine 2007
==> Prancing Wolf Kabinett 2002
```

Since varietal and friendsuggest are just normal Pipe-building steps, you can chain them together to make more interesting queries. The following finds the varietals that Patty's friends like best:

```
g.V.filter{it.name=='Patty'}.friendsuggest.varietal.name
```

```
==> riesling
```

Using Groovy metaprogramming to create new steps is a powerful force for crafting domain-specific languages. But like Gremlin itself, the practice can take some getting used to.

Update, Delete, Done

You've inserted and stepped through a graph, but what about updating and deleting data? It's easy enough, once you find the vertex or edge you want to alter. Let's add a weight to how much Alice likes the Prancing Wolf Ice Wine 2007.

```
gremlin> e=g.V.filter{it.name=='Alice'}.outE('likes').next()
gremlin> e.weight = 95
gremlin> e.save
```

We can remove the value just as easily.

```
gremlin> e.removeProperty('weight')
gremlin> e.save
```

Before we call it a day and go into some homework, we should cover how to clean up our database.

Don't run these commands until you've finished the homework for the day!

The graph object has functions to remove vertices and edges, removeVertex and removeEdge, respectively. We could destroy our graph by removing all vertices and edges.

```
gremlin> g.V.each{ g.removeVertex(it) }
gremlin> g.E.each{ g.removeEdge(it) }
```

You can validate they are gone by calling g.V and g.E. Or you can achieve the same thing with the ridiculously dangerous clear() method.

```
gremlin> g.clear()
```

If you're running your own Gremlin instance (outside of the web interface), it's a good idea to cleanly shut down the graph connection with the shutdown() method.

```
gremlin> g.shutdown()
```

If you don't, it may corrupt the database. But usually it will just yell at you the next time you connect to the graph.

Day 1 Wrap-Up

Today we got to peek at the graph database Neo4j—and what a different beast it is. Although we didn't cover specific design patterns, our brains were buzzing with possibilities when we first began working with Neo4j. If you can draw it on a whiteboard, you can store it in a graph database.

Day 1 Homework

Find

1. Bookmark the Neo4j wiki.
2. Bookmark the Gremlin steps from the wiki or API.
3. Find two other Neo4j shells (such as the Cypher shell in the admin console).

Do

1. Query all node names with another shell (such as the Cypher query language).
2. Delete all the nodes and edges in your database.
3. Create a new graph that represents your family.

7.3 Day 2: REST, Indexes, and Algorithms

Today we'll start with Neo4j's REST interface. We'll create nodes and relationships using REST and then use REST to index and execute a full-text search. We'll then look at a plug-in that lets us execute Gremlin queries on the server through REST, freeing our code from the confines of the Gremlin console—or even running Java at all in our application server or clients.

Taking a REST

Just like Riak, HBase, Mongo, and CouchDB, Neo4j ships with a REST interface. One of the reasons all of these databases support REST is because it allows language-agnostic interactions in a standard connection interface. We can connect to Neo4j—which requires Java to work—from a separate machine with no trace of Java whatsoever. And with the Gremlin plug-in, we'll see how to gain the power of its terse query syntax over REST.

First you might want to check that the REST server is running by issuing a GET against the base URL, which retrieves the root node. It runs on the same port as the web admin tool you used yesterday, at the /db/data/ path. We'll use our trusty friend curl to issue the REST commands.

```
$ curl http://localhost:7474/db/data/
{
  "relationship_index" : "http://localhost:7474/db/data/index/relationship",
  "node" : "http://localhost:7474/db/data/node",
  "relationship_types" : "http://localhost:7474/db/data/relationship/types",
  "extensions_info" : "http://localhost:7474/db/data/ext",
  "node_index" : "http://localhost:7474/db/data/index/node",
  "extensions" : {
  }
}
```

It will return a nice JSON object describing the URLs of other commands, like node actions or indices.

Creating Nodes and Relationships Using REST

It's as easy to create nodes and relationships in Neo4j REST as in CouchDB or Riak. Creating a node is a POST to the /db/data/node path with JSON data. As matter of convention, it pays to give each node a name property. This makes viewing any node's information easy: just call name.

```
$ curl -i -X POST http://localhost:7474/db/data/node \
-H "Content-Type: application/json" \
-d '{"name": "P.G. Wodehouse", "genre": "British Humour"}'
```

When posted, you'll get the node path in the header and a body of metadata about the node (both are truncated here for brevity). All of this data is retrievable by calling GET on the given header Location value (or the self property in the metadata).

```
HTTP/1.1 201 Created
Location: http://localhost:7474/db/data/node/9
Content-Type: application/json

{
  "outgoing_relationships" :
    "http://localhost:7474/db/data/node/9/relationships/out",
  "data" : {
    "genre" : "British Humour",
    "name" : "P.G. Wodehouse"
  },
  "traverse" : "http://localhost:7474/db/data/node/9/traverse/{returnType}",
  "all_typed_relationships" :
    "http://localhost:7474/db/data/node/9/relationships/all/{-list|&|types}",
  "property" : "http://localhost:7474/db/data/node/9/properties/{key}",
  "self" : "http://localhost:7474/db/data/node/9",
  "properties" : "http://localhost:7474/db/data/node/9/properties",
  "outgoing_typed_relationships" :
    "http://localhost:7474/db/data/node/9/relationships/out/{-list|&|types}",
  "incoming_relationships" :
    "http://localhost:7474/db/data/node/9/relationships/in",
  "extensions" : {
  },
  "create_relationship" : "http://localhost:7474/db/data/node/9/relationships",
  "paged_traverse" :
    "http://localhost:7474/db/.../{returnType}{?pageSize,leaseTime}",
  "all_relationships" : "http://localhost:7474/db/data/node/9/relationships/all",
  "incoming_typed_relationships" :
    "http://localhost:7474/db/data/node/9/relationships/in/{-list|&|types}"
}
```

If you just want the node properties (not the metadata), you can GET that by appending /properties to the node URL or even an individual property by further appending the property name.

```
$ curl http://localhost:7474/db/data/node/9/properties/genre
"British Humour"
```

One node doesn't do us much good, so go ahead and create another one with the properties ["name" : "Jeeves Takes Charge", "style" : "short story"].

Since P.G. Wodehouse wrote the short story "Jeeves Takes Charge," we can make a relationship between them.

```
$ curl -i -X POST http://localhost:7474/db/data/node/9/relationships \
-H "Content-Type: application/json" \
-d '{"to": "http://localhost:7474/db/data/node/10", "type": "WROTE",
  "data": {"published": "November 28, 1916"}}'
```

A nice thing about the REST interface is that it actually reported on how to create a relationship early in the body metadata's create_relationship property. In this way, the REST interfaces tend to be mutually discoverable.

Finding Your Path

Through the REST interface, you can find the path between two nodes by posting the request data to the starting node's /paths URL. The POST request data must be a JSON string denoting the node you want the path to, the type of relationships you want to follow, and the path-finding algorithm to use.

For example, here we're looking for a path following relationships of the type WROTE from node 1 using the shortestPath algorithm and capping out at a depth of 10.

```
$ curl -X POST http://localhost:7474/db/data/node/9/paths \
-H "Content-Type: application/json" \
-d '{"to":"http://localhost:7474/db/data/node/10",
  "relationships": {"type" : "WROTE"},
  "algorithm":"shortestPath", "max_depth":10}'
[ {
  "start" : "http://localhost:7474/db/data/node/9",
  "nodes" : [
    "http://localhost:7474/db/data/node/9",
    "http://localhost:7474/db/data/node/10"
  ],
  "length" : 1,
  "relationships" : [ "http://localhost:7474/db/data/relationship/14" ],
  "end" : "http://localhost:7474/db/data/node/10"
} ]
```

The other path algorithm choices are allPaths, allSimplePaths, and dijkstra. Details on these algorithms can be found in the online documentation,[1] but covering them in detail is outside the scope of this book.

---

1. http://api.neo4j.org/current/org/neo4j/graphalgo/GraphAlgoFactory.html

Indexing

Like other databases we've seen, Neo4j supports fast data lookups by constructing indexes. There is a twist, though. Unlike other database indexes where you perform queries in much the same way as without one, Neo4j indexes have a different path. This is because the indexing service is actually a separate service.

The simplest index is the key-value or hash style. You key the index by some node data, and the value is a REST URL, which points to the node in the graph. You can have as many indexes as you like, so we'll name this one "authors." The end of the URL will contain the author name we want to index and pass in node 1 as the value (or whatever your Wodehouse node was).

```
$ curl -X POST http://localhost:7474/db/data/index/node/authors \
-H "Content-Type: application/json" \
-d '{ "uri" : "http://localhost:7474/db/data/node/9",
"key" : "name", "value" : "P.G.+Wodehouse"}'
```

Retrieving the node is simply a call to the index, which you'll notice doesn't return the URL we set but instead the actual node data.

```
$ curl http://localhost:7474/db/data/index/node/authors/name/P.G.+Wodehouse
```

Besides key-value, Neo4j provides a full-text search inverted index, so you can perform queries like this: "Give me all books that have names beginning with 'Jeeves.'" To build this index, we need to build it against the entire dataset, rather than our one-offs earlier. Like Riak, Neo4j incorporates Lucene to build our inverted index.

```
$ curl -X POST http://localhost:7474/db/data/index/node \
-H "Content-Type: application/json" \
-d '{"name":"fulltext", "config":{"type":"fulltext","provider":"lucene"}}'
```

The POST will return a JSON response containing information about the newly added index.

```
{
  "template" : "http://localhost:7474/db/data/index/node/fulltext/{key}/{value}",
  "provider" : "lucene",
  "type" : "fulltext"
}
```

Now if we add Wodehouse to the full-text index, we get this:

```
curl -X POST http://localhost:7474/db/data/index/node/fulltext \
-H "Content-Type: application/json" \
-d '{ "uri" : "http://localhost:7474/db/data/node/9",
"key" : "name", "value" : "P.G.+Wodehouse"}'
```

Then a search is as easy as a Lucene syntax query on the index URL.

```
$ curl http://localhost:7474/db/data/index/node/fulltext?query=name:P*
```

Indexes can also be built on edges like earlier; just replace the instances of *node* in the URLs with *relationship*, for example http://localhost:7474/db/data/index/relationship/published/date/1916-11-28.

REST and Gremlin

We spent much of Day 1 using Gremlin and the first half of today using the REST interface. If you wondered which you should use, fear not. The Neo4j REST interface has a Gremlin plug-in (which is installed by default in the version of Neo4j we're using).[2] You can send through REST any commands you could in the Gremlin console. This allows you the power and flexibility of both tools in production. This is a great combination, since Gremlin is better geared toward powerful queries, where REST is geared toward deployment and language flexibility.

The following code will return all vertex names. You only need to send the data to the plug-in URL as a JSON string value, under the field script.

```
$ curl -X POST \
http://localhost:7474/db/data/ext/GremlinPlugin/graphdb/execute_script \
-H "content-type:application/json" \
-d '{"script":"g.V.name"}'

[ "P.G. Wodehouse", "Jeeves Takes Charge" ]
```

Although code samples from here on out will use Gremlin, bear in mind that you could instead choose to use REST.

Big Data

Up until now we've dealt with very small data sets, so now it's time to see what Neo4j can do with some big data.

Let's explore some movie data by grabbing a dataset from Freebase.com. We'll be using the "performance" tab-separated set.[3] Download the file and use the following script, which iterates through each line and creates a relationship between new or existing nodes (matches are found by name in the index).

Be warned, this dataset contains a vast amount of movie information, from blockbusters to foreign films to, well, adult entertainment. You will need the json and faraday Ruby gems installed to run this script.

---

2.   http://docs.neo4j.org/chunked/stable/gremlin-plugin.html

3.   http://download.freebase.com/datadumps/latest/browse/film/performance.tsv

neo4j/importer.rb
```ruby
REST_URL = 'http://localhost:7474/'
HEADER = { 'Content-Type' => 'application/json' }

%w{rubygems json cgi faraday}.each{|r| require r}

# make a connection to the Neo4j REST server
conn = Faraday.new(:url => REST_URL) do |builder|
  builder.adapter :net_http
end

# method to get existing node from the index, or create one
def get_or_create_node(conn, index, value)
  # look for node in the index
  r = conn.get("/db/data/index/node/#{index}/name/#{CGI.escape(value)}")
  node = (JSON.parse(r.body).first || {})['self'] if r.status == 200
  unless node
    # no indexed node found, so create a new one
    r = conn.post("/db/data/node", JSON.unparse({"name" => value}), HEADER)
    node = (JSON.parse(r.body) || {})['self'] if [200, 201].include? r.status
    # add new node to an index
    node_data = "{\"uri\" : \"#{node}\", \"key\" : \"name\",
      \"value\" : \"#{CGI.escape(value)}\"}"
    conn.post("/db/data/index/node/#{index}", node_data, HEADER)
  end
  node
end

puts "begin processing..."

count = 0
File.open(ARGV[0]).each do |line|
  _, _, actor, movie = line.split("\t")
  next if actor.empty? || movie.empty?

  # build the actor and movie nodes
  actor_node = get_or_create_node(conn, 'actors', actor)
  movie_node = get_or_create_node(conn, 'movies', movie)

  # create relationship between actor and movie
  conn.post("#{actor_node}/relationships",
    JSON.unparse({ :to => movie_node, :type => 'ACTED_IN' }), HEADER)

  puts "  #{count} relationships loaded" if (count += 1) % 100 == 0

end

puts "done!"
```

With everything set up, just run the script and point it to the downloaded performance.tsv file.

```
$ ruby importer.rb performance.tsv
```

This can take hours to run the whole dataset, but you can stop the process at any time for a partial movie/actor list. If you're running Ruby 1.9, you might have better luck replacing the line builder.adapter :net_http with builder.adapter :em_synchrony, which creates a nonblocking connection.

Fancy Algorithms

With our big movie dataset, it's time to hang up our REST interface for a while and jump back into Gremlin.

Of Course, Kevin Bacon

Let's have a little fun implementing one of the more famous graph algorithms in existence: the Kevin Bacon algorithm. This algorithm is based on a game to find the shortest distance between any actor and Kevin Bacon through commonly acted movies. For instance, Alec Guinness acted in *Kafka* with Theresa Russell, who was in *Wild Things* with Kevin Bacon.

Before continuing, fire up your Gremlin console and start up the graph. Then we'll create the costars custom step with the following code. This is similar to the friendsuggest from yesterday. It finds the costars of an actor node (actors who share an edge with the initial actor's movies).

```
neo4j/costars.groovy
Gremlin.defineStep( 'costars',
  [Vertex, Pipe],
  {
    _().sideEffect{start = it}.outE('ACTED_IN').
    inV.inE('ACTED_IN').outV.filter{
      !start.equals(it)
    }.dedup
  }
)
```

In Neo4j you don't so much "query" for a set of values as you "walk" the graph. The nice thing about this concept is that generally the first node walked to will be the closest to your starting node (in terms of raw edge/node distance, not of weighted distance). Let's begin by finding our starting and ending nodes.

```
gremlin> bacon = g.V.filter{it.name=='Kevin Bacon'}.next()
gremlin> elvis = g.V.filter{it.name=='Elvis Presley'}.next()
```

We start by finding an actor's costars' costars' costars...the classic stopping distance is six degrees, but practically we can stop at four (if you don't find a match, you can try again). Here we can loop through the graph four times, which finds all actors with "four degrees of separation." We'll use the costars step we just created.

```
elvis.costars.loop(1){it.loops < 4}
```

Only vertices that end with Bacon are to be retained. All others are ignored.

```
elvis.costars.loop(1){
  it.loops < 4
}.filter{it.equals(bacon)}
```

Just to ensure we don't want to continue looping back to the Kevin Bacon node for a second pass, hitting the bacon node short-circuits the loop. Or, in other words, loop as long as the loop hasn't occurred four times and we are not on the bacon node. Then we can output the paths taken to arrive at each bacon node.

```
elvis.costars.loop(1){
  it.loops < 4 & !it.object.equals(bacon)
}.filter{it.equals(bacon)}.paths
```

With that, we only need to pop the first path off the top of the list of possible paths—the shortest path will be arrived at first. The >> nomenclature just pops the first item off the list of all nodes.

```
(elvis.costars.loop(1){
  it.loops < 4 & !it.object.equals(bacon)
}.filter{it.equals(bacon)}.paths >> 1)
```

Finally, we get the name of each vertex and filter out any null edge data using the Groovy grep command.

```
(elvis.costars.loop(1){
  it.loops < 4 & !it.object.equals(bacon)
}.filter{it.equals(bacon)}.paths >> 1).name.grep{it}
```

```
==>Elvis Presley
==>Double Trouble
==>Roddy McDowall
==>The Big Picture
==>Kevin Bacon
```

We didn't know who Roddy McDowall was, but that's the beauty of our graph database. We didn't have to know to get a good answer. Feel free to sharpen your Groovy-foo if you want the output to be fancier than our simple list, but the data is all there.

Random Walk

When looking for good sample from a large data set, a useful trick is the "random walk." You start with a random number generator.

```
rand = new Random()
```

Then you filter out some target ratio of the total. If we want to return only about one-third of Kevin Bacon's ~60 movies, we could filter out any random number less than 0.33.

```
bacon.outE.filter{rand.nextDouble() <= 0.33}.inV.name
```

The count should be somewhere around twenty random titles from the Bacon canon.

Taking a second-degree step away from Kevin Bacon, his costars' costars, creates quite a list (more than 300,000 in our data set).

```
bacon.outE.inV.inE.outV.loop(4){
  it.loops < 3
}.count()

==> 316198
```

But if you need only about 1 percent of that list, add a filter. Also note the filter is itself a step, so you'll need to add one more to your loop number.

```
bacon.outE{
  rand.nextDouble() <= 0.01
}.inV.inE.outV.loop(5){
  it.loops < 3
}.name
```

We received Elijah Wood, who we can run through our Bacon path algorithm and reasonably expect two steps (Elijah Wood acted in *Deep Impact* with Ron Eldard, who was in *Sleepers* with Kevin Bacon).

Centrality Park

Centrality is a measure of individual nodes against a full graph. For example, if we wanted to measure how important each node in a network is based on its distance to all the other nodes, that would require a centrality algorithm.

The most famous centrality algorithm is probably Google's PageRank, but there are several styles. We'll execute a simple version called *eigenvector centrality*, which just counts the number of in or out edges related to a node. We're going to give each actor a number related to how many roles they have played.

We need a map for groupCount() to populate and a count to set a maximum number or loops.

```
role_count = [:]; count = 0
g.V.in.groupCount(role_count).loop(2){ count++ < 1000 }; ''
```

The role_count map will be keyed by vertices, with values of the count of edges the vertex has. The easiest way to read the output is by sorting the map.

```
role_count.sort{a,b -> a.value <=> b.value}
```

The last value will be the actor with the greatest number of acting credits. In our dataset that honor belonged to legendary voice actor Mel Blanc with 424 credits (which you can list by running g.V.filter{it.name=='Mel Blanc'}.out.name).

External Algorithms

Writing your own algorithms is fine, but most of this work has already been done for you. The Java Universal Network/Graph (JUNG) Framework is a collection of common graph algorithms and other tools for modeling and visualizing graphs. Thanks to the Gremlin/Blueprint project, it's easy to access JUNG's algorithms, such as PageRank, HITS, Voltage, centrality algorithms, and graph-as-a-matrix tools.

To use JUNG, we need to wrap the Neo4j Graph into a new JUNG Graph.[4] To access the JUNG graph, we need to do one of two options: download and install all of the Blueprint and JUNG jars into your Neo4j server libs directory and restart the server, or download the prepackaged Gremlin console. We recommend the latter option for this project, since it will save you the hassle of hunting down several Java archive files (jars).

Assuming you've downloaded the gremlin console, shut down your neo4j server and start up Gremlin. You'll have to create the Neo4jGraph object and point it to your installation's data/graph directory.

```
g = new Neo4jGraph('/users/x/neo4j-enterprise-1.7/data/graph.db')
```

We'll keep the Gremlin graph named g. The Neo4jGraph object needs to be wrapped in a GraphJung object, which we'll call j.

```
j = new GraphJung( g )
```

Part of the reason Kevin Bacon was chosen as the ultimate path destination is his relative closeness to other actors. He has starred in movies with other popular stars. To be important, he didn't need to be in many roles himself but simply be connected to those who are well connected.

---

4.   http://blueprints.tinkerpop.com

This raises the question: can we find a better actor than Kevin Bacon, in terms of distance from other actors?

JUNG contains a scoring algorithm called BarycenterScorer that gives a score to each vertex based on its distance to all other vertices. If Kevin Bacon is indeed the best choice, we would expect his score to be the lowest, meaning he is "closest" to all other actors.

Our JUNG algorithm should apply only to actors, so we construct a *transformer* to filter only actor nodes. The EdgeLabelTransformer permits only those nodes with an edge of ACTED_IN to the algorithm.

```
t = new EdgeLabelTransformer(['ACTED_IN'] as Set, false)
```

Next, we need to import the algorithm itself, passing in our GraphJung and transformer.

```
import edu.uci.ics.jung.algorithms.scoring.BarycenterScorer
barycenter = new BarycenterScorer<Vertex,Edge>( j, t )
```

With that, we can get the BarycenterScorer score of any node. Let's find out what Kevin Bacon's score is.

```
bacon = g.V.filter{it.name=='Kevin Bacon'}.next()
bacon_score = barycenter.getVertexScore(bacon)
```

```
~0.0166
```

Once we have Kevin Bacon's score, we can go through every vertex and store any that have a score lower than his.

```
connected = [:]
```

It could take a really long time to execute the BarycenterScorer score for each actor in our database. So, instead, let's just run the algorithm against each of Kevin's costars. This may take a few minutes, depending on your hardware. BarycenterScorer is fast, but executing over each of Bacon's costars adds up.

```
bacon.costars.each{
  score = b.getVertexScore(it);
  if(score < bacon_score) {
    connected[it] = score;
  }
}
```

All of the keys that exist in the connected map represent a better choice than Kevin Bacon. But it's good to have a name we recognize, so let's output them all and pick one we like. Your output will vary from ours, since the public movie dataset is always in flux.

```
connected.collect{k,v -> k.name + " => " + v}

==> Donald Sutherland => 0.00925
==> Clint Eastwood => 0.01488
...
```

Donald Sutherland appeared in the list with a respectable ~0.00925. So, hypothetically, the Six Degrees of Donald Sutherland should be an easier game to play with your friends than the traditional Six Degrees of Kevin Bacon.

With our j graph we can now run any JUNG algorithm on our dataset, for example PageRank. Like BarycenterScorer, you need to import the class first.

```
import edu.uci.ics.jung.algorithms.scoring.PageRank
pr = new PageRank<Vertex,Edge>( j, t, 0.25d )
```

The full list of JUNG algorithms can be found in their online Javadoc API. More are added all the time, so it's a good place to look before implementing your own.

Day 2 Wrap-Up

On Day 2 we broadened our ability to interact with Neo4j by taking a look at the REST interface. We saw how, using the Gremlin plug-in, we can execute Gremlin code on the server and have the REST interface return results. We played around with a larger dataset and finally finished up with a handful of algorithms for diving into that data.

Day 2 Homework

Find

1. Bookmark the documentation for the Neo4j REST API.
2. Bookmark the API for the JUNG project and the algorithms it implements.
3. Find a binding or REST interface for your favorite programming language.

Do

1. Turn the path-finding portion of the Kevin Bacon algorithm into its own step. Then implement a general-purpose Groovy function (for example, def actor_path(g, name1, name2) {...}) that accepts the graph and two names and compares the distance.

2. Choose and run one of the many JUNG algorithms on a node (or the data set, if the API demands it).

3. Install your driver of choice, and use it to manage your company graph with the people and the roles they play, with edges describing their interactions (reports to, works with). If your company is huge, just try

your close teams; if you're with a small organization, try including some customers. Find the most well-connected person in the organization by closest distance to all other nodes.

7.4 Day 3: Distributed High Availability

We're going to wrap up our Neo4j investigation by learning how to make Neo4j more attuned to mission-critical uses. We'll see how Neo4j keeps data stable via ACID-compliant transactions. Then we'll install and configure a Neo4j high availability (HA) cluster to improve availability when serving high-read traffic. Then we're going to look into backup strategies to ensure our data remains safe.

Transactions

Neo4j is an Atomic, Consistent, Isolated, Durable (ACID) transaction database, similar to PostgreSQL. This makes it a good option for important data you may have otherwise picked a relational database for. Just like transactions we've seen before, Neo4j transactions are all-or-nothing operations. When a transaction starts, every following operation will succeed or fail as an atomic unit—failure of one means failure of all.

The details of how transactions are handled goes beyond Gremlin into the underlying Neo4j wrapper project called Blueprint. Specific details can change from version to version. We're using Gremlin 1.3, which uses Blueprints 1.0. If you're using a different version of either, you can find the specifics in the Blueprint API Javadocs.

Just like PostgreSQL, basic one-line functions are automatically wrapped in an implicit transaction. To demonstrate multiline transactions, we need to flag the graph object to turn off automatic transaction mode, letting Neo4j know that we plan to handle transactions manually. You can change the transaction mode through the setTransactionMode() function.

```
gremlin> g.setTransactionMode(TransactionalGraph.Mode.MANUAL)
```

You start and stop the transaction on the graph object using startTransaction() and stopTransaction(conclusion). When you stop the transaction, you also need to mark whether the transaction was successful. If not, Neo4j can roll back all commands executed since the start. It's a good idea to wrap the transaction within a try/catch block to ensure that any exceptions will trigger a rollback.

```
g.startTransaction()
try {
  // execute some multi-step graph stuff here...
  g.stopTransaction(TransactionalGraph.Conclusion.SUCCESS)
} catch(e) {
  g.stopTransaction(TransactionalGraph.Conclusion.FAILURE)
}
```

If you want to operate outside the Gremlin confines and work directly with the Neo4j EmbeddedGraphDatabase, you can use the Java API syntax for transactions. You may have to use this style if you write Java code or use a language that is Java under the covers—like JRuby.

```
r = g.getRawGraph()
tx = r.beginTx()
try {
  // execute some multistep graph stuff here...
  tx.success()
} finally {
  tx.finish()
}
```

Both varieties provide you with full ACID transaction guarantees. Even system failure will ensure any writes are rolled back when the server is fired back up. If you don't need to manually handle transactions, you're better off keeping the transaction mode on TransactionalGraph.Mode.AUTOMATIC.

High Availability

High availability mode is Neo4j's answer to the question, "Can a graph database scale?" Yes, but with some caveats. A write to one slave is not immediately synchronized with all other slaves, so there is a danger of losing consistency (in the CAP sense) for a brief moment (making it eventually consistent). HA will lose pure ACID-compliant transactions. It's for this reason that Neo4j HA is touted as a solution largely for increasing capacity for reads.

Just like Mongo, the servers in the cluster will elect a master that is the gold copy of data. Unlike Mongo, however, slaves accept writes. Slave writes will synchronize with the master node, which then propagates those changes to the other slaves.

HA Cluster

To use Neo4j HA, we must first set up a cluster. Neo4j uses an external cluster coordinator service called Zookeeper. Zookeeper is yet another excellent project to arise from the Apache Hadoop project. It's a general-purpose service to coordinate distributed applications. Neo4j HA uses this to manage its life-cycle activities. Each Neo4j server has its own related coordinator—tasked with managing its place in the cluster—as shown in Figure 36, *A three-server Neo4j cluster and their coordinators*, on page 253.

Happily, Neo4j Enterprise comes bundled with Zookeeper as well as some files to help us configure a cluster. We're going to run three instances of Neo4j Enterprise version 1.7. You can download a copy from the website for your operating system (be sure you select the correct edition)[5] and then unzip it and create two more copies of the directory. We suffixed ours with 1, 2, and 3 and will refer to them as such.

```
tar fx neo4j-enterprise-1.7-unix.tar
mv neo4j-enterprise-1.7 neo4j-enterprise-1.7-1
cp -R neo4j-enterprise-1.7-1 neo4j-enterprise-1.7-2
cp -R neo4j-enterprise-1.7-1 neo4j-enterprise-1.7-3
```

Now we have three identical copies of our database.

Normally you would unpack one copy per server and configure the cluster to be aware of the other servers. But since we're running them locally, we'll instead run them on different directories using different ports.

We will follow five steps to create our cluster, starting by configuring the Zookeeper cluster coordinators and then the Neo4j servers.

1. Set unique IDs for each coordinator server.

2. Configure each coordinator server to communicate with the other servers and its hosted Neo4j server.

3. Start up all three coordinator servers.

4. Configure each Neo4j server to run in HA mode, give them unique ports, and make them aware of the coordinator cluster.

---

5.   http://neo4j.org/download/

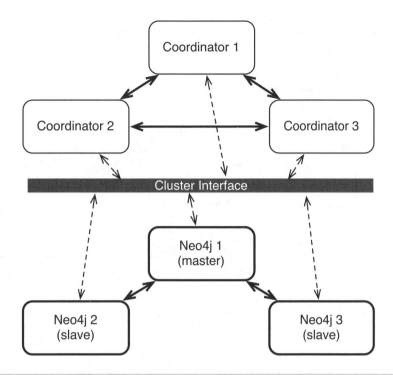

Figure 36—A three-server Neo4j cluster and their coordinators

5. Start up all three Neo4j servers.

Zookeeper tracks each server by way of an ID unique to the cluster. This number is the only value in the file data/coordinator/myid. For server 1 we'll keep it at the default 1; for server 2 we'll set it to 2 and set server 3 to contain 3.

```
echo "2" > neo4j-enterprise-1.7-2/data/coordinator/myid
echo "3" > neo4j-enterprise-1.7-3/data/coordinator/myid
```

We must also indicate some communication settings internal to the cluster. Each server will have a file named conf/coord.cfg. By default, notice the server.1 variable has the server as localhost and two ports set: the quorum election port (2888) and the master election port (3888).

Building the Cluster

A Zookeeper quorum is a group of servers in the cluster and the ports they communicate through (this should not to be confused with a Riak quorum, which is a minimal majority for enforcing consistency). The master election port is used when the master goes down—this special port is used so the remaining servers can elect a new master. We'll keep server.1 as is and add server.2 and server.3 to use successive ports. The coord.cfg files under servers 1, 2, and 3 must all contain the same three lines.

```
server.1=localhost:2888:3888
server.2=localhost:2889:3889
server.3=localhost:2890:3890
```

Finally, we must set the public port to which Neo4j may connect. This clientPort defaults to 2181, so for server 1 we'll leave it alone. We set clientPort=2182 for server 2 and clientPort=2183 for server 3. If any of these ports are in use on your machine, feel free to change this as necessary, but we'll assume the previous ports are in use for the remaining steps.

Coordinate

We start up the Zookeeper coordinator with a handy script provided by the Neo4j team. Run the following command in each of the three server directories:

```
bin/neo4j-coordinator start
Starting Neo4j Coordinator...WARNING: not changing user
  process [36542]... waiting for coordinator to be ready. OK.
```

The coordinator is now running, but Neo4j is not.

Wiring in Neo4j

Next we need to set up Neo4j to run in high availability mode and then connect to a coordinator server. Open conf/neo4j-server.properties, and add the following line under each server:

```
org.neo4j.server.database.mode=HA
```

This sets Neo4j to run in high availability mode; up until now we've been running in SINGLE mode. While we're in this file, let's set the web server port to a unique number. Normally the default port 7474 is fine, but since we're running three neo4j instances on one box, we can't let them overlap for http/https. We chose ports 7471/7481 for server 1, 7472/7482 for server 3, and 7473/7483 for server 3.

```
org.neo4j.server.webserver.port=7471
org.neo4j.server.webserver.https.port=7481
```

Finally, we set each Neo4j instance to connect to one of the coordinator servers. If you open the conf/neo4j.properties file for server 1, you should see a few commented lines starting with ha. These are high availability settings that convey three things: the current cluster machine number, the list of zookeeper servers, and the port that the neo4j servers will use to communicate with each other. For server 1, add the following fields to neo4j.properties:

```
ha.server_id=1
ha.coordinators=localhost:2181,localhost:2182,localhost:2183
ha.server=localhost:6001
ha.pull_interval=1
```

These settings will be similar on the other two servers, with two provisos: ha.server_id=2 for server 2 and ha.server_id=3 for server 3. And the ha.server must use a different port (we chose 6002 for server 2 and 6003 for server 3). Again, the server ports needn't change when you run them on separate machines. Server 2 will contain the following (and so on for server 3):

```
ha.server_id=2
ha.coordinators=localhost:2181,localhost:2182,localhost:2183
ha.server=localhost:6002
ha.pull_interval=1
```

We set pull_interval to 1, which means each slave should check the master for updates every second. Generally, you won't go this low, but it lets us see updates for the example data we'll soon insert.

With our Neo4j HA servers configured, it's time to start them up. Just like the coordinator server startup script, start the neo4j server in each install directory.

```
bin/neo4j start
```

You can watch the server output by tailing the log file.

```
tail -f data/log/console.log
```

Each server will attach to its configured coordinator.

Verifying Cluster Status

Whatever coordinator was first launched will be the master server—probably server 1. You can verify this by opening the attached Neo4j instance's web admin (previously we set server 1 to port 7471). Click the Server Info link at the top and then High Availability on the side menu.[6]

The properties under High Availability list information about this cluster. If this server is the master server, the property will be true. If not, you can find which server has been elected master by looking under InstancesInCluster. This lists each connected server, its machine ID, whether it is the master server, and other info.

---

6.   http://localhost:7471/webadmin/#/info/org.neo4j/High%20Availability/

Verifying Replication

With our cluster up and running, you can verify that your servers are replicating correctly. If all goes according to plan, any writes to a slave should propagate to the master node and then eventually to the other slave server. If you open the web consoles for each of the three servers, you can use the built-in Gremlin consoles in the web admin. Notice that the Gremlin graph object has changed to wrap a HighlyAvailableGraphDatabase.

```
g = neo4jgraph[HighlyAvailableGraphDatabase [/.../neo4j-ent-1.7-2/data/graph.db]]
```

To test our servers, we're going to populate our new graph with some nodes containing the names of some famous paradoxes. In one of the slave consoles, let's set the root node to store Zeno's paradox.

```
gremlin> root = g.v(0)
gremlin> root.paradox = "Zeno's"
gremlin> root.save
```

Now let's switch to the master server's console and output the vertex paradox values.

```
gremlin> g.V.paradox
==> Zeno's
```

Now if you switch to the other slave server and add Russell's paradox, a quick look at our list will reveal both nodes exist in the second slave, having added only one directly to this server.

```
gremlin> g.addVertex(["paradox" : "Russell's"])
gremlin> g.V.paradox
==> Zeno's
==> Russell's
```

If one of your slave servers does not yet have the changes propagated to it, you can go back to the Server Info, High Availability screen. Look for all instances of lastCommittedTransactionId. When these values are equal, the system data is consistent. The lower the number, the older the version of data in that server.

Master Election

If you shut down the master server and refresh the server info in one of the remaining servers, you will see that another server has been elected the new master. Starting the server again will add it back to the cluster, but now the old master will remain a slave (until another server goes down).

High availability allows very read-heavy systems to deal with replicating a graph across multiple servers and thus sharing the load. Although the cluster as a whole is only eventually consistent, there are tricks you can apply to reduce the chance of reading stale data in your own applications, such as assigning a session to one server. With the right tools, planning, and a good setup, you can build a graph database large enough to handle billions of nodes and edges and nearly any number of requests you may need. Just add regular backups, and you have the recipe for a solid production system.

Backups

Backups are a necessary aspect of any professional database use. Although backups are effectively built in when using replication, nightly backups that are stored off-site are always a good idea for disaster recovery. It's hard to plan for a server room fire or an earthquake shaking a building to rubble.

Neo4j Enterprise offers a simple backup tool named neo4j-backup.

The most powerful method when running an HA server is to craft a full backup command to copy the database file from the cluster to a date-stamped file on a mounted drive. Pointing the copy to every server in the cluster will ensure you get the most recent data available. The backup directory created is a fully usable copy. If you need to recover, just replace each installation's data directory with the backup directory, and you're ready to go.

You must start with a full backup. Here we back up our HA cluster to a directory that ends with today's date (uses the *nix date command).

```
bin/neo4j-backup -full -from ha://localhost:2181,localhost:2182,localhost:2183 \
-to /mnt/backups/neo4j-`date +%Y.%m.%d`.db
```

If you're not running in HA mode, just change the mode in the URI to single. Once you have done a full backup, you can choose to do an incremental backup that will store changes only since the last backup. If we want to do a full backup on a single server at midnight and then grab the incremental changes every two hours, you could execute this command:

```
bin/neo4j-backup -incremental -from single://localhost \
-to /mnt/backups/neo4j-`date +%Y.%m.%d`.db
```

But keep in mind incremental works only on a fully backed-up directory, so ensure the previous command is run on the same day.

Day 3 Wrap-Up

Today we spent some time keeping Neo4j data stable via ACID-compliant transactions, high availability, and backup tools.

It's important to note that all of the tools we used today require the Neo4j Enterprise edition, and so use a dual license—GPL/AGPL. If you want to keep your server closed source, you should look into switching to the Community edition or getting an OEM from Neo Technology (the company behind Neo4j). Contact the Neo4j team for more information.

Day 3 Homework

Find

1. Find the Neo4j licensing guide.

2. Answer the question, "What is the maximum number of nodes supported?" (Hint: it's in Questions & Answers in the website docs.)

Do

1. Replicate Neo4j across three physical servers.

2. Set up a load balancer using a web server like Apache or Nginx, and connect to the cluster using the REST interface. Execute a Gremlin script command.

7.5 Wrap-Up

Neo4j is a top open source implementation of the (relatively rare) class of graph databases. Graph databases focus on the relationships between data, rather than the commonalities among values. Modeling graph data is simple. You just create nodes and relationships between them and optionally hang key-value pairs from them. Querying is as easy as declaring how to walk the graph from a starting node.

Neo4j's Strengths

Neo4j is one of the finest examples of open source graph databases. Graph databases are perfect for unstructured data, in many ways even more so than document datastores. Not only is Neo4j typeless and schemaless, but it puts no constraints on how data is related. It is, in the best sense, a free-for-all. Currently, Neo4j can support 34.4 billion nodes and 34.4 billion relationships, which is more than enough for most uses (Neo4j could hold more than 42 nodes for each of Facebook's 800 million users in a single graph).

The Neo4j distributions provide several tools for fast lookups with Lucene and easy-to-use (if sometimes cryptic) language extensions like Gremlin and the REST interface. Beyond ease of use, Neo4j is fast. Unlike join operations in relational databases or map-reduce operations in other databases, graph traversals are constant time. Like data is only a node step away, rather than joining values in bulk and filtering the desired results—as most of the databases we've seen operate. It doesn't matter how large the graph becomes; moving from node A to node B is always one step if they share a relationship. Finally, the Enterprise edition provides for highly available and high read-traffic sites by way of Neo4j HA.

Neo4j's Weaknesses

Neo4j does have a few shortcomings. Edges in Neo4j cannot direct a vertex back on itself. We also found its choice of nomenclature (*node* rather than *vertex*, and *relationship* rather than *edge*) to add complexity when communicating. Although HA is excellent at replication, it can only replicate a full graph to other servers. It cannot currently shard subgraphs, which still places a limit on graph size (though, to be fair, that limit measures in the tens of billions). Finally, if you are looking for a business-friendly open source license (like MIT), Neo4j may not be for you. Where the Community edition (everything we used in the first two days) is GPL, if you want to run a production environment using the Enterprise tools (which includes HA and backups), you'll probably need to purchase a license.

Neo4j on CAP

If you choose to distribute, the name "high availability" cluster should give away their strategy. Neo4j HA is available and partition tolerant (AP). Each slave will return only what it currently has, which may be out of sync with the master node temporarily. Although you can reduce the update latency by increasing a slave's pull interval, it's still technically eventually consistent. This is why Neo4j HA is recommended for read-mostly requirements.

Parting Thoughts

Neo4j's simplicity can be off-putting if you're not used to modeling graph data. It provides a powerful open source API with years of production use and yet still has relatively few users. We chalk this up to lack of knowledge, since graph databases mesh so naturally with how humans tend to conceptualize data. We imagine our families as trees, or our friends as graphs; most of us don't imagine personal relationships as self-referential datatypes. For certain classes of problems, like social networks, Neo4j is an obvious choice. But you should give it some serious consideration for nonobvious problems as well— it just may surprise you how powerful and easy it is.

## CHAPTER 8

Redis

Redis is like grease. It's most often used to lubricate moving parts and keep them working smoothly by reducing friction and speeding up their overall function. Whatever the machinery of your system, it could very well be improved with a bit poured over it. Sometimes the answer to your problem is simply a judicious use of more Redis.

First released in 2009, Redis (REmote DIctionary Service) is a simple-to-use key-value store with a sophisticated set of commands. And when it comes to speed, Redis is hard to beat. Reads are fast, and writes are even faster, handling upwards of 100,000 SET operations per second by some benchmarks. Redis creator Salvatore Sanfilippo refers to his project as a "data structure server" to capture its nuanced handling of complex datatypes and other features. Exploring this super-fast, more-than-just-a-key-value-store will round out our view of the modern database landscape.

8.1 Data Structure Server Store

It can be a bit difficult to classify exactly what Redis *is*. At a basic level, it's a key-value store, of course, but that simple label doesn't really do it justice. Redis supports advanced data structures, though not to the degree that a document-oriented database would. It supports set-based query operations but not with the granularity or type support you'd find in a relational database. And, of course, it's *fast*, trading durability for raw speed.

In addition to being an advanced data structure server, Redis is a blocking queue (or stack) and a publish-subscribe system. It features configurable expiry policies, durability levels, and replication options. All of this makes Redis more of a toolkit of useful data structure algorithms and processes than a member of any specific database genre.

Redis' expansive list of client libraries makes it a drop-in option for many programming languages. It's not simply easy to use; it's a joy. If an API is UX for programmers, then Redis should be in the Museum of Modern Art alongside the Mac Cube.

In Days 1 and 2 we'll explore Redis's features, conventions, and configuration. Starting with simple CRUD operations like always, we'll quickly move on to more advanced operations involving more powerful data structures: lists, hashes, sets, and sorted sets. We'll create transactions and manipulate data expiry characteristics. We'll use Redis to create a simple message queue and explore its publish-subscribe functionality. Then we'll dive into Redis's configuration and replication options, learning how to strike an application-appropriate balance between data durability and speed.

Databases are often and increasingly used in concert with each other. Redis is introduced last in this book so that we can use it in just such a manner. In Day 3, we'll build our capstone system, a rich multidatabase music solution including Redis, CouchDB, Neo4J, and Postgres—using Node.js to cement it together.

8.2 Day 1: CRUD and Datatypes

Since the command-line interface (CLI) is of such primary importance to the Redis development team—and loved by users everywhere—we're going to spend Day 1 looking at many of the 124 commands available. Of primary importance is its sophisticated datatypes and how they can query in more ways than simply "retrieve the value of this key."

Getting Started

Redis is available through a few package builders like Homebrew for Mac but is also rather painless to build.[1] We'll be working off version 2.4. Once you have it installed, you can start up the server by calling this:

```
$ redis-server
```

It won't run in the background by default, but you can make that happen by appending &, or you can just open another terminal. Next run the command-line tool, which should connect to the default port 6379 automatically.

After you connect, let's try to ping the server.

---

1. http://redis.io

```
$ redis-cli
```

```
redis 127.0.0.1:6379> PING
PONG
```

If you cannot connect, you'll receive an error message. Typing *help* will display a list of help options. Type *help* followed by a space and then start typing any command. If you don't know any Redis commands, just start pressing Tab to cycle through your options.

```
redis 127.0.0.1:6379> help
Type: "help @<group>" to get a list of commands in <group>
      "help <command>" for help on <command>
      "help <tab>" to get a list of possible help topics
      "quit" to exit
```

Today we're going to use Redis to build the back end for a URL shortener, like tinyurl.com or bit.ly. A URL shortener is a service that takes a really long URL and maps it to a shorter version on their own domain—like mapping http://www.myveryververylongdomain.com/somelongpath.php to http://bit.ly/VLD. Visiting that short URL redirects users to the longer mapped URL, saves the visitors from text messaging long strings, and also provides the short URL creator some statistics like a count of visits.

In Redis we can use SET to key a short code like 7wks to a value like http://www.sevenweeks.org. SET always requires two parameters, a key and a value. Retrieving the value just needs GET and the key name.

```
redis 127.0.0.1:6379> SET 7wks http://www.sevenweeks.org/
OK
redis 127.0.0.1:6379> GET 7wks
"http://www.sevenweeks.org/"
```

To reduce traffic, we can also set multiple values with MSET, like any number of key-value pairs. Here we map Google.com to gog and Yahoo.com to yah.

```
redis 127.0.0.1:6379> MSET gog http://www.google.com yah http://www.yahoo.com
OK
```

Correlatively, MGET grabs multiple keys and returns values as an ordered list.

```
redis 127.0.0.1:6379> MGET gog yah
1) "http://www.google.com/"
2) "http://www.yahoo.com/"
```

Although Redis stores strings, it recognizes integers and provides some simple operations for them. If we want to keep a running total of how many short keys are in our dataset, we can create a count and then increment it with the INCR command.

```
redis 127.0.0.1:6379> SET count 2
OK
redis 127.0.0.1:6379> INCR count
(integer) 3
redis 127.0.0.1:6379> GET count
"3"
```

Although GET returns count as a string, INCR recognized it as an integer and added one to it. Any attempt to increment a noninteger ends poorly.

```
redis 127.0.0.1:6379> SET bad_count "a"
OK
redis 127.0.0.1:6379> INCR bad_count
(error) ERR value is not an integer or out of range
```

If the value can't be resolved to an integer, Redis rightly complains. You can also increment by any integer (INCRBY) or decrement (DECR, DECRBY).

Transactions

We've seen transactions in previous databases (Postgres and Neo4j), and Redis' MULTI block atomic commands are a similar concept. Wrapping two operations like SET and INCR in a single block will complete either successfully or not at all. But you will never end up with a partial operation.

Let's key another short code to a URL and also increment the count all in one transaction. We begin the transaction with the MULTI command and execute it with EXEC.

```
redis 127.0.0.1:6379> MULTI
OK
redis 127.0.0.1:6379> SET prag http://pragprog.com
QUEUED
redis 127.0.0.1:6379> INCR count
QUEUED
redis 127.0.0.1:6379> EXEC
1) OK
2) (integer) 2
```

When using MULTI, the commands aren't actually executed when we define them (similar to Postgres transactions). Instead, they are queued and then executed in sequence.

Similar to ROLLBACK in SQL, you can stop a transaction with the DISCARD command, which will clear the transaction queue. Unlike ROLLBACK, it won't revert the database; it will simply not run the transaction at all. The effect is identical, although the underlying concept is a different mechanism (transaction rollback vs. operation cancellation).

Complex Datatypes

So far, we haven't seen much complex behavior. Storing string and integer values under keys—even as transactions—is all fine and good, but most programming and data storage problems deal with many types of data. Storing lists, hashes, sets, and sorted sets natively helps explain Redis' popularity, and after exploring the complex operations you can enact on them, you may find you agree.

These collection datatypes can contain a huge number of values (up to 2^32 elements or more than 4 billion) per key. That's more than enough for all Facebook accounts to live as a list under a single key.

While some Redis commands may appear cryptic, they generally follow a good pattern. SET commands begin with S, hashes with H, and sorted sets with Z. List commands generally start with either an L (for left) or an R (for right), depending on the direction of the operation (such as LPUSH).

Hash

Hashes are like nested Redis objects that can take any number of key-value pairs. Let's use a hash to keep track of users who sign up for our URL-shortening service.

Hashes are nice because they help you avoid storing data with artificial key prefixes. (Note that we used colons [:] within our key. This is a valid character that often logically separates a key into segments. It's merely a matter of convention, with no deeper meaning in Redis.)

```
redis 127.0.0.1:6379> MSET user:eric:name "Eric Redmond" user:eric:password s3cret
OK
redis 127.0.0.1:6379> MGET user:eric:name user:eric:password
1) "Eric Redmond"
2) "s3cret"
```

Instead of separate keys, we can create a hash that contains its own key-value pairs.

```
redis 127.0.0.1:6379> HMSET user:eric name "Eric Redmond" password s3cret
OK
```

We need only keep track of the single Redis key to retrieve all values of the hash.

```
redis 127.0.0.1:6379> HVALS user:eric
1) "Eric Redmond"
2) "s3cret"
```

Or we can retrieve all hash keys.

```
redis 127.0.0.1:6379> HKEYS user:eric
1) "name"
2) "password"
```

Or we can get a single value, by passing in the Redis key, followed by the hash key. Here we get just the password.

```
redis 127.0.0.1:6379> HGET user:eric password
"s3cret"
```

Unlike the document datastores Mongo and CouchDB, hashes in Redis cannot nest (nor can any other complex datatype such as lists). In other words, hashes can store only string values.

More commands exist to delete hash fields (HDEL), increment an integer field value by some count (HINCRBY), or retrieve the number of fields in a hash (HLEN).

List

Lists contain multiple ordered values that can act both as queues (first value in, first value out) and as stacks (last value in, first value out). They also have more sophisticated actions for inserting somewhere in the middle of a list, constraining list size, and moving values between lists.

Since our URL-shortening service can now track users, we want to allow them to keep a wishlist of URLs they'd like to visit. To create a list of short-coded websites we'd like to visit, we set the key to USERNAME:wishlist and push any number of values to the right (end) of the list.

```
redis 127.0.0.1:6379> RPUSH eric:wishlist 7wks gog prag
(integer) 3
```

Like most collection value insertions, the Redis command returns the number of values pushed. In other words, we pushed three values into the list so it returns 3. You can get the list length at any time with LLEN.

Using the list range command LRANGE, we can retrieve any part of the list by specifying the first and last positions. All list operations in Redis use a zero-based index. A negative position means the number of steps from the end.

```
redis 127.0.0.1:6379> LRANGE eric:wishlist 0 -1
1) "7wks"
2) "gog"
3) "prag"
```

LREM removes from the given key some matching values. It also requires a number to know how many matches to remove. Setting the count to 0 as we do here just removes them all:

```
redis 127.0.0.1:6379> LREM eric:wishlist 0 gog
```

Setting the count greater than 0 will remove only that number of matches, and setting the count to a negative number will remove that number of matches but scan the list from the end (right side).

To remove and retrieve each value in the order we added them (like a queue), we can pop them off from the left (head) of the list.

```
redis 127.0.0.1:6379> LPOP eric:wishlist
"7wks"
```

To act as a stack, after you RPUSH the values, you would RPOP from the end of the list. All of these operations are performed in constant time.

On the previous combination of commands, you can use LPUSH and RPOP to similar effect (a queue) or LPUSH and LPOP to be a stack.

Suppose we wanted to remove values from our wishlist and move them to another list of visited sites. To execute this move atomically, we could wrap pop and push actions within a multiblock. In Ruby these steps might look something like this (you can't use the CLI here because you must save the popped value, so we used the redis-rb gem):

```
redis.multi do
  site = redis.rpop('eric:wishlist')
  redis.lpush('eric:visited', site)
end
```

But Redis provides a single command for popping values from the tail of one list and pushing to the head of another. It's called RPOPLPUSH (right pop, left push).

```
redis 127.0.0.1:6379> RPOPLPUSH eric:wishlist eric:visited
"prag"
```

If you find the range of the wishlist, prag will be gone; it now lives under visited. This is a useful mechanism for queuing commands.

If you looked through the Redis docs to find RPOPRPUSH, LPOPLPUSH, and LPOPRPUSH commands, you may be dismayed to learn they don't exist. RPOPLPUSH is your only option, and you must build your list accordingly.

Blocking Lists

Now that our URL shortener is taking off, let's add some social activities—like a real-time commenting system—where people can post about the websites they have visited.

Let's write a simple messaging system where multiple clients can push comments and one client (the digester) pops messages from the queue. We'd like the digester to just listen for new comments and pop them as they arrive. Redis provides a few blocking commands for this sort of purpose.

First open another terminal and start another redis-cli client. This will be our digester. The command to block until a value exists to pop is BRPOP. It requires the key to pop a value from and a timeout in seconds, which we'll set to five minutes.

```
redis 127.0.0.1:6379> BRPOP comments 300
```

Then switch back to the first console and push a message to comments.

```
redis 127.0.0.1:6379> LPUSH comments "Prag is great! I buy all my books there."
```

If you switch back to the digester console, two lines will be returned: the key and the popped value. The console will also output the length of time it spent blocking.

```
1) "comments"
2) "Prag is great! I buy all my books there."
(50.22s)
```

There's also a blocking version of left pop (BLPOP) and right pop, left push (BRPOPLPUSH).

Set

Our URL shortener is shaping up nicely, but it would be nice to group common URLs in some way.

Sets are unordered collections with no duplicate values and are an excellent choice for performing complex operations between two or more key values, such as unions or intersections.

If we wanted to categorize sets of URLs with a common key, we can add multiple values with SADD.

```
redis 127.0.0.1:6379> SADD news nytimes.com pragprog.com
(integer) 2
```

Redis added two values. We can retrieve the full set, in no particular order, via SMEMBERS.

```
redis 127.0.0.1:6379> SMEMBERS news
1) "pragprog.com"
2) "nytimes.com"
```

Let's add another category called *tech* for technology-related sites.

```
redis 127.0.0.1:6379> SADD tech pragprog.com apple.com
(integer) 2
```

To find the intersection of websites that both provide news and are technology focused, we use the SINTER command.

```
redis 127.0.0.1:6379> SINTER news tech
1) "pragprog.com"
```

Just as easily, we can remove any matching values in one set from another. To find all news sites that are not tech sites, use SDIFF:

```
redis 127.0.0.1:6379> SDIFF news tech
1) "nytimes.com"
```

We can also build a union of websites that are either news or tech. Since it's a set, any duplicates are dropped.

```
redis 127.0.0.1:6379> SUNION news tech
1) "apple.com"
2) "pragprog.com"
3) "nytimes.com"
```

That set of values can also be stored directly into a new set (SUNIONSTORE destination key [key ...]).

```
redis 127.0.0.1:6379> SUNIONSTORE websites news tech
```

This also provides a useful trick for cloning a single key's values to another key, such as SUNIONSTORE news_copy news. Similar commands exist for storing intersections (SINTERSTORE) and diffs (SDIFFSTORE).

Just like RPOPLPUSH moved values from one list to another, SMOVE does the same for sets; it's just easier to remember.

And like LLEN finds the length of a list, SCARD (set cardinality) counts the set; it's just harder to remember.

Since sets are not ordered, there are no left, right, or other positional commands. Popping a random value from a set just requires SPOP key, and removing values is SREM key value [value ...].

Unlike lists, there are no blocking commands for sets.

Sorted Sets

Whereas other Redis datatypes we've looked at so far easily map to common programming language constructs, sorted sets take something from each of the previous datatypes. They are ordered like lists and are unique like sets. They have field-value pairs like hashes, but rather than string fields, they are instead numeric scores that denote the order of the values. You can think of sorted sets as like a random access priority queue. This power has a trade-off, however. Internally, sorted sets keep values in order, so inserts can take log(N) time to insert (where N is the size of the set), rather than the constant time complexity of hashes or lists.

Next we want to keep track of the popularity of specific shortcodes. Every time someone visits a URL, the score gets increased. Like a hash, adding a value to a sorted set requires two values after the Redis key name: the score and the member.

```
redis 127.0.0.1:6379> ZADD visits 500 7wks 9 gog 9999 prag
(integer) 3
```

To increment a score, we can either re-add it with the new score, which just updates the score but does not add a new value, or increment by some number, which will return the new value.

```
redis 127.0.0.1:6379> ZINCRBY visits 1 prag
"10000"
```

You can decrement also by setting a negative number for ZINCRBY.

Ranges

To get values from our visits set, we can issue a range command, ZRANGE, which returns by position, just like the list datatype's LRANGE command. Except in the case of a sorted set, the position is ordered by score from lowest to highest. So, to get the top two scoring visited sites (zero-based), use this:

```
redis 127.0.0.1:6379> ZRANGE visits 0 1
1) "gog"
2) "7wks"
```

To get the scores of each element as well, append WITHSCORES to the previous code. To get them in reverse, insert the word REV, as in ZREVRANGE.

```
redis 127.0.0.1:6379> ZREVRANGE visits 0 -1 WITHSCORES
1) "prag"
2) "10000"
3) "7wks"
4) "500"
5) "gog"
6) "9"
```

But if we're using a sorted set, it's more likely we want to range by score, rather than by position. ZRANGEBYSCORE has a slightly different syntax from ZRANGE. Since the low and high range numbers are *inclusive* by default, we can make a score number *exclusive* by prefixing it with an opening paren: (. So, this will return all scores where 9 <= score <= 10,000:

```
redis 127.0.0.1:6379> ZRANGEBYSCORE visits 9 9999
1) "gog"
2) "7wks"
```

But the following will return 9 < score <= 10,000:

```
redis 127.0.0.1:6379> ZRANGEBYSCORE visits (9 9999
1) "7wks"
```

We can also range by both positive and negative values, including infinities. This returns the entire set.

```
redis 127.0.0.1:6379> ZRANGEBYSCORE visits -inf inf
```

You can list them in reverse too, with ZREVRANGEBYSCORE.

Along with retrieving a range of values by rank (index) or score, ZREMRANGE-BYRANK and ZREMRANGEBYSCORE, respectively, remove values by rank or score.

Unions

Just like the set datatype, we can create a destination key that contains the union or intersection of one or more keys. This is one of the more complex commands in Redis, since it must not only join the keys—a relatively simple operation—but also merge (possibly) differing scores. The union operation looks like this:

```
ZUNIONSTORE destination numkeys key [key ...]
  [WEIGHTS weight [weight ...]] [AGGREGATE SUM|MIN|MAX]
```

destination is the key to store into, and key is one or more keys to union. numkeys is simply the number of keys you're about to join, while weight is the optional number to multiply each score of the relative key by (if you have two keys, you can have two weights, and so on). Finally, aggregate is the optional rule for resolving each weighted score and summing by default, but you can also choose the min or max between many scores.

Let's use this command to measure the importance of a sorted set of short-codes.

First we'll create another key that scores our short codes by votes. Each visitor to a site can vote if they like the site or not, and each vote adds a point.

```
redis 127.0.0.1:6379> ZADD votes 2 7wks 0 gog 9001 prag
(integer) 3
```

We want to figure out the most important websites in our system, as some combination of votes and visits. Votes are important, but to a lesser extent, website visits also carry some weight (perhaps people are so enchanted by the website, they simply forget to vote). We want to add the two types of scores together to compute a new importance score, while giving votes a weight of double importance—multiplied by two.

```
ZUNIONSTORE importance 2 visits votes WEIGHTS 1 2 AGGREGATE SUM
(integer) 3
redis 127.0.0.1:6379> ZRANGEBYSCORE importance -inf inf WITHSCORES
1) "gog"
2) "9"
3) "7wks"
4) "504"
5) "prag"
6) "28002"
```

This command is powerful in other ways too. For example, if we need to double all scores of a set, we can union a single key with a weight of 2 and store it back into itself.

```
redis 127.0.0.1:6379> ZUNIONSTORE votes 1 votes WEIGHTS 2
(integer) 2
redis 127.0.0.1:6379> ZRANGE votes 0 -1 WITHSCORES
1) "gog"
2) "0"
3) "7wks"
4) "4"
5) "prag"
6) "18002"
```

Sorted sets contain a similar command (ZINTERSTORE)to perform intersections.

Expiry

A common use case for a key-value system like Redis is as a fast-access cache for data that's more expensive to retrieve or compute. Expiration helps keep the total key set from growing unbounded, by tasking Redis to delete a key-value after a certain time has passed.

Marking a key for expiration requires the EXPIRE command, an existing key, and a time to live in seconds. Here we set a key and set it to expire in ten seconds. We can check whether the key EXISTS within ten seconds and it returns a 1 (true). If we wait to execute, it will eventually return a 0 (false).

```
redis 127.0.0.1:6379> SET ice "I'm melting…"
OK
redis 127.0.0.1:6379> EXPIRE ice 10
(integer) 1
```

```
redis 127.0.0.1:6379> EXISTS ice
(integer) 1
redis 127.0.0.1:6379> EXISTS ice
(integer) 0
```

Setting and expiring keys is so common that Redis provides a shortcut command called SETEX.

```
redis 127.0.0.1:6379> SETEX ice 10 "I'm melting…"
```

You can query the time a key has to live with TTL. Setting ice to expire as shown earlier and checking its TTL will return the number of seconds left.

```
redis 127.0.0.1:6379> TTL ice
(integer) 4
```

At any moment before the key expires, you can remove the timeout by running PERSIST key.

```
redis 127.0.0.1:6379> PERSIST ice
```

For marking a countdown to a specific time, EXPIREAT accepts a Unix timestamp (as seconds since January 1, 1970) rather than a number of seconds to count up to. In other words, EXPIREAT is for absolute timeouts, and EXPIRE is for relative timeouts.

A common trick for keeping only recently used keys is to update the expire time whenever you retrieve a value. This is the most recently used (MRU) caching algorithm to ensure your most recently used keys will remain in Redis, while the neglected keys will just expire as normal.

Database Namespaces

So far, we've interacted only with a single namespace. Just like buckets in Riak, sometimes we need to separate keys by namespace. For example, if you wrote an internationalized key-value store, you could store different translated responses in different namespaces. The key greeting could be set to "guten tag" in a German namespace and "bonjour" in French. When a user selects their language, the application just pulls all values from the namespace assigned.

In Redis nomenclature, a namespace is called a *database* and is keyed by number. So far, we've always interacted with the default namespace 0 (also known as database 0). Here we set greeting to the English hello.

```
redis 127.0.0.1:6379> SET greeting hello
OK
redis 127.0.0.1:6379> GET greeting
"hello"
```

But if we switch to another database via the SELECT command, that key is unavailable.

```
redis 127.0.0.1:6379> SELECT 1
OK
redis 127.0.0.1:6379[1]> GET greeting
(nil)
```

And setting a value to this database's namespace will not affect the value of the original.

```
redis 127.0.0.1:6379[1]> SET greeting "guten tag"
OK
redis 127.0.0.1:6379[1]> SELECT 0
OK
redis 127.0.0.1:6379> GET greeting
"hello"
```

Since all databases are running in the same server instance, Redis lets us shuffle keys around with the MOVE command. Here we move greeting to database 2:

```
redis 127.0.0.1:6379> MOVE greeting 2
(integer) 2
redis 127.0.0.1:6379> SELECT 2
OK
redis 127.0.0.1:6379[2]> GET greeting
"hello"
```

This can be useful for running different applications against a single Redis server but still allow these multiple applications to trade data between each other.

And There's More

Redis has plenty of other commands for actions such as renaming keys (RENAME), determining the type of a key's value (TYPE), and deleting a key-value (DEL). There's also the painfully dangerous FLUSHDB, which removes all keys from this Redis database, and its apocalyptic cousin, FLUSHALL, which removes all keys from all Redis databases. Check out the online documentation for the full list of Redis commands.

Day 1 Wrap-Up

The datatypes of Redis and the complex queries it can perform make it much more than a standard key-value store. It can act as a stack, queue, or priority queue; can be an object store (via hashes); and even can perform complex set operations such as unions, intersections, and subtractions (diff). It provides many atomic commands, and for those multistep commands, it provides a transaction mechanism. It has a built-in ability to expire keys, which is useful as a cache.

Day 1 Homework

Find

Find the complete Redis commands documentation, as well as the Big-O notated (O(x)) time complexity under the command details.

Do

1. Install your favorite programming language driver and connect to the Redis server. Insert and increment a value within a transaction.

2. Using your driver of choice, create a program that reads a blocking list and outputs somewhere (console, file, Socket.io, and so on) and another that writes to the same list.

8.3 Day 2: Advanced Usage, Distribution

Day 1 introduced us to Redis as a data structure server. Today we'll build on that foundation by looking at some of the advanced functions provided by Redis, such as pipelining, the publish-subscribe model, system configuration, and replication. Beyond that, we'll look at how to create a Redis cluster, store a lot of data quickly, and use an advanced technique introducing Bloom filters.

A Simple Interface

At 20,000 lines of source code, Redis is a fairly simple project. But beyond code size, it has a simple interface that accepts the very strings we have been writing in the console.

Telnet

We can interact without the command-line interface by streaming commands through TCP on our own via telnet and terminating the command with a carriage return line feed (CRLF, or \r\n).

```
redis/telnet.sh
$ telnet localhost 6379
Trying 127.0.0.1...
Connected to localhost.
Escape character is '^]'.
SET test hello
① +OK
GET test
② $5
hello
SADD stest 1 99
③ :2
SMEMBERS stest
④ *2
$1
1
$2
99

CTRL-]
```

We can see that our input is the same as we provided to the console, but the console cleaned up the responses a bit.

① Redis streams the OK status prefixed by a + sign.

② Before it returned the string *hello*, it sent $5, which means "the following string is five characters."

③ The number 2 after we add two set items to the test key is prefixed by : to represent an integer (two values were added successfully).

④ Finally, when we requested two items, the first line returned begins with an asterisk and the number 2—meaning there are two complex values about to be returned. The next two lines are just like the *hello* string but contain the string *1*, followed by the string *99*.

Pipelining

We can also stream our own strings one at a time by using the BSD netcat (nc) command, which you may find is already installed on many Unix machines. With netcat, we must specifically end a line with CRLF (telnet did this for us implicitly). We also sleep for a second after the echo command has finished to give some time for the Redis server to return. Some nc implementations have a -q option, thus negating the need for a sleep, but not all do, so feel free to try it.

```
$ (echo -en "ECHO hello\r\n"; sleep 1) | nc localhost 6379
$5
hello
```

We can take advantage of this level of control by *pipelining* our commands, or streaming multiple commands in a single request.

```
$ (echo -en "PING\r\nPING\r\nPING\r\n"; sleep 1) | nc localhost 6379
+PONG
+PONG
+PONG
```

This can be far more efficient than pushing a single command at a time and should always be considered if it makes sense to do so—especially in transactions. Just be sure to end every command with \r\n, which is a required delimiter for the server.

publish-subscribe

Yesterday we were able to implement a rudimentary blocking queue using the list datatype. We queued data that could be read by a blocking pop command. Using that queue, we made a very basic publish-subscribe model. Any number of messages could be pushed to this queue, and a single queue reader would pop messages as they were available. This is powerful but limited. Under many circumstances we want a slightly inverted behavior, where several subscribers want to read the announcements of a single publisher, as shown in Figure 37, *A publisher sends a message to all subscribers*, on page 278. Redis provides some specialized publish-subscribe (or pub-sub) commands.

Let's improve on the commenting mechanism we made yesterday using blocking lists, by allowing a user to post a comment to multiple subscribers (as opposed to just one). We start with some subscribers that connect to a key, known as a *channel* in pub-sub nomenclature. Let's start two more clients and subscribe to the comments channel. Subscribing will cause the CLI to block.

```
redis 127.0.0.1:6379> SUBSCRIBE comments
Reading messages... (press Ctrl-C to quit)
1) "subscribe"
2) "comments"
3) (integer) 1
```

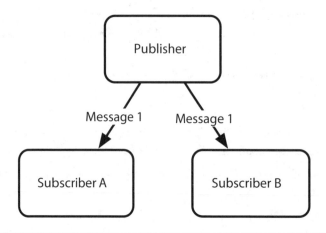

Figure 37—A publisher sends a message to all subscribers.

With two subscribers, we can publish any string we want as a message to the comments channel. The PUBLISH command will return the integer 2, meaning two subscribers received it.

```
redis 127.0.0.1:6379> PUBLISH comments "Check out this shortcoded site! 7wks"
(integer) 2
```

Both of the subscribers will receive a *multibulk reply* (a list) of three items: the string "message," the channel name, and the published message value.

```
1) "message"
2) "comments"
3) "Check out this shortcoded site! 7wks"
```

When your clients want to no longer receive correspondence, they can execute the UNSUBSCRIBE comments command to disconnect from the comments channel or simply UNSUBSCRIBE alone to disconnect from all channels. However, note in redis-cli that you will have to press CTRL+C to break the connection.

Server Info

Before getting into changing Redis's system settings, it's worth taking a quick look at the INFO command, since changing settings values will alter some of these values as well. INFO outputs a list of server data, including version, process ID, memory used, and uptime.

```
redis 127.0.0.1:6379> INFO
redis_version:2.4.5
redis_git_sha1:00000000
redis_git_dirty:0
```

```
arch_bits:64
multiplexing_api:kqueue
process_id:54046
uptime_in_seconds:4
uptime_in_days:0
lru_clock:1807217
…
```

You may want to revisit this command again in this chapter, because it provides a useful snapshot of this server's global information and settings. It even provides information on durability, memory fragmentation, and replication server status.

Redis Configuration

So far, we've only used Redis out of the box. Much of Redis's power comes from its configurability, allowing you to tailor settings to your use case. The redis.conf file that comes with the distribution—found in /etc/redis on *nix systems —is fairly self-explanatory, so we're going to cover only a portion of the file. We'll go through a few of the common settings in order.

```
daemonize no
port 6379
loglevel verbose
logfile stdout
database 16
```

By default daemonize is set to *no*, which is why the server always starts up in the foreground. This is nice for testing but not very production friendly. Changing this value to *yes* will run the server in the background while setting the server's process ID in a pid file.

The next line is the default port number for this server, port 6379. This can be especially useful when running multiple Redis servers on a single machine.

loglevel defaults to verbose, but it's good to set it to notice or warning in production. logfile outputs to stdout (standard output, the console), but a filename is necessary if you run in daemonize mode.

database sets the number of Redis databases we have available. We saw how to switch between databases yesterday. If you plan to only ever use a single database namespace, it's not a bad idea to set this to 1.

Durability

Redis has a few persistence options. First is no persistence at all, which will simply keep all values in main memory. If you're running a basic caching server, this is a reasonable choice since durability always increases latency.

One of the things that sets Redis apart from other fast-access caches like memcached[2] is its built-in support for storing values to disk. By default, key-value pairs are only occasionally saved. You can run the LASTSAVE command to get a Unix timestamp of the last time a Redis disk write succeeded, or you can read the last_save_time field from the server INFO output.

You can force durability by executing the SAVE command (or BGSAVE, to asynchronously save in the background).

```
redis 127.0.0.1:6379> SAVE
```

If you read the redis-server log, you will see lines similar to this:

```
[46421] 10 Oct 19:11:50 * Background saving started by pid 52123
[52123] 10 Oct 19:11:50 * DB saved on disk
[46421] 10 Oct 19:11:50 * Background saving terminated with success
```

Another durability method is to alter the snapshotting settings in the configuration file.

Snapshotting

We can alter the rate of storage to disk by adding, removing, or altering one of the save fields. By default there are three, prefixed by the save keyword followed by a time in seconds and a minimum number of keys that must change before a write to disk occurs.

For example, to trigger a save every 5 minutes (300 seconds) if any keys change at all, you would write the following:

```
save 300 1
```

The configuration has a good set of defaults. The set means if 10,000 keys change, save in 60 seconds; if 10 keys change, save in 300 seconds, and any key changes will be saved in at least 900 seconds (15 minutes).

```
save 900 1
save 300 10
save 60 10000
```

You can add as many or few save lines as necessary to specify precise thresholds.

Append-Only File

Redis is *eventually durable* by default, in that it asynchronously writes values to disk in intervals defined by our save settings, or it is forced to write by

---

2.   http://www.memcached.org/

client-initiated commands. This is acceptable for a second-level cache or session server but is insufficient for storing data you need to be durable, like financial data. If a Redis server crashes, our users might not appreciate having lost money.

Redis provides an append-only file (appendonly.aof) that keeps a record of all write commands. This is like the write-ahead logging we saw in Chapter 4, *HBase*, on page 93. If the server crashes before a value is saved, it executes the commands on startup, restoring its state; appendonly must be enabled by setting it to yes in the redis.conf file.

```
appendonly yes
```

Then we must decide how often a command is appended to the file. Setting always is the more durable, since every command is saved. It's also slow, which often negates the reason people have for using Redis. By default everysec is enabled, which saves up and writes commands only once a second. This is a decent trade-off, since it's fast enough, and worst case you'll lose only the last one second of data. Finally, no is an option, which just lets the OS handle flushing. It can be fairly infrequent, and you're often better off skipping the append-only file altogether rather than choosing it.

```
# appendfsync always
appendfsync everysec
# appendfsync no
```

Append-only has more detailed parameters, which may be worth reading about in the config file when you need to respond to specific production issues.

Security

Although Redis is not natively built to be a fully secure server, you may run across the requirepass setting and AUTH command in the Redis documentation. These can be safely ignored, since they are merely a scheme for setting a plain-text password. Since a client can try nearly 100,000 passwords a second, it's almost a moot point, beyond the fact that plain-text passwords are inherently unsafe anyway. If you want Redis security, you're better off with a good firewall and SSH security.

Interestingly, Redis provides command-level security through obscurity, by allowing you to hide or suppress commands. This will rename the FLUSHALL command (remove all keys from the system) into some hard-to-guess value like c283d93ac9528f986023793b411e4ba2:

```
rename-command FLUSHALL c283d93ac9528f986023793b411e4ba2
```

If we attempt to execute FLUSHALL against this server, we'll be hit with an error. The secret command works instead.

```
redis 127.0.0.1:6379> FLUSHALL
(error) ERR unknown command 'FLUSHALL'
redis 127.0.0.1:6379> c283d93ac9528f986023793b411e4ba2
OK
```

Or better yet, we can disable the command entirely by setting it to a blank string.

```
rename-command FLUSHALL ""
```

You can set any number of commands to a blank string, allowing you a modicum of customization over your command environment.

Tweaking Parameters

There are several more advanced settings for speeding up slow query logs, encoding details, making latency tweaks, and importing external config files. Keep in mind, though, that if you run across some documentation about Redis virtual memory, you're best to avoid it if possible. It's been deprecated in Redis 2.4 and may be removed in future versions.

To aid in testing your server configuration, Redis provides an excellent benchmarking tool. It connects locally to port 6379 by default and issues 10,000 requests using 50 parallel clients. We can execute 100,000 requests with the -n argument.

```
$ redis-benchmark -n 100000
====== PING (inline) ======
  100000 requests completed in 3.05 seconds
  50 parallel clients
  3 bytes payload
  keep alive: 1
5.03% <= 1 milliseconds
98.44% <= 2 milliseconds
99.92% <= 3 milliseconds
100.00% <= 3 milliseconds
32808.40 requests per second
...
```

Other commands are tested as well, like SADD and LRANGE; the more complex ones generally taking more time.

Master-Slave Replication

Just like other NoSQL databases we've seen (such as MongoDB and Neo4j), Redis supports master-slave replication. One server is the master by default if you don't set it as a slave of anything. Data will be replicated to any number of slave servers.

Making slave servers is easy. We first need a copy of our redis.conf file.

```
$ cp redis.conf redis-s1.conf
```

The file will remain largely the same but with the following changes:

```
port 6380
slaveof 127.0.0.1 6379
```

If all went according to plan, you should see something similar to the following in the slave server's log when you start it:

```
$ redis-server redis-s1.conf
```

```
[9003] 16 Oct 23:51:52 * Connecting to MASTER...
[9003] 16 Oct 23:51:52 * MASTER <-> SLAVE sync started
[9003] 16 Oct 23:51:52 * Non blocking connect for SYNC fired the event.
[9003] 16 Oct 23:51:52 * MASTER <-> SLAVE sync: receiving 28 bytes from master
[9003] 16 Oct 23:51:52 * MASTER <-> SLAVE sync: Loading DB in memory
[9003] 16 Oct 23:51:52 * MASTER <-> SLAVE sync: Finished with success
```

And you should see the string 1 slaves output in the master log.

```
redis 127.0.0.1:6379> SADD meetings "StarTrek Pastry Chefs" "LARPers Intl."
```

If we connect the command line to our slave, we should receive our meeting list.

```
redis 127.0.0.1:6380> SMEMBERS meetings
1) "StarTrek Pastry Chefs"
2) "LARPers Intl."
```

In production, you'll generally want to implement replication for availability or backup purposes and thus have Redis slaves on different machines.

Data Dump

So far, we've talked a lot about how fast Redis is, but it's hard to get a feel for it without playing with a bit more data.

Let's insert a large dataset into our Redis server. You can keep the slave running if you like, but a laptop or desktop might run quicker if you have just a single master server. We're going to grab a list of more than 2.5 million published book titles, keyed by their International Standard Book Number (ISBN) from Freebase.com.[3]

---

3. http://download.freebase.com/datadumps/latest/browse/book/isbn.tsv

You'll first need the redis Ruby gem.

```
$ gem install redis
```

There are several ways to go about inserting a large dataset, and they get progressively faster but more complex.

The simplest method is to simply iterate through a list of data and execute SET for each value using the standard redis-rb client.

redis/isbn.rb
```
LIMIT = 1.0 / 0  # 1.0/0 is Infinity in Ruby
# %w{rubygems hiredis redis/connection/hiredis}.each{|r| require r}
%w{rubygems time redis}.each{|r| require r}

$redis = Redis.new(:host => "127.0.0.1", :port => 6379)
$redis.flushall
count, start = 0, Time.now
File.open(ARGV[0]).each do |line|
  count += 1
  next if count == 1
  isbn, _, _, title = line.split("\t")
  next if isbn.empty? || title == "\n"

  $redis.set(isbn, title.strip)

  # set the LIMIT value if you do not wish to populate the entire dataset
  break if count >= LIMIT
end
puts "#{count} items in #{Time.now - start} seconds"
```

```
$ ruby isbn.rb isbn.tsv
2456384 items in 266.690189 seconds
```

If you want to speed up insertion and are not running JRuby, you can optionally install the hiredis gem. It's a C driver that is considerably faster than the native Ruby driver. Then uncomment the hiredis require line in order to load the driver. You may not see a large improvement for this type of CPU-bound operation, but we highly recommend hiredis for production Ruby use.

You will see a big improvement with pipelining. Here we batch 1,000 lines at a time and pipeline their insertion. It reduced our insertion time by more than 300 percent.

redis/isbn_pipelined.rb
```
BATCH_SIZE = 1000
LIMIT = 1.0 / 0  # 1.0/0 is Infinity in Ruby

# %w{rubygems hiredis redis/connection/hiredis}.each{|r| require r}
%w{rubygems time redis}.each{|r| require r}
```

```ruby
$redis = Redis.new(:host => "127.0.0.1", :port => 6379)
$redis.flushall

# set line data as a single batch update
def flush(batch)
  $redis.pipelined do
    batch.each do |saved_line|
      isbn, _, _, title = line.split("\t")
      next if isbn.empty? || title == "\n"
      $redis.set(isbn, title.strip)
    end
  end
  batch.clear
end

batch = []
count, start = 0, Time.now
File.open(ARGV[0]).each do |line|
  count += 1
  next if count == 1

  # push lines into an array
  batch << line

  # if the array grows to BATCH_SIZE, flush it
  if batch.size == BATCH_SIZE
    flush(batch)
    puts "#{count-1} items"
  end

  # set the LIMIT value if you do not wish to populate the entire dataset
  break if count >= LIMIT
end
# flush any remaining values
flush(batch)

puts "#{count-1} items in #{Time.now - start} seconds"
```

```
$ ruby isbn_pipelined.rb isbn.tsv
2666642 items in 79.312975 seconds
```

This reduces the number of Redis connections required, but building the pipelined dataset has some overhead of its own. You should experiment with different numbers of batched operations when pipelining in production.

As a side note to Ruby users, if your application is nonblocking via Event Machine, the Ruby driver can use em-synchrony via EM::Protocols::Redis.connect.

Redis Cluster

Beyond simple replication, many Redis clients provide an interface for building a simple ad hoc distributed Redis cluster. The Ruby client redis-rb supports a consistent-hashing managed cluster. You may recall consistent hashing from the Riak chapter, where nodes can be added and dropped without having to expire most keys. This is the same idea, only managed via a client rather than by the servers themselves.

First we need another server. Unlike the master-slave setup, both of our servers will take the master (default) configuration. We copied the redis.conf file and changed the port to 6380. That's all that's required for the servers.

```
redis/isbn_cluster.rb
LIMIT = 10000
%w{rubygems time redis}.each{|r| require r}
require 'redis/distributed'

$redis = Redis::Distributed.new([
  "redis://localhost:6379/", "redis://localhost:6380/"
])
$redis.flushall

count, start = 0, Time.now
File.open(ARGV[0]).each do |line|
  count += 1
  next if count == 1
  isbn, _, _, title = line.split("\t")
  next if isbn.empty? || title == "\n"

  $redis.set(isbn, title.strip)

  # set the LIMIT value if you do not wish to populate the entire dataset
  break if count >= LIMIT
end
puts "#{count} items in #{Time.now - start} seconds"
```

Bridging between two or more servers requires only some minor changes to our existing ISBN client. First we need to require the redis/distributed file from the redis gem.

```
require 'redis/distributed'
```

Then replace the Redis client with Redis::Distributed and pass in an array of server URIs. Each URI requires the redis scheme, server (localhost), and port.

```
$redis = Redis::Distributed.new([
  "redis://localhost:6379/",
  "redis://localhost:6380/"
])
```

Running the client is the same as before.

```
$ ruby isbn_cluster.rb isbn.tsv
```

But a lot more work is being done by the client, since it handles computing which keys are stored on which servers. You can validate that keys are stored on separate servers by attempting to retrieve the same ISBN key from each server through the CLI. Only one client will GET a value. But as long as you retrieve keys set through the same Redis::Distributed configuration, the client will access the values from the correct servers.

Bloom Filters

Owning a unique term is an excellent strategy for making something easily findable online. If you were to write a book named *The Jabbyredis*, you would be fairly certain any search engine would link to you. Let's write a script that lets someone quickly check whether a word is unique against all words used in all titles in the ISBN catalog. We can use a Bloom filter to test whether a word is used.

A Bloom filter is a probabilistic data structure that checks for the nonexistence of an item in a set, first covered in *Compression and Bloom Filters*, on page 109. Although it can return a false positive, it cannot return a false negative. This is a useful when you need to quickly discover whether a value does not exist in a system.

Bloom filters succeed at discovering nonexistence by converting a value to a very sparse sequence of bits and comparing that to a union of every value's bits. In other words, when a new value is added, it is OR'd against the current Bloom filter bit sequence. When you want to check whether the value is already in the system, you perform an AND against the Bloom filter's sequence. If the value has any true bits that aren't also true in the Bloom filter's corresponding buckets, then the value was never added. In other words, this value is definitely not in the Bloom filter. Following is a graphic representation of this concept.

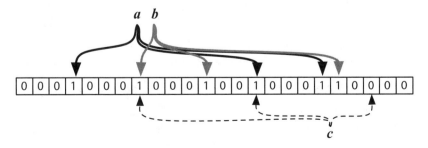

Let's write a program that loops through a bunch of ISBN book data, extracts and simplifies each book's title works, and splits them into individual words. Each new word encountered is checked against the Bloom filter. If the Bloom filter returns false, meaning the word does not exist in our Bloom filter, then go ahead and add it. Just to follow along, we can output any new word that's added.

```
$ gem install bloomfilter-rb
```

redis/isbn_bf.rb
```ruby
# LIMIT = 1.0 / 0  # 1.0/0 is Infinity in Ruby
LIMIT= 10000
%w{rubygems time bloomfilter-rb}.each{|r| require r}
bloomfilter = BloomFilter::Redis.new(:size => 1000000)

$redis = Redis.new(:host => "127.0.0.1", :port => 6379)
$redis.flushall

count, start = 0, Time.now
File.open(ARGV[0]).each do |line|
  count += 1
  next if count == 1
  _, _, _, title = line.split("\t")
  next if title == "\n"

  words = title.gsub(/[^\w\s]+/, '').downcase
  # puts words
  words = words.split(' ')
  words.each do |word|
    # skip any keyword already in the bloomfilter
    next if bloomfilter.include?(word)
    # output the very unique word
    puts word
    # add the new word to the bloomfilter
    bloomfilter.insert(word)
  end
  # set the LIMIT value if you do not wish to populate the entire dataset
  break if count >= LIMIT
end
puts "Contains Jabbyredis? #{bloomfilter.include?('jabbyredis')}"
puts "#{count} lines in #{Time.now - start} seconds"
```

Ruby wunderkind Ilya Grigorik created this Redis-backed Bloom filter, but the concepts are transferable to any language.

Running the client uses the same ISBN file but needs only the book titles.

```
$ ruby isbn_bf.rb isbn.tsv
```

At the start of the output you should see plenty of common words, like *and* and *the*. Near the end of the set, the words become increasingly esoteric, like *unindustria*.

The upside with this approach is the ability to detect duplicate words. The downside is that a few false positives will seep through—the Bloom filter may flag a word we have never seen before. This is why in a real-world use case you would perform some secondary check, such as a slower database query to a system of record, which should happen only a small percentage of the time, presuming a large enough filter size, which is computable.[4]

SETBIT and GETBIT

As we mentioned earlier, Bloom filters function by flipping certain bits in a sparse binary field. The Redis Bloom filter implementation we just used takes advantage of two relatively recent Redis commands that perform just such actions: SETBIT and GETBIT.

Like all Redis commands, SETBIT is fairly descriptive. The command sets a single bit (either 1 or 0) at a certain location in a bit sequence, starting from zero. It's a common use case for high-performance multivariate flagging—it's faster to flip a few bits than write a set of descriptive strings.

If we want to keep track of the toppings on a hamburger, we can assign each type of topping to a bit position, such as ketchup = 0, mustard = 1, onion = 2, lettuce = 3. So, a hamburger with only mustard and onion could be represented as 0110 and set in the command line:

```
redis 127.0.0.1:6379> SETBIT my_burger 1 1
(integer) 0
redis 127.0.0.1:6379> SETBIT my_burger 2 1
(integer) 0
```

Later, a process can check whether my burger should have lettuce or mustard. If zero is returned, the answer is false—one if true.

```
redis 127.0.0.1:6379> GETBIT my_burger 3
(integer) 0
redis 127.0.0.1:6379> GETBIT my_burger 1
(integer) 1
```

The Bloom filter implementation takes advantage of this behavior by hashing a value as a multibit value. It calls SETBIT X 1 for each on position in an insert() (where X is the bit position) and verifies existence by calling GETBIT X on include?() —returning false if any GETBIT position returns 0.

---

4.   http://en.wikipedia.org/wiki/Bloom_filter

Bloom filters are excellent for reducing unnecessary traffic to a slower underlying system, be it a slower database, limited resource, or network request. If you have a slower database of IP addresses and you want to track all new users to your site, you can use a Bloom filter to first check whether the IP address exists in your system. If the Bloom filter returns false, you know the IP address has yet to be added and can respond accordingly. If the Bloom filter returns true, this IP address may or may not exist on the back end and requires a secondary lookup to be sure. This is why computing the correct size is important—a well-sized Bloom filter can reduce (but not eliminate) the error rate or the likelihood of a false positive.

Day 2 Wrap-Up

Today we rounded out our Redis investigation by moving beyond simple operations into squeezing every last bit of speed out of a very fast system. Redis provides for fast and flexible data structure storage and simple manipulations as we saw in Day 1 but is equally adept at more complex behaviors by way of built-in publish-subscribe functions and bit operations. It's also highly configurable, with many durability and replication settings that conform to whatever your needs may be. It also supports some nice third-party enhancements, like Bloom filters and clustering.

This also concludes major operations for the Redis data structure store. Tomorrow we're going to do something a bit different, by using Redis as the cornerstone of a polyglot persistence setup along with CouchDB and Neo4j.

Day 2 Homework

Find

Find out what messaging patterns are, and discover how many Redis can implement.

Do

1. Run the ISBN populator script with all snapshotting and the append-only file turned off. Then try running with appendfsync set to always, marking the speed difference.

2. Using your favorite programming language's web framework, try to build a simple URL-shortening service backed by Redis with an input box for the URL and a simple redirect based on the URL. Back it up with a Redis master-slave replicated cluster across multiple nodes as your back end.

8.4 Day 3: Playing with Other Databases

Today we're wrapping up our final database chapter by inviting some previous databases to play. Yet Redis will hold a starring role by making our interaction with other databases faster and easier.

We've learned throughout this book that different databases have different strengths, so many modern system designs have moved toward a polyglot persistence model, where many databases each play a role in the system. You'll learn how to build one of these projects using CouchDB as the system of record (the canonical data source), Neo4j to handle data relationships, and Redis to help with data population and caching. Consider this your final exam.

Note that this project is not the authors' endorsement of any specific set of databases, languages, or frameworks over another but rather a showcase of how multiple databases can work together, leveraging the capabilities of each in pursuit of a single goal.

A Polyglot Persistent Service

Our polyglot persistence service will act as a front end to a band information service. We want to store a list of musical band names, the artists who performed in those bands, and any number of roles each artist played in the band, from lead singer to backup keytar player. Each of three databases—Redis, CouchDB, and Neo4j—will handle a different aspect of our band management system.

Redis plays three important roles in our system: to assist in data populating CouchDB, as a cache for recent Neo4j changes, and as a quick lookup for partial value searches. Its speed and ability to store multiple data formats make it well suited for population, and its built-in expiry policies are perfect for handling cached data.

CouchDB is our system of record (SOR), or authoritative data source. CouchDB's document structure is an easy way to store band data with nested artist and role information, and we will take advantage of the Changes API in CouchDB to keep our third data source in sync.

Neo4j is our relationship store. Although querying the CouchDB SOR directly is perfectly reasonable, a graph datastore allows us a simplicity and speed in walking node relationships that other databases have a difficult time matching. We'll store relationships between bands, band members, and the roles the members play.

The Rise of Polyglot Persistence

Like the growing phenomenon of polyglot programming, polyglot persistence is now gaining ground.

If you are unfamiliar with the practice, polyglot programming is whereby a team uses more than one programming language in a single project. Contrast this with the convention of using one general-purpose language throughout a project. This is useful because of the different inherent strengths of languages. A framework like Scala may be better suited for server-side stateless transactions on the Web, but a language like Ruby may be friendlier for business logic. Used together, they create a synergy. A polyglot language system like this was famously used at Twitter.

Some of the databases we've seen themselves support polyglot programming—Riak supports both JavaScript and Erlang when writing mapreduce, and a single request can execute both.

Similar to its language-centric cousin, polyglot persistence is where you can leverage the strengths of many kinds of databases in the same system, as opposed to the currently familiar practice of a single database, probably a relational style. A basic variant of this is already common: using a key-value store (like Redis) that acts as a cache for relatively slower relational database (like PostgreSQL) queries. Relational, as we've seen in previous chapters, is suboptimally suited for a growing host of problems, such as graph traversal. But even these new databases shine only as a few stars in the full galaxy of requirements.

Why the sudden interest in polyglot? Martin Fowler noted[a] that having a single central database where multiple applications could integrate was a common pattern in software design. This once popular database integration pattern has given way to a middleware layer pattern, where multiple applications instead communicate to a service layer over HTTP. This frees up the middleware service itself to rely on any number of databases or, in the case of polyglot persistence, any type.

a.   http://martinfowler.com/bliki/DatabaseThaw.html

Each database has a specific role to play in our system, but they don't natively communicate. We use the Node.js JavaScript framework to populate the databases, communicate between them, and act as a simple front-end server. Since gluing multiple databases together requires a bit of code, this last day will have much more code than we have seen so far in this book.

Population

The first item of business is to populate our datastores with the necessary data. We take a two-phased approach here, by first populating Redis and then populating our CouchDB SOR.

As in earlier sections, we download a dataset from Freebase.com. We'll be using the group_membership tab-separated set.[5] This file contains a lot of information, but we are interested only in extracting the member or artist name, the group or band name, and their roles in that band stored as a comma-separated list. For example, *John Cooper* played in the band *Skillet* as the *Lead vocalist*, *Acoustic guitar* player, and *Bassist*.

```
/m/0654bxy  John Cooper Skillet Lead vocalist,Acoustic guitar,Bass  1996
```

Ultimately we want to structure John Cooper and the other members of Skillet into a single CouchDB document like the following, stored at the URL http://localhost:5984/bands/Skillet:

```
{
  "_id": "Skillet",
  "name": "Skillet"
  "artists": [
    {
      "name": "John Cooper",
      "role": [
        "Acoustic guitar",
        "Lead vocalist",
        "Bass"
      ]
    },
    ...
    {
      "name": "Korey Cooper",
      "role": [
        "backing vocals",
        "Synthesizer",
        "Guitar",
        "Keyboard instrument"
      ]
    }
  ]
}
```

This file contains well over 100,000 band members and more than 30,000 bands. That's not many, but it's a good starting point to build your own system. Note that not every artist's roles are documented. This is an incomplete dataset, but we can deal with that later.

---

5. http://download.freebase.com/datadumps/latest/browse/music/group_membership.tsv

Phase 1: Data Transformation

You may wonder why we bother populating Redis and not just dive right into populating CouchDB. Acting as an intermediary, Redis adds structure to the flat TSV data so that subsequent insertion into another database is fast. Since our plan is to create a single record per band name, Redis allows us to make a single pass through our TSV file (which lists the same band for each band member—each band member is represented in a line). Adding single members directly to CouchDB for each line in the file can cause update thrashing, where two band member lines attempt to create/update the same band document at the same time, forcing the system to reinsert when one of them fails CouchDB's version check.

The catch with this strategy is that you're limited to the constraints of Redis to hold an entire dataset in RAM—though this limit could be overcome by the simple consistent-hashing cluster we saw on Day 2.

With our data file in hand, ensure you have Node.js installed as well as the Node Package Manager (npm). Once that's all done, we need to install three NPM projects: redis, csv, and hiredis (the optional Redis C-driver we learned about yesterday that can greatly speed up Redis interactions).

```
$ npm install hiredis redis csv
```

Then, check that your Redis server is running on the default port 6379, or alter each script's createClient() function to point to your Redis port.

You can populate Redis by running the following Node.js script in the same directory as your TSV file, which we assume is named group_membership.tsv. (All of the JavaScript files we'll look at are fairly verbose, so we don't show them in their entirety. All of the code can be downloaded from the Pragmatic Bookshelf website. Here we'll just stick to the meat of each file.) Download and run the following file:

```
$ node pre_populate.js
```

This script basically iterates through each line of the TSV and extracts the artist name, the band name, and the roles they play in that band. Then it adds those values to Redis (skipping any blank values).

The format of each Redis band key is "band:Band Name". The script will add this artist name to the set of artist names. So, the key "band:Beatles" will contain the set of values ["John Lennon", "Paul McCartney", "George Harrison", "Ringo Starr"]. The artist keys will also contain the band name and similarly contain a set of roles. "artist:Beatles:Ringo Starr" will contain the set ["Drums"].

The other code just keeps track of how many lines we've processed and outputs the results to the screen.

```
redis/pre_populate.js
csv().
fromPath( tsvFileName, { delimiter: '\t', quote: '' }).
on('data', function(data, index) {
  var
    artist = data[2],
    band = data[3],
    roles = buildRoles(data[4]);
  if( band === '' || artist === '' ) {
    trackLineCount();
    return true;
  }
  redis_client.sadd('band:' + band, artist);
  roles.forEach(function(role) {
    redis_client.sadd('artist:' + band + ':' + artist, role);
  });
  trackLineCount();
}).
```

You can test that the code has been populating Redis by launching redis-cli and executing RANDOMKEY. We should expect a key prefixed by band: or artist:...any value but (nil) is good.

Now that Redis is populated, proceed immediately to the next section. Turning off Redis could lose data, unless you chose to set a higher durability than the default or initiated a SAVE command.

Phase 2: SOR Insertion

CouchDB will play the role of our system of record (SOR). If any data conflicts arise between Redis, CouchDB, or Neo4j, CouchDB wins. A good SOR should contain all of the data necessary to rebuild any other data source in its domain.

Ensure CouchDB is running on the default port 5984, or change the require('http').createClient(5984, 'localhost') line in the following code to the port number you require. Redis should also still be running from the previous section. Download and run the following file:

```
$ node populate_couch.js
```

Since phase 1 was all about pulling data from a TSV and populating Redis, this phase is all about pulling data from Redis and populating CouchDB. We don't use any special drivers for CouchDB, since it's a simple REST interface and Node.js has a simple built-in HTTP library.

Eric says:
Nonblocking Code

Before starting this book, we were only passingly familiar with writing event-driven nonblocking applications. *Nonblocking* means precisely that: rather than waiting for a long-running process to complete, the main code will continue executing. Whatever you need to do in response to a blocking event you put inside a function or code block to be executed later. This can be by spawning a separate thread or, in our case, implementing a reactor pattern event-driven approach.

In a blocking program, you can write code that queries a database, waits, and loops through the results.

```
results = database.some_query()
for value in results
  # do something with each value
end
# this is not executed until after the results are looped...
```

In a event-driven program, you would pass in the loop as a function/code block. While the databases is doing its thing, the rest of the program can continue running. Only after the database returns the result does the function/code block get executed.

```
database.some_query do |results|
  for value in results
    # do something with each value
  end
end
# this continues running while the database performs its query...
```

It took us quite some time to realize the benefits here. The rest of the program can run rather than sitting idle while it waits on the database, sure, but is this common? Apparently so, because when we began coding in this style, we noticed an order-of-magnitude decrease in latency.

We try to keep the code as simple as we can, but interacting with databases in a nonblocking way is an inherently complex process. But as we learned, it's generally a very good method when dealing with databases. Nearly every popular programming language has some sort of nonblocking library. Ruby has EventMachine, Python has Twisted, Java has the NIO library, C# has Interlace, and of course JavaScript has Node.js.

In the following block of code, we perform a Redis KEYS bands:* to get a list of all band names in our system. If we had a *really* big dataset, we could add more scoping (for example, bands:A* to get only band names starting with *a*, and so on). Then for each of those bands we fetch the set of artists and extract the band name from the key, by removing the prefix *bands:* from the key string.

```
redis/populate_couch.js
redisClient.keys('band:*', function(error, bandKeys) {
  totalBands = bandKeys.length;
  var
    readBands = 0,
    bandsBatch = [];

  bandKeys.forEach(function(bandKey) {
    // substring of 'band:'.length gives us the band name
    var bandName = bandKey.substring(5);
    redisClient.smembers(bandKey, function(error, artists) {
```

Next we get all of the roles for every artist in this band, which Redis returns as an array of arrays (each artists role is its own array). We can do this by batching up Redis SMEMBERS commands into an array called roleBatch and executing them in a single MULTI batch. Effectively, that would be executing a single pipelined request like this:

```
MULTI
  SMEMBERS "artist:Beatles:John Lennon"
  SMEMBERS "artist:Beatles:Ringo Starr"
EXEC
```

From there, a batch of 50 CouchDB documents are made. We build a batch of 50, because we then send the entire set to CouchDB's /_bulk_docs command, allowing us very, very fast insertion.

```
redis/populate_couch.js
redisClient.
  multi(roleBatch).
  exec(function(err, roles)
  {
    var
      i = 0,
      artistDocs = [];

    // build the artists sub-documents
    artists.forEach( function(artistName) {
      artistDocs.push({ name: artistName, role : roles[i++] });
    });

    // add this new band document to the batch to be executed later
    bandsBatch.push({
      _id: couchKeyify( bandName ),
      name: bandName,
      artists: artistDocs
    });
```

With the population of the bands database, we now have in a single location all of the data our system requires. We know the names of many bands, the artists who performed in them, and the roles they played in those bands.

Now would be a good time to take a break and play around with our newly populated bands system of record in CouchDB at http://localhost:5984/_utils/ database.html?bands.

Relationship Store

Next on the docket is our Neo4j service that we'll use to track relationships between artists and the roles they play. We could certainly query CouchDB outright by creating views, but we are rather limited on complex queries based on relationships. If Wayne Coyne from the Flaming Lips loses his theremin before a show, he could ask Charlie Clouser from Nine Inch Nails, who also plays a theremin. Or we could discover artists who have many overlapping talents, even if they performed different roles in different bands—all with a simple node walk.

With our initial data in place, now we need to keep Neo4j in sync with CouchDB should any data ever change on our system of record. So, we'll kill two birds by crafting a service that populates Neo4j on any changes to CouchDB since the database was created.

We also want to populate Redis with keys for our bands, artists, and role so we can quickly access this data later. Happily, this includes all data that we've already populated in CouchDB, thus saving us a separate initial Neo4j and Redis population step.

Ensure that Neo4j is running on port 7474, or change the appropriate create-Client() function to use your correct port. CouchDB and Redis should still be running. Download and run the following file. This file will continue running until you shut it down.

```
$ node graph_sync.js
```

This server just uses the continuous polling example we saw in the CouchDB chapter to track all CouchDB changes. Whenever a change is detected, we do two things: populate Redis and populate Neo4j. This code populates Redis by cascading callback functions. First it populates the band as "band-name:Band Name". It follows this pattern for artist name and roles.

This way, we can search with partial strings. For example, KEYS band-name:Bea* could return this: Beach Boys, Beastie Boys, Beatles, and so on.

```
redis/graph_sync.js
function feedBandToRedis(band) {
  redisClient.set('band-name:' + band.name, 1);
  band.artists.forEach(function(artist) {
    redisClient.set('artist-name:' + artist.name, 1);
    artist.role.forEach(function(role){
      redisClient.set('role-name:' + role, 1);
```

The next block is how we populate Neo4j. We created a driver that you can download as part of this book's code, named neo4j_caching_client.js. It just uses Node.js's HTTP library to connect to the Neo4j REST interface with a bit of rate-limiting built in so the client doesn't open too many connections at once. Our driver also uses Redis to keep track of changes made to the Neo4j graph without having to initiate a separate query. This is our third separate use for Redis—the first being as a data transformation step for populating CouchDB, and the second we just saw earlier, to quickly search for band values.

This code creates band nodes (if they need to be created), then artist nodes (if they need to be created), and then roles. Each step along the way creates a new relationship, so The Beatles node will relate to John, Paul, George, and Ringo nodes, who in turn each relate to the roles they play.

```
redis/graph_sync.js
function feedBandToNeo4j(band, progress) {
  var
    lookup = neo4jClient.lookupOrCreateNode,
    relate = neo4jClient.createRelationship;

  lookup('bands', 'name', band.name, function(bandNode) {
    progress.emit('progress', 'band');
    band.artists.forEach(function(artist) {
      lookup('artists', 'name', artist.name, function(artistNode){
        progress.emit('progress', 'artist');
        relate(bandNode.self, artistNode.self, 'member', function(){
          progress.emit('progress', 'member');
        });
        artist.role.forEach(function(role){
          lookup('roles', 'role', role, function(roleNode){
            progress.emit('progress', 'role');
            relate(artistNode.self, roleNode.self, 'plays', function(){
              progress.emit('progress', 'plays');
```

Let this service keep running in its own window. Every update to CouchDB that adds a new artist or role to an existing artist will trigger a new relationship in Neo4j and potentially new keys in Redis. As long as this service runs, they should be in sync.

Open your CouchDB web console and open a band. Make any data change you want to the database: add a new band member (make yourself a member of the Beatles!), or add a new role to an artist. Keep an eye on the graph_sync output. Then fire up the Neo4j console and try finding any new connections in the graph. If you added a new band member, they should now have a relationship with the band node or new role if that was altered. The current implementation does not remove relationships—though it would not be a complete modification to add a Neo4j DELETE operation to the script.

The Service

This is the part we've been building up to. We're going to create a simple web application that allows users to search for a band. Any band in the system will list all of the band members as links, and any clicked band member link will list some information about the artist—namely, the roles they play. In addition, each role the artist plays will list every other artist in the system who also plays that role.

For example, searching for Led Zeppelin would give you Jimmy Page, John Paul Jones, John Bonham, and Robert Plant. Clicking Jimmy Page will list that he plays guitar and also many other artists who play guitar, like The Edge from U2.

To simplify our web app creation a bit, we'll need two more node packages: bricks (a simple web framework) and mustache (a templating library).

```
$ npm install bricks mustache
```

Like in the previous sections, ensure you have all of the databases running, and then start up the server. Download and run the following code:

```
$ node band.js
```

The server is set to run on port 8080, so if you point your browser to http://localhost:8080/, you should see a simple search form.

Let's take a look at the code that will build a web page that lists band information. Each URL performs a separate function in our little HTTP server. The first is at http://localhost:8080/band and accepts any band name as a parameter.

redis/bands.js
```
appServer.addRoute("^/band$", function(req, res) {
  var
    bandName = req.param('name'),
    bandNodePath = '/bands/' + couchUtil.couchKeyify( bandName ),
    membersQuery = 'g.V[[name:"'+bandName+'"]]'
              + '.out("member").in("member").uniqueObject.name';
```

```
getCouchDoc( bandNodePath, res, function( couchObj ) {
  gremlin( membersQuery, function(graphData) {
    var artists = couchObj && couchObj['artists'];
    var values = { band: bandName, artists: artists, bands: graphData };
    var body = '<h2>{{band}} Band Members</h2>';
    body += '<ul>{{#artists}}';
    body += '<li><a href="/artist?name={{name}}">{{name}}</a></li>';
    body += '{{/artists}}</ul>';
    body += '<h3>You may also like</h3>';
    body += '<ul>{{#bands}}';
    body += '<li><a href="/band?name={{.}}">{{.}}</a></li>';
    body += '{{/bands}}</ul>';
    writeTemplate( res, body, values );
```

If you enter in the band *Nirvana* in the search form, your URL request will be
http://localhost:8080/band?name=Nirvana. This function will render an HTML page
(the overall template is in an external file named template.html). This web page
lists all artists in a band, which it pulls directly from CouchDB. It also lists
some suggested bands, which it retrieves from a Gremlin query against the
Neo4j graph. The Gremlin query is like this for Nirvana:

```
g.V.filter{it.name=="Nirvana"}.out("member").in("member").dedup.name
```

Or in other words, from the Nirvana node, get all unique names whose
members are connected to Nirvana members. For example, Dave Grohl played
in Nirvana and the Foo Fighters, so Foo Fighters will be returned in this list.

The next action is the http://localhost:8080/artist URL. This page will output information about an artist.

redis/bands.js
```
appServer.addRoute("^/artist$", function(req, res) {
  var
    artistName = req.param('name'),
    rolesQuery = 'g.V[[name:"'+artistName+'"]].out("plays").role.uniqueObject',
    bandsQuery = 'g.V[[name:"'+artistName+'"]].in("member").name.uniqueObject';
  gremlin( rolesQuery, function(roles) {
    gremlin( bandsQuery, function(bands) {
      var values = { artist: artistName, roles: roles, bands: bands };
      var body = '<h3>{{artist}} Performs these Roles</h3>';
      body += '<ul>{{#roles}}';
      body += '<li>{{.}}</li>';
      body += '{{/roles}}</ul>';
      body += '<h3>Play in Bands</h3>';
      body += '<ul>{{#bands}}';
      body += '<li><a href="/band?name={{.}}">{{.}}</a></li>';
      body += '{{/bands}}</ul>';
      writeTemplate( res, body, values );
```

Two Gremlin queries are executed here. This first outputs all roles a member plays, and the second is a list of bands that person played in. For example, Jeff Ward (http://localhost:8080/artist?name=Jeff%20Ward) would be listed as playing the role Drummer and in the bands Nine Inch Nails and Ministry.

A cool feature of the previous two pages is that we render links between these values. The artist list in the /bands page links to the chosen /artist page, and vice versa. But we could make searching a bit easier.

```
redis/bands.js
appServer.addRoute("^/search$", function(req, res) {
  var query = req.param('term');

  redisClient.keys("band-name:"+query+"*", function(error, keys) {
    var bands = [];
    keys.forEach(function(key){
      bands.push(key.replace("band-name:", ''));
    });
    res.write( JSON.stringify(bands) );
    res.end();
```

Here we just pull all keys from Redis that match the first part of the string, such as "Bea*" as described previously. It then outputs the data as JSON. The template.html file links to the jQuery code necessary to make this function as an autocomplete feature on the rendered search box.

Expanding the Service

This is a fairly little script for all of the bare-bones work we're doing here. You may find many places you want to extend. Notice that the band suggestion is only first-order bands (bands the current band's members have performed in); you can get interesting results by writing a query to walk second-order bands, like this: g.V.filter{it.name=='Nine Inch Nails'}.out('member').in('member').dedup. loop(3){ it.loops <= 2 }.name.

You may also note that we do not have a form where someone can update band information. Adding this functionality could be fairly simple, since we already wrote CouchDB population code in the populate_couch.js script, and populating CouchDB will automatically keep Neo4j and Redis eventually consistent as long as the graph_sync.js service is running.

If you enjoy playing with this kind of polyglot persistence, you could take this even further. You could add a PostgreSQL data warehouse[6] to transform this data into a star schema—allowing for different dimensions of analysis, such

---

6. http://en.wikipedia.org/wiki/Data_warehouse

as most commonly played instrument or average numbers of total members in a band vs. total instruments. You could add a Riak server to store samples of bands' music, an HBase server to build a messaging system where users can keep track of their historical likes/dislikes, or a MongoDB extension to add a geographic element to this service.

Or, redesign this project entirely with a different language, web framework, or dataset. There are as many opportunities to extend this project as there are combinations of databases and technologies to create it—a Cartesian product of all open source.

Day 3 Wrap-Up

Today was a big day—so big, in fact, we wouldn't be surprised if it took several days to complete. But this is a little taste of the future of data management systems, as the world strolls away from the *one large relational database* model to a *several specialized databases* model. We also glued these databases together with some nonblocking code, which, though not a focus of this book, also seems to be where database interaction is headed in the development space.

The importance of Redis in this model should not be missed. Redis certainly doesn't provide any functionality these databases don't supply individually, but it does supply speedy data structures. We were able to organize a flat file into a series of meaningful data structures, which is an integral part of both data population and transportation. And it did this in a fast and simple-to-use way.

Even if you're not sold on the whole polyglot persistence model, you should certainly consider Redis for any system.

Day 3 Homework

Do

1. Alter the importer steps to also track a band member's start and end dates with the band. Track that data in the artist's CouchDB subdocument. Display this information on the artist's page.

2. Add MongoDB into the mix by storing a few music samples into GridFS, whereby users can hear a song or two related to a band. If any songs exists for a band, add a link to the web app. Ensure the Riak data and CouchDB remain in sync.

8.5 Wrap-Up

The Redis key-value (or data structure) store is light and compact, with a variety of uses. It's akin to one of those multitools composed of a knife, can opener, and other bits and bobs like a corkscrew—Redis is good to have around for solving a variety of odd tasks. Above all, Redis is fast, simple, and as durable as you choose. While rarely a stand-alone database, Redis is a perfect complement to any polyglot ecosystem as an ever-present helper for transforming data, caching requests, or managing messages by way of its blocking commands.

Redis's Strengths

The obvious strength of Redis is speed, like so many key-value stores of its ilk. But more than most key-value stores, Redis provides the ability to store complex values like lists, hashes, and sets, and retrieve them based through operations specific to those datatypes. Beyond even a data structure store, however, Redis's durability options allow you to trade speed for data safety up to a fairly fine point. Built-in master-slave replication is another nice way of ensuring better durability without requiring the slowness of syncing an append-only file to disk on every operation. Additionally, replication is great for very high-read systems.

Redis's Weaknesses

Redis is fast largely because it resides in memory. Some may consider this cheating, since of course a database that never hits the disk will be fast. A main memory database has an inherent durability problem; namely, if you shut down the database before a snapshot occurs, you can lose data. Even if you set the append-only file to disk sync on every operation, you run a risk with playing back expiry values, since time-based events can never be counted on to replay in exactly the same manner—though in fairness this case is more hypothetical than practical.

Redis also does not support datasets larger than your available RAM (Redis is removing virtual memory support), so its size has a practical limitation. Although there is a Redis Cluster currently in development to grow beyond a single-machine's RAM requirements, anyone wanting to cluster Redis must currently roll their own with a client that supports it (like the Ruby driver we used in Day 2).

Parting Thoughts

Redis is chock-full of commands—more than 120 of them. Most commands are straightforward enough to understand by their names alone, once you get used to the idea that seemingly random letters will be removed (for example, INCRBY) or that mathematical precision can sometimes be more confusing than helpful (for example, ZCOUNT, or sorted set count, vs. SCARD, or set cardinality).

Redis is already becoming an integral part of many systems. Several open source projects rely on Redis, from Resque, a Ruby-based asynchronous job queueing service, to session management in the Node.js project SocketStream. Regardless of the database you choose as your SOR, you should certainly add Redis to the mix.

CHAPTER 9

Wrapping Up

Now that we've made it through the databases, congratulations are in order!

We hope you've gained an appreciation for these seven databases. If you use one in a project, we'll be happy. And if you decide to use multiple databases, like we saw at the end of the Redis chapter, we'll be ecstatic. We believe the future of data management lies in the polyglot persistence model (using more than one database in a project)—while the worldview of the general-purpose RDBMS fog drifts away.

Let's take this opportunity to see where our seven databases fit together in the greater database ecosystem. By this point, we have explored the details of each and mentioned a few commonalities and differences. We'll see how they contribute to the vast and expanding landscape of data storage options.

9.1 Genres Redux

We've seen that how databases store their data can be largely divided into five genres: relational, key-value, columnar, document, and graph. Let's take a moment and recap their differences and see what each style is good for and not so good for—when you'd want to use them and when to avoid them.

Relational

This is the most common classic database pattern. Relational database management systems (RDBMSs) are set-theory-based systems implemented as two-dimensional tables with rows and columns. Relational databases strictly enforce type and are generally numeric, strings, dates, and uninterpreted blobs, but as we saw, PostgreSQL provided extensions such as array or cube.

Good For:

Because of the structured nature of relational databases, they make sense when the layout of the data is known in advance but how you plan to use that data later may not be. Or, in other words, you pay the organizational complexity up front to achieve query flexibility later. Many business problems are aptly modeled this way, from orders to shipments and from inventory to shopping carts. You may not know in advance how you'll want to query the data later—how many orders did we process in February?—but the data is quite regular in nature, so enforcing that regularity is helpful.

Not-So-Good For:

When your data is highly variable or deeply hierarchical, relational databases aren't the best fit. Because you must specify a schema up front, data problems that exhibit a high degree of record-to-record variation will be problematic. Consider developing a database to describe all the creatures in nature. Creating a full list of all features to account for (hasHair, numLegs, laysEggs, and so on) would be intractable. In such a case, you'd want a database that makes less restrictions in advance on what you can put into it.

Key-Value

The key-value (KV) store was the simplest model we covered. KV maps simple keys to (possibly) more complex values like a huge hashtable. Because of their relative simplicity, this genre of database has the most flexibility of implementation. Hash lookups are fast, so in the case of Redis, speed was its primary concern. Hash lookups are also easily distributed, and so Riak took advantage of this fact for focusing on simple-to-manage clusters. Of course, its simplicity can be a downside for any data with complex modeling requirements.

Good For:

With little or no need to maintain indexes, key-value stores are often designed to be horizontally scalable, extremely fast, or both. They're particularly suited for problems where the data are not highly related. For example, in a web application, users' session data meet this criteria; each user's session activity will be different and largely unrelated to the activity of other users.

Not-So-Good For:

Often lacking indexes and scanning capabilities, KV stores won't help you if you need to be able to perform queries on your data, other than basic CRUD operations (Create, Read, Update, Delete).

Columnar

Columnar databases (aka *column-oriented*, aka *column family*) share many similarities with both KV and RDBMS stores. Like with a key-value database, values are queried by matching keys. Like relational, their values are groups of zero or more columns, though each row is capable of populating however many it wants. Unlike either, columnar databases store like data by columns, rather than keeping data together by rows. Columns are inexpensive to add, versioning is trivial, and there is no real storage cost for unpopulated values. We saw how HBase is a classic implementation of this genre.

Good For:

Columnar databases have been traditionally developed with horizontal scalability as a primary design goal. As such, they're particularly suited to "Big Data" problems, living on clusters of tens, hundreds, or thousands of nodes. They also tend to have built-in support for features such as compression and versioning. The canonical example of a good columnar data storage problem is indexing web pages. Pages on the Web are highly textual (benefits from compression), somewhat interrelated, and change over time (benefits from versioning).

Not-So-Good For:

Different columnar databases have different features and therefore different drawbacks. But one thing they have in common is that it's best to design your schema based on how you plan to query the data. This means you should have some idea in advance of how your data will be used, not just what it'll consist of. If data usage patterns can't be defined in advance—for example, fast ad hoc reporting—then a columnar database may not be the best fit.

Document

Document databases allow for any number of fields per object and even allow objects to be nested to any depth as values of other fields. The common representation of these objects is as JavaScript Object Notation (JSON), adhered to by both MongoDB and CouchDB—though this is by no means a conceptual requirement. Since documents don't relate to each other like relational databases, they are relatively easy to shard and replicate across several servers, making distributed implementations fairly common. MongoHQ tends to tackle availability by supporting the creation of datacenters that manage huge datasets for the Web. Meanwhile, CouchDB focuses on being simple and durable, where availability is achieved by master-master replication of fairly autonomous nodes. There is high overlap between these projects.

Good For:

Document databases are suited to problems involving highly variable domains. When you don't know in advance what exactly your data will look like, document databases are a good bet. Also, because of the nature of documents, they often map well to object-oriented programming models. This means less impedance mismatch when moving data between the database model and application model.

Not-So-Good For:

If you're used to performing elaborate join queries on highly normalized relational database schemas, you'll find the capabilities of document databases lacking. A document should generally contain most or all of the relevant information required for normal use. So while in a relational database you'd naturally normalize your data to reduce or eliminate copies that can get out of sync, with document databases, denormalized data is the norm.

Graph

Graph databases are an emerging class of database that focuses more on the free interrelation of data than the actual values. Neo4j, as our open source example, is growing in popularity for many social network applications. Unlike other database styles that group collections of like objects into common buckets, graph databases are more free-form—queries consist of following edges shared by two nodes or, namely, *traversing* nodes. As more projects use them, graph databases are growing the straightforward social examples to occupy more nuanced use cases, such as recommendation engines, access control lists, and geographic data.

Good For:

Graph databases seem to be tailor-made for networking applications. The prototypical example is a social network, where nodes represent users who have various kinds of relationships to each other. Modeling this kind of data using any of the other styles is often a tough fit, but a graph database would accept it with relish. They are also perfect matches for an object-oriented system. If you can model your data on a whiteboard, you can model it in a graph.

Not-So-Good For:

Because of the high degree of interconnectedness between nodes, graph databases are generally not suitable for network partitioning. Spidering the graph quickly means you can't afford network hops to other database nodes, so graph databases don't scale out well. It's likely that if you use a graph database, it'll be one piece of a larger system, with the bulk of the data stored elsewhere and only the relationships maintained in the graph.

9.2 Making a Choice

As we said at the beginning, data is the new oil. We sit upon a vast ocean of data, yet until it's refined into information, it's unusable (and with a more crude comparison, there's a lot of money in data these days). The ease of collecting and ultimately storing, mining, and refining the data out there starts with the database you choose.

Deciding which database to choose is often more complex than merely considering which genre maps best to a given domain's data. Though a social graph may seem to clearly function best with a graph database, if you're Facebook, you simply have far too much data to choose one. You are more likely going to choose a "Big Data" implementation, such as HBase or Riak. This will force your hand into choosing a columnar or key-value store. In other cases, though you may believe a relational database is clearly the best option for bank transactions, it's worth knowing that Neo4j also supports ACID transactions, expanding your options.

These examples serve to point out that there are other avenues beyond genre to consider when choosing which database—or databases—best serve your problem scope. As a general rule, as the size of data increases, the capacity of certain database styles wane. Column-oriented datastore implementations are often built to scale across datacenters and support the largest "Big Data" sets, while graphs generally support the smallest. This is not always the case, however. Riak is a large-scale key-value store meant to shard data across hundreds or thousands of nodes, while Redis was built to run on one—with the possibility of a few master-slave replicas or client-managed shards.

There are several more dimensions to consider when choosing a database, such as durability, availability, consistency, scalability, and security. You have to decide whether ad hoc queryability is important or if mapreduce will suffice. Do you prefer to use an HTTP/REST interface, or are you willing to require a driver for a custom binary protocol? Even smaller scope concerns, such as the existence of bulk data loaders, might be important for you to think about.

To simplify the comparison between these databases, we created a table in Appendix 1, *Database Overview Tables*, on page 313. The table is not meant to be an exhaustive list of features. Instead, it's meant to be a tool to quickly compare these databases we've already covered. Note the versions of each database. These features change in the blink of an eye, so we highly recommend double-checking these values for more recent versions.

9.3 Where Do We Go from Here?

Modern application scaling problems now fall largely in the realm of data management. We've reached a point in application evolution where programming language, framework, and operating system choice—even hardware and operations (thanks to virtual machine hosts and "the cloud")—are becoming so cheap and easy as to become largely trivial problems driven as much by preference as necessity. If you want to scale your application in this age, you should think quite a bit about which database, or databases, you choose—it's more than likely your true bottleneck. Helping you make this choice correctly was a leading purpose of this book.

Although the book has come to a close, we trust your interest in polyglot persistence is wide open. The next steps from here are to pursue in detail the databases that piqued your interest or continue learning about other options like Cassandra, Drizzle, or OrientDB.

It's time to get your hands dirty.

Database Overview Tables

This book contains a wealth of information about each of the seven databases we discuss: PostgreSQL, Riak, HBase, MongoDB, CouchDB, Neo4j, and Redis. In the pages that follow, you'll find tables that tally up these databases along a number of dimensions to present an overview of what's covered in more detail elsewhere in the book. Although the tables are not a replacement for a true understanding, they should provide you with an at-a-glance sense of what each database is capable of, where it falls short, and how it fits into the modern database landscape.

	Genre	Version	Datatypes	Data Relations
MongoDB	Document	2.0	Typed	None
CouchDB	Document	1.1	Typed	None
Riak	Key-value	1.0	Blob	Ad hoc (Links)
Redis	Key-value	2.4	Semi-typed	None
PostgreSQL	Relational	9.1	Predefined and typed	Predefined
Neo4j	Graph	1.7	Untyped	Ad hoc (Edges)
HBase	Columnar	0.90.3	Predefined and typed	None

	Standard Object	Written in Language	Interface Protocol	HTTP/REST
MongoDB	JSON	C++	Custom over TCP	Simple
CouchDB	JSON	Erlang	HTTP	Yes
Riak	Text	Erlang	HTTP, protobuf	Yes
Redis	String	C/C++	Simple text over TCP	No
PostgreSQL	Table	C	Custom over TCP	No
Neo4j	Hash	Java	HTTP	Yes
HBase	Columns	Java	Thrift, HTTP	Yes

	Ad Hoc Query	Mapreduce	Scalable	Durability
MongoDB	Commands, mapreduce	JavaScript	Datacenter	Write-ahead journaling, Safe mode
CouchDB	Temporary views	JavaScript	Datacenter (via BigCouch)	Crash-only
Riak	Weak support, Lucene	JavaScript, Erlang	Datacenter	Durable write quorum
Redis	Commands	No	Cluster (via master-slave)	Append-only log
PostgreSQL	SQL	No	Cluster (via add-ons)	ACID
Neo4j	Graph walking, Cypher, search	No (in the distributed sense)	Cluster (via HA)	ACID
HBase	Weak	Hadoop	Datacenter	Write-ahead logging

	Secondary Indexes	Versioning	Bulk Load	Very Large Files
MongoDB	Yes	No	mongoimport	GridFS
CouchDB	Yes	Yes	Bulk Doc API	Attachments
Riak	Yes	Yes	No	Lewak (deprecated)
Redis	No	No	No	No
PostgreSQL	Yes	No	COPY command	BLOBs
Neo4j	Yes (via Lucene)	No	No	No
HBase	No	Yes	No	No

	Requires Compaction	Replication	Sharding	Concurrency
MongoDB	No	Master-slave (via replica sets)	Yes	Write lock
CouchDB	File rewrite	Master-master	Yes (with filters in BigCouch)	Lock-free MVCC
Riak	No	Peer-based, master-master	Yes	Vector-clocks
Redis	Snapshot	Master-slave	Add-ons (e.g., client)	None
PostgreSQL	No	Master-slave	Add-ons (e.g., PL/Proxy)	Table/row writer lock
Neo4j	No	Master-slave (in Enterprise Edition)	No	Write lock
HBase	No	Master-slave	Yes via HDFS	Consistent per row

	Transactions	Triggers	Security	Multitenancy
MongoDB	No	No	Users	Yes
CouchDB	No	Update validation or Changes API	Users	Yes
Riak	No	Pre/post-commits	None	No
Redis	Multi operation queues	No	Passwords	No
PostgreSQL	ACID	Yes	Users/groups	Yes
Neo4j	ACID	Transaction event handlers	None	No
HBase	Yes (when enabled)	No	Kerberos via Hadoop security	No

	Main Differentiator	Weaknesses
MongoDB	Easily query *Big Data*	Embed-ability
CouchDB	Durable and embeddable clusters	Query-ability
Riak	Highly available	Query-ability
Redis	Very, very fast	Complex data
PostgreSQL	Best of OSS RDBMS model	Distributed availability
Neo4j	Flexible graph	BLOBs or terabyte scale
HBase	Very large-scale, Hadoop infrastructure	Flexible growth, query-ability

The CAP Theorem

Understanding the five database genres is an important selection criterion, but it's not the only one. Another recurring theme in this book is the CAP theorem, which lays bare an unsettling truth about how distributed database systems behave in the face of network instability.

CAP proves that you can create a distributed database that is *consistent* (writes are atomic and all subsequent requests retrieve the new value), *available* (the database will always return a value as long as a single server is running), or *partition tolerant* (the system will still function even if server communication is temporarily lost—that is, a network partition), but you can have only two at once.

In other words, you can create a distributed database system that is *consistent* and *partition tolerant*, a system that is *available* and *partition tolerant*, or a system that is *consistent* and *available* (but not *partition tolerant*—which basically means not distributed). But it is not possible to create a distributed database that is consistent and available and partition tolerant at the same time.

The CAP theorem is pertinent when considering a distributed database, since you must decide what you are willing to give up. The database you choose will lose availability or consistency. Partition tolerance is strictly an architectural decision (will the database be distributed or not). It's important to understand the CAP theorem to fully grok your options. The trade-offs made by the database implementations in this book are largely influenced by it.

A2.1 Eventual Consistency

Distributed databases must be partition tolerant, so the choice between availability and consistency can be difficult. However, while CAP dictates that

A CAP Adventure, Part I: CAP

Imagine the world as a giant distributed database system. All of the land in the world contains information about certain topics, and as long as you're somewhere near people or technology, you can find an answer to your questions.

Now, for the sake of argument, imagine you are a passionate Beyoncé Knowles fan and the date is September 5, 2006. Suddenly, at your friend's beach house party celebrating the release of Beyoncé's second studio album, a freak tidal wave sweeps across the dock and drags you out to sea. You fashion a makeshift raft and wash up on a desert island days later. Without any means of communication, you are effectively *partitioned* from the rest of the system (the world). There you wait for five long years....

One morning in 2011 you are awakened by shouts from the sea. A salty old schooner captain has discovered you! After five years alone, the captain leans over the bow and bellows: "How many studio albums does Beyoncé have?"

You now have a decision to make. You can answer the question with the most recent value you have (which is now five years old). If you answer his query, you are *available*. Or, you can decline to answer the question, knowing since you are partitioned, your answer may not be *consistent* with the rest of the world. The captain won't get his answer, but the state of the world remains consistent (if he sails back home, he can get the correct answer). As your role of queried node, you can either help keep the world's data *consistent* or be *available*, but *not both*.

if you pick availability you cannot have true consistency, you can still provide *eventual consistency*.

The idea behind eventual consistency is that each node is always available to serve requests. As a trade-off, data modifications are propagated in the background to other nodes. This means that at any time the system may be inconsistent, but the data is still largely accurate.

The Internet's Domain Name Service (DNS) is a prime example of an eventually consistent system. You register a domain, and it may take a few days to propagate to all DNS servers across the Internet. But at no time is any particular DNS server unavailable (assuming you can connect to it, that is).

A2.2 CAP in the Wild

Some partition-tolerant databases can be tuned to be more or less consistent or available on a per-request basis. Riak works like this, allowing clients to decide at request time what level of consistency they require. The other databases in this book largely occupy one corner or another of the CAP trade-off triangle.

A CAP Adventure, Part II: Eventual Consistency

Let's rewind two years, back to 2009. You've been on the island for three years at this point, and you spot a bottle in the sand—precious contact with the outside world. You uncork it and rejoice! You've just received an integral piece of knowledge...

The number of studio albums Beyoncé has is of utmost importance to the world's aggregate knowledge. It's so important, in fact, that every time she releases a new album, someone writes the current date and the number on a piece of paper. They place that paper in a bottle and throw it out to sea. If someone, like yourself, is partitioned from the rest of the world on a desert island, they can *eventually* have the correct answer.

Skip forward to the present. When the ship captain asks, "How many studio albums does Beyoncé have?" you remain *available* and answer "three." You may be *inconsistent* with the rest of the world, but you are reasonably certain of your answer, having not yet received another bottle.

The story ends with the captain rescuing you, and you return home to find her new album and live happily ever after. As long as you remain on land, you needn't be partition tolerant and can remain consistent and available until the end of your days.

Redis, PostgreSQL, and Neo4J are consistent and available (CA); they don't distribute data and so partitioning is not an issue (though arguably, CAP doesn't make much sense in non-distributed systems). MongoDB and HBase are generally consistent and partition tolerant (CP). In the event of a network partition, they can become unable to respond to certain types of queries (for example, in a Mongo replica set you flag slaveok to false for reads). In practice, hardware failure is handled gracefully—other still-networked nodes can cover for the downed server—but strictly speaking, in the CAP theorem sense, they are unavailable. Finally, CouchDB is available and partition tolerant (AP). Even though two or more CouchDB servers can replicate data between them, CouchDB doesn't guarantee consistency between any two servers.

It's worth noting that most of these databases can be configured to change CAP type (Mongo can be CA, CouchDB can be CP), but here we've noted their default or common behaviors.

A2.3 The Latency Trade-Off

There is more to distributed database system design than CAP, however. For example, low latency (speed) is a chief concern for many architects. If you read the Amazon Dynamo[1] paper, you'll notice a lot of talk about availability

---

1. http://allthingsdistributed.com/files/amazon-dynamo-sosp2007.pdf

but also Amazon's latency requirements. For a certain class of applications, even a small latency change can translate to a large costs. Yahoo's PNUTS database famously gives up both availability on normal operation and consistency on partitions in order to squeeze a lower latency out of its design.[2] It's important to consider CAP when dealing with distributed databases, but it's equally important to be aware that distributed database theory does not stop there.

---

2.   http://dbmsmusings.blogspot.com/2010/04/problems-with-cap-and-yahoos-little.html

Bibliography

[TH01]   David Thomas and Andrew Hunt. *Programming Ruby: The Pragmatic Programmer's Guide*. Addison-Wesley, Reading, MA, 2001.

[Tat10]   Bruce A. Tate. *Seven Languages in Seven Weeks: A Pragmatic Guide to Learning Programming Languages*. The Pragmatic Bookshelf, Raleigh, NC and Dallas, TX, 2010.

Index

SYMBOLS

! (exclamation sign), in regular expression searches, 37

% (percent sign), as wildcard on LIKE searches, 22

* (star)
in regular expression searches, 37
in Riak searches, 88

-> (arrow operator), in Groovy, 234

<> (not equal sign), in PostgreSQL, 14

? (question mark), in Riak searches, 88

@- command, cURL, 66

\ (backslash) commands, for psql shell, 11

{...} curly braces, Groovy code use of, 225

~ operator, in regular expression searches, 37

A

abstract syntax tree (query tree), 31

ACID compliance, 25

ACID transaction database, Neo4j as, 250–251

aggregate functions, 21–23

aggregated queries, in MongoDB, 155–157

algebra, relational, SQL and, 13

Amazon
Dynamo paper, Riak and, 52
Elastic Compute Cloud (EC2), 126

Amazon's Web Services (AWS), 126, 129

Apache Hadoop, 94, 119

Apache Hadoop project, 252

Apache Incubator project, 122

Apache Solr, 87

append only file, in Redis, 280

application code, choosing to execute database code, 29

arbiters and voting, in MongoDB, 169

Array Value, CouchDB Futon document with, 181

arrow operator (->), in Groovy, 234

atomicity, verifying, 25

attributes
mapping, 12
in PostgreSQL (COLUMNs), 11

AUTO_INCREMENT, MySQL, 16

Avro protocol, HBase, 122

AWS (Amazon's Web Services), 126, 129

B

B-tree
definition of, 21
index in PostgreSQL, 19
in MongoDB, 152–155

B-tree index, in PostgreSQL, 20

backslash (\) commands, for psql shell, 11

Big Data implementation, 106–111, 311

Big Table, 94

big_vclock, 84

BigCouch, vs. CouchDB, 212

Bloom filters, 287–290
about, 109, 111

Bloom, Burton Howard, 109

BSD netcat (nc), 276–277

bucket values, storing map functions in, 67–68

buckets, populating Riak, 55

built-in functions, in Riak, 68

C

CAP theorem
about, 317–320
adventure, 318–319
in HBase, 132
in Neo4j, 259
in Riak, 72, 92

Cartesian products, 12

Cassandra database, 5, 125

centrality, meaning of, 246

Changes API interface, 203, 291

characters, regular expression, 37

CLI (command-line interface), connecting to MySQL, 137

Cloud Servers, RackSpace, 125

cloud service providers, 125

cluster
  checking health of, 128
  configuring, 127–128
  connecting to, 128
  HA, 252
  launching, 128–129
  Redis, 286–287
  setting up, 125–126
code, choosing to execute database, 29
collect(), as Groovy map function, 233
collection
  in Gremlin, 226
  in MongoDB, 150
column families, HBase, 97–99, 104, 116
column-oriented databases, 94
columnar databases
  about, 309
  strengths of, 309
  weaknesses of, 309
columnar databases (column-oriented databases), about, 5
columns
  definition of, 21
  in PostgreSQL, 11
command line shell, in PostgreSQL, 10–11
command line, Redis commands
  DEL command, 274
  DISCARD command, 264
  EXPIRE command, 272–273
  FLUSHALL command, 274, 281
  FLUSHDB command, 274
  GET command, 264
  GETBIT command, 287–290
  INCR command, 263
  INFO command, 278–279
  LASTSAVE command, 280
  LRANGE command, 270, 282
  MGET command, 263
  MOVE command, 274
  MULTI command in, 264
  RENAME command, 274
  SADD command, 282
  SAVE command, 280
  SDIFF command, 269
  SET command, 263
  SETBIT command, 287–290
  SETEX command, 273
  SINTER command, 269
  TYPE command, 274
  ZRANGE command, 270–271
command-line interface (CLI)
  connecting to MySQL, 137
  Redis and, 262
compression algorithms, in HBase, 110
conflicts, resolving with vector clocks, 80
constraints
  foreign key, 13
  primary key, 11
  REFERENCES keyword as, 15
CouchDB, see also polyglot persistence service example
  _all_docs view, 191
  _changes field, 205
  _id field in, 180
  _rev field, 181
  about, 6, 177–178
  accessing documents through views, 186–188
  Changes API interface, 203, 291
  communication with, 182
  CouchDB, 217
  creating documents with POST, 183–184
  creating views with reducers, 200–202
  developing application specific view, 191–192
  field names, 180
  filtering changes, 210–211
  handling conflicts, 213–216
  importing data using, 194–199
  issuing GET requests, 183
  JSON structure nested in, 180, 182
  modifying records, 180
  polling for changes with Node.js, 206–209
  querying design documents with curl, 192–194
  removing documents with DELETE, 185
  replicating data in, 212–213
  role in polyglot persistence service example, 291
  saving view as design document, 191
  strengths of, 217
  total_rows field, 194
  updating documents with PUT, 183–184
  vs. BigCouch, 212
  vs. MongoDB, 178
  watching for changes, 203–206
  watching for changes continuously, 209–210
  weaknesses of, 217
  writing views, 188–190
CouchDB Futon
  creating documents, 179–181
  document with Array Value, 181
  replicator, 213
count() function
  about, 22
  using HAVING with, 23
count()function, aggregating results, 156
CREATE INDEX command, SQL, 19
CREATE TABLE command, SQL, 11, 18
crosstab(), using in PostgreSQL, 33–34
Crow's-Feet Entity Relationship Diagram, 17–18
CRUD
  about, 14
  definition of, 21
  verbs, 54
cURL
  @- command, 66
  issuing GET requests, 182
  querying CouchDB design documents with, 192
  REST and, 54
  Riak and, 52

-v (verbose) attribute in, 55

-X PUT parameter, 55

curly braces {...}, Groovy code use of, 225

D

database code, choosing to execute, 29

databases
  choosing correct, 1–3
  genres of, 3–7
  listing languages available in, 28

datastores, genres of, 1–2

datatypes
  PostgreSQL, 14
  Redis, 263, 265–267

default values, in HBase, 101

DEL command, in Redis, 274

DELETE (Delete)
  as CRUD verb, 54
  removing documents with, 185
  removing value using, 56

DELETE FROM command, SQL, 13

describe command, 116

dictionaries
  installing language, 41
  Postgres use of, 41
  simple, 40

DISCARD command
  in Redis, 264
  vs. ROLLBACK (SQL), 264

DISTINCT keyword, SQL, 23

distinct() function
  in aggregated queries, 157
  aggregating results, 156

document databases
  about, 309
  strengths of, 310
  uniqueness of, 165
  weaknesses of, 310

document datastore, MongoDB as, 151

document oriented databases, about, 5–6

domain specific languages, conversing in, 235

dynamic programming languages, vs. static programming languages, 149

E

EC2 (Elastic Compute Cloud), Amazon, 126

edges, in Gremlin, 223

Elastic Compute Cloud (EC2), Amazon, 125–126

elemMatch directive, MongoDB, 143–145

Entity Relationship Diagram (ERD), 17–18

ERD (Entity Relationship Diagram), 17–18

Erlang, 52, 78, 86–87
  CouchDB written in, 177
  downloading, 52

eval() function, MongoDB, 160

event-driven nonblocking applications, 296

exclamation sign (!), in regular expression searches, 37

EXPIRE command, in Redis, 272–273

EXPLAIN command, SQL, 42–43

extract(), in PostgreSQL, 33

F

Facebook, messaging index table of, 100

filters
  definition of, 210
  using, 211

find function, in MongoDB, 140–141, 148–149

FLUSHALL command, in Redis, 274, 281

FLUSHDB command, in Redis, 274

foreign key constraint, 13

foreign keys, building indexes on, 35

freebase.com, 293

full table scans, 18

full text search, inverted index in Neo4j, 241–242

Full-text searches, 39–48

Fully distributed mode, HBase, 95

functions, creating functions in Riak, 66–67

Futon web interface
  creating Admin, 180
  creating documents, 181
  creating documents in CouchDB, 179–181

fuzzy searching, about, 36

G

Generalized Index Search Tree (GIST), 39

Generalized Inverted iNdex (GIN), 42–43

genre graph, two-dimensional, 46

genres, as multidimensional cube, 45–48

GeoSpatial indexes, spherical, 152

GeoSpatial Queries, MongoDB, 171–172

German dictionary, installing, 41

GET (Read)
  as CRUD verb, 54
  issuing requests, 182–183
  reading documents with, 183
  in Redis, 264
  request for _changes field, 205
  retrieving value using, 56
  using in Neo4j, 238–240

get command, in HBase, 100

getLast(collection), calling in MongoDB, 160

GETBIT command, 287–290

GIN (Generalized Inverted iNdex), 42–43

GIST (Generalized Index Search Tree), 39

Git, downloading, 52

Google, MapReduce, 132

graph, Gremlin terms in, 223

graph databases
  about, 6, 310
  Neo4j as, 219–220
  strengths of, 310
  weaknesses of, 310

Gremlin
  about, 223
  as Pipe building language, 226–228
  as general-purpose graph traversal language, 223
  calling loop(), 230–232

conversing in domain specific languages, 235
edges in, 223
graph algorithms in, 244–245
Groovy programming language and, 233–235
jQuery and, 228
Java libraries in, 223
REST and, 242
Gremlin/Blueprint project, 247–249
GridFS, in MongoDB, 172–173
Groovy programming language, 223–226
closure in, 224
map function in, 233
method parentheses in, 225
reduce function in, 233
GROUP BY clause
in MySQL, 24
SQL, 23
vs. PARTITION BY, 24
vs. Window functions, 24–25
group() function
in aggregated queries, 157
aggregating results, 156
in MongoDB, 163
groupCount(), in Neo4j, 246
group()function, aggregate query in MongoDB, 156

H

HA cluster, using in Neo4j, 252–253, 255
Hadoop distributed file system (HDFS), 132
Hadoop, Apache, 94, 119, 125, 252
hash datatype, Redis, 265–267
hash index, creating, 19
HAVING clause, using with count(), 23
HBase
about, 93–94
adding data programmatically, 103–104
altering tables, 101–102
as columnar database, 5
Big Data implementation, 106–111

Bloom filter support, 110
capturing data contained in links, 116
column families, 97, 99, 104, 116
compression algorithms in, 110
configuring, 95–96
constructing scanner, 116–118
creating tables, 96–99
datatypes, 132
default values in, 101
developing Thrift HBase application, 124–125
disk usage, 111–112
get command in, 100
importing data, 106–107
inserting data in, 99
invoking scripts, 106–107
map, 96
on CAP, 132
properties, 97
protocols for client connectivity, 122
put command in, 100
regions, 111, 113–115
retrieving data in, 99
running modes, 95
setting up cloud service, 126–129
shell in, 96–97, 103
shutting down, 96
starting, 96
streaming Wikipedia, 107–109
strengths of, 131
timestamp in, 100
timestamps in, 99
updating data in, 99
weaknesses of, 132
Whirr setting up clusters in, 125
HBase Network Settings, 97
HBase shell, 96
HBaseMaster, 115
HDFS (Hadoop distributed file system), 132
Homebrew for Mac, 262
hooks, pre/post commit, 84–86
HTTP Etags, 83
HTTP headers and error codes, in Riak, 55
HTTP PUT action, 55
HTTP Solr interface, Riak, 87

HTTP/REST interface, 52, 311
humongous, 135–136
Hypertable database, 5

I

ILIKE searches, 37
INCR command, in Redis, 263–264
index, as URL parameter for Riak searches, 88
indexed lookup points, 19
indexes
about, 18
building on foreign keys, 35
definition of, 21
inverted, 42–43
in PostgreSQL, 18–20
in Riak, 89–90
indexing
lexemes, 42–43
in MongoDB, 152
in Neo4j, 241
values in Redis, 271
INFO command, in Redis, 278–279
inject(), as reduce function in Groovy, 233
inner joins, 15–17
INSERT INTO, SQL commands, 14
INSERT INTO command
INSERT INTO command, 14
SQL, 13
inverted indexes, GIN, 42–43

J

jQuery, Gremlin and, 228
Jamendo data, 200
Java, support in PostgreSQL for, 28
Java API protocol, HBase, 122
Java libraries, in Gremlin, 223
Java Virtual Machine (JVM), 103
JavaScript
as native tongue of MongoDB, 138–140
reduce function in, 69
Riak precommit property to use function name, 85

JavaScript framework
    in polyglot persistence service exam, 292
    relationship store, 298–300
joins
    about, 15
    definition of, 21
    inner, 15–17
    left, 21
    left joins, 17
    MongoDB and, 148
    outer, 17–18
    right, 18
journaling, WAL, 112
JRuby
    Apache Hadoop and, 119
    based command line program, HBase and, 96
JSON
    based document database, CouchDB as, 178
    documents, 136
    Riak search returning, 88
    structure nested in CouchDB, 180, 182
JSON objects
    in CouchDB, 187
    key/value pairs in, 180
    in Neo4j, 238
    serialized change notification, 209
JUNG (Java Universal Network/Graph) Framework, 247–249
JVM (Java Virtual Machine), 103

K

Kevin Bacon algorithm, 244–245
key events, 80
key filters, in Riak, 69
key name, creating using Post, 56
key-value (KV) store
    about, 4, 308
    Redis as, 261
    strengths of, 308
    weaknesses of, 308
key/value index, in Neo4j, 241
key/values, Neo4j data as set of, 222

keys, in HBase, 97
KV (key-value) store, about, 4

L

large-scale deployments, in Riak, 72
LASTSAVE command, in Redis, 280
left joins, 17, 21
levenshtein, searches, 38
lexemes, indexing, 42–43
LIKE searches
    % as wildcard on, 22
    about, 37
link walking, 57–60
    with mapreduce, 70–71
Links
    about, 57
    metadata, 58
    using next_to in, 57
links, capturing data contained in, 116
Linls, metadata, 57
list datatype, Redis, 266–267
listCommands() function, MongoDB, 158
logs, table, 28–29
lookups with indexing, in PostgreSQL, 18–20
loopback interface, 97
loops(), Neo4j calling, 230–232
LRANGE command, in Redis, 270, 282
Lucene, Erlang module, 86

M

map function
    following pattern of reduce function, 70
    in Groovy, 233
    outputs in Riak, 65
    storing in bucked value, 67–68
    storing in bucket value, 68
map functions, mapreduce converting data using, 63–64
map() function, in MongoDB, 163
mapping object to common key, 64–66

/mapred command, 67
MapReduce, Google, 132
mapreduce
    about, 63–66
    in CouchDB, 200, 202–203
    creating in Riak, 66–67
    link walking, 70–71
    mapping object to common key, 64–66
    in MongoDB, 160–164
    retrieving objects using, 156
mapreduce functions, creating in Riak, 66–67
max(), 22
membase database, 4
memcached database, 4
Mercurial, downloading, 52
metadata
    Links as, 57
    storing, 58
metaphones, using in searches, 43–44
MGET command, using in Redis, 263
MIME types
    multipart/mixed, 58
    in Riak, 60–61
min(), 22
misspellings, MongoDB warning about, 149
MongoDB
    about, 6, 135–136
    aggregated queries, 155–157
    building index on nested values, 154
    collection in, 150
    command line reading, 140–142
    commands, 139
    constructing ad-hoc queries, 141–142
    count() function, 156
    creating, 137–138
    creating JavaScript functions, 139–140
    deleting documents, 149–150
    distinct() function, 156
    elemMatch directive, 143–145
    eval() function, 160
    find function in, 140–141, 148–149

GeoSpatial Queries, 171–172
getLast(collection), 160
GridFS, 172–173
group() function, 156–157
indexing in, 152–155
installing, 136
joins and, 148
listCommands() function, 158
mapreduce in, 160–164
MongoDB, 139
nested array data in, 142–143
ObjectId, 138
operators, 145–148
problem with even nodes, 168
reading with code, 150
reducers, 163–164
references, 148
replica sets, 165–168
retrieving documents in, 140–141
runCommand() function, 157–159
server-side commands, 158–159
sharding in, 169–171
shortcut for simple decision functions, 150
strengths of, 174
updating, 146–148
use of JavaScript in, 138–140
voting and arbiters in, 169
vs. CouchDB, 178
vs. mongoconfig, 170
warning about misspellings, 149
MOVE command, in Redis, 274
movie suggestion system schema, 35–36
MULTI command, in Redis, 264
multidimensional cubes, 45–48
genres as, 45–48
multipart/mixed MIME type, 58
MySQL
AUTO_INCREMENT, 16
connecting to command-line interface, 137
GROUP BY in, 24

N

namespaces, in Redis, 273–274
Neo4j, random walk in, 246
Neo4j database
about, 7, 219
adding nodes in, 222, 224
adding subset of nodes to graph, 230–232
as ACID transaction database, 250–251
as whiteboard friendly, 219–221
backups, 257
building cluster, 253
calling loop(), 230–232
conversing in domain specific languages, 235
dealing with large data sets, 242–244
deleting, 236
finding path between two nodes, 240
graph algorithms in, 244–245
graph of nodes, 227
Gremlin and REST, 242
Groovy programming language and, 233–235
groupCount() in, 246
high availability mode and, 251, 254
indexing in, 241–242
process called walking, 220
process stepping forward and back, 231
REST interface of, 238
role in polyglot persistence service example, 291
role_count map in, 246
shutting down master servers, 256
strengths of, 258
suggested schema, 220
updating, 236
using HA cluster in, 252–253, 255
using JUNG in, 247–249
using REST in, 238–240
using pipes in Gremlin, 226–228
verifying cluster status, 255
verifying replication, 256
via Gremlin, 223–227
weaknesses of, 259
web interface, 221–222
Zookeeper coordinator in, 252, 254
nested array data, in MongoDB, 142–143
nested values, building MongoDB index on, 154
next_to, using in links, 57
*nix pipes, 110–111
*nix systems, 279
Node.js
JavaScript framework in polyglot persistence service example, 292
polling for changes with, 206–209
nodes
adding in Neo4j, 222, 224
consistency by quorum in Riak, 77
consistency by reads in Riak, 76
consistency by writes in Riak, 76
durable writes in Riak, 78–79
eventual consistency in Riak, 76
finding in Neo4j path between two in, 240
in Neo4j, 221
Neo4j graph of, 224
Riak, 72–78
server, 221
using REST in Neo4j to create, 238
non-blocking, meaning of, 296
NoSQL, vs. relational databases RDBMS, 1
not equal sign (<>), in PostgreSQL, 14
Null values
about, 14
disallowing, 14

O

ObjectId, MongoDB, 138–139
old_vclock, 84
ON keyword, 15
operators
MongoDB, 145–148
in regular expression searches, 37
outer joins, 17–18

P

PageRank, Google, 246
parsers, in Postgres, 41
PARTITION BY clause, *vs.*
  GROUP BY, 24
percent sign (%), as wildcard
  on LIKE searches, 22
Perl, 28
PERSIST key, in Redis, 273
PHP, 28
Pipe, processing units, 231
pipeline
  Gremlin operations as,
    226
  meaning of, 226
  streaming strings, 276–
    277
  vs. vertex, 228
pivot tables, in PostgreSQL,
  33–34
PL/pgSQL, 28
polling interface, accessing
  Changes API interface
  through, 204
polyglot persistence, about, 7
polyglot persistence service
  example, 291–303
  phase 1, data transforma-
    tion, 294–295
  phase 2, system of
    record(SOR) insertion,
    295–298
  populate datastores, 292–
    293
  rise of, 292
  service of searching for
    bands, 300–303
population script, using Ruby, 62–63
POST (Create)
  as CRUD verb, 54
  creating documents with,
    183–184
  creating key name using,
    56
PostgreSQL, SQL executed to,
  32
PostgreSQL database
  about, 4, 9–10
  aggregate functions, 21–
    23
  as relational database, 9
  built-in documentation,
    11
  creating table logs, 28–29

creating views in, 30–31
datatypes, 14
generating tsvector lex-
  emes, 41
installing, 10
joining tables, 15–18
lookups with indexing,
  18–20
parsers in, 41
pivot tables in, 33–34
searching, 37–38
shell in, 11
SQL executed to, 31
strengths of, 49
templates in, 41
transactions in, 25–26
using Window functions,
  24–25
using crosstab() in, 33–34
using extract() in, 33
views as RULES, 31–33
weaknesses of, 49
working with tables, 11–
  15
writing procedures in, 28
pre/post commit hooks, 84–
  86
precommit functions, Erlang
  module, 86–87
primary key, 21
  as SQL identifier, 11
  constraints, 11
  creating compound key
    using, 14
  definition of, 21
  index, 19
  ObjectId in MongoDB as,
    138–139
  setups, 16
protocols for client connectivity, HBase, 122
Pseudodistributed mode,
  HBase, 95
psql shell
  backslash (/) commands,
    11
  connecting to, 11
PUT (Update)
  as CRUD verb, 54
  creating Riak buckets,
    55–57
  updating documents with
    PUT, 184–185
put and get commands, in
  HBase, 100

put command, in HBase,
  100, 103
Python, 28

Q

q and q.op, as URL parameter
  for Riak searches, 88
query parameter values, Riak,
  77
query tree (abstract syntax
  tree), 31
question mark (?), in Riak
  searches, 88

R

RackSpace Cloud Servers,
  125
random walk, in Neo4j, 246
RDBMS databases
  about, 2–3, 307
  mathematical relations
    in, 12
  strengths of, 308
  transactions in, 25–26
  vs. NoSQL, 1
  weaknesses of, 308
RDBMS databases), *vs.*
  columnar databases, 5
reading, in MongoDB
  with code, 150
  command line, 140–142
Redis Bloom filter, 287–290
Redis database, *see also* polyglot persistence service example
  , 287
  about, 5, 261
  as key-value store, 261–
    262
  blocking lists, 267
  building backend for a,
    263–264
  cluster, 282
  command-line interface
    and, 262
  configuration of, 279
  connecting to server,
    262–263
  data dumps, 283–285
  datatypes, 263
  DEL command, 274
  DISCARD command, 264
  durability of, 280
  EXPIRE command, 272–
    273
  FLUSHALL command,
    274, 281

FLUSHDB command, 274
GET command, 264
GETBIT command, 287–290
getting ranges in, 270–271
INCR command, 263
INFO command, 278–279
LASTSAVE command, 280
LRANGE command, 270, 282
master/slave replication, 282
MGET command, 263
MOVE command, 274
MULTI command in, 264
namespaces in, 273–274
PERSIST key in, 273
persistence options, 279
publishing and subscribing, 276–278
RENAME command, 274
role in polyglot persistence service example, 291
SADD command, 282
SAVE command, 280
SDIFF command, 269
security of, 281–282
server information, 278–279
SET command, 263
SETBIT command, 291
SETEX command, 273
SINTER command, 269
sorting sets, 269–272
streaming commands via telnet, 276
streaming strings, 276–277
strengths of, 304
transactions in, 264
tweaking parameters, 282
TYPE command, 274
using Bloom filter, 287–290
weaknesses of, 304
ZRANGE command, 270–271
Redis Ruby gem, 282
reduce function
in CouchDB, 202
following pattern of map function, 70
in Groovy, 233

in JavaScript, 69
mapreduce converting scalar values using, 63–64
reduce() function, in MongoDB, 163
reducers
in CouchDB, 200–202
in MongoDB, 163
running on separate servers, 163
REFERENCES, SQL keyword, 13–14
REFERENCES keyword, as constraint, 15
regex (regular expression) searches, 37
regioninfo scans, TABLE schema, 116
regions, HBase, 111, 113–115
regular expression (regex) searches, 37
relational algebra, SQL and, 13
relational databases
about, 2–3, 307
mathematical relations in, 12
Neo4j as, 219–220
strengths of, 308
transactions in, 25–26
vs. NoSQL, 1
vs. Riak database, 91
vs. columnar databases, 5
weaknesses of, 308
relations, in PostgreSQL (TABLES), 11
relationship, vs. vertex, 223
RENAME command, in Redis, 274
replicating data, in CouchDB, 212–213
Representational State Transfer (REST), about, 54–55
REST (Representational State Transfer)
about, 54–55
based document database, CouchDB as, 178
communication with CouchDB, 182
Gremlin and, 242

Neo4j interface of, 238
using in Neo4j, 238–240
REST protocol, HBase, 122
restart argument, in Riak, 85
RETURNING statement, SQL, 16
Riak database
about, 4, 51
Amazon Dynamo paper, 52
as NoSQL style database, 91
as key value store, 55
built-in functions, 68
creating mapreduce functions in Riak, 66–67
cURL and, 52
indexes in, 89–90
installing, 52–54
key filters in, 69
mapreduce in, 66
MIME types in, 58
on CAP, 92
populating buckets, 55–57
query parameter values, 77
restart argument, 85
ring, 72–74
searching, 86–88
stored functions in, 67–68
strengths of, 91
timeout option, 71
timestamps in, 80
valid bucket properties, 77
vs. relational databases, 91
weaknesses of, 91
web and, 51–52
-X PUT parameter, 55
Riak servers
app. config, 84
configuring partitions, 72–74
durable writes in, 78–79
large-scale deployments and, 72
nodes and vnodes, 72–78
resolving with vector clocks, 80–84
Riak, HTTP Solr interface, 87
right joins, 18
role_count map, in Neo4j, 246

ROLLBACK command
    SQL, 25
    vs. ROLLBACK (SQL)
        DISCARD (Redis), 264

rows
    as URL parameter for Ri-
        ak searches, 88
    definition of, 21
    in PostgreSQL, 11

Ruby
    importing data into
        CouchDB using, 194–
        199
    population script using,
        62–63
    support in PostgreSQL
        for, 28

Ruby on Rails system, grab-
    bing data via ActiveRecord
    interface, 64

RULES, in PostgreSQL, 31–33

runCommand() function,
    MongoDB, 157–159

S

SADD command, in Redis,
    282

SAVE command, in Redis,
    280

scalability, about, 2–3

scanner, constructing HBase,
    116–118

scanning tables to build other
    tables
    about, 115–116
    examining output, 119–
        120
    running script, 118
    using mapreduce for, 119

schema definition diagram,
    18

schemas
    definition diagram, 17
    movie suggestion system,
        35–36
    in Neo4j, 220
    for PostgreSQL, 11–14

Scheme, 28

scripts
    HBase Big Data imple-
        mentation, 106–111
    for scanning all rows of
        table, 116–118

SDIFF command, in Redis,
    269

searches
    about, 36
    combining string match-
        es, 44
    Full-text, 39–48
    ILIKE, 37
    levenshtein, 38
    LIKE, 22, 37
    regular expression
        (regex), 37
    in Riak, 86–88
    trigram, 38–39
    TSQuery, 39–41
    TSVector, 39–41
    using metaphones, 43–44
    using wildcards in Riak,
        88

secondary indexes, in Riak,
    89–90

SELECT...FROM table com-
    mand
    , 13
    SQL, 13

SERIAL integers, 17

SERIAL keyword, 16

server-side commands, in
    MongoDB, 158–159

servers, nodes in, 221

servers, Riak
    configuring partitions,
        72–74
    durable writes in, 78–79
    large-scale deployments
        and, 72
    nodes and vnodes, 72–78
    pruning vector clocks, 84
    resolving with vector
        clocks, 80–84

SET command, using in Re-
    dis, 263

$set operation, in MongoDB,
    147–148

SETBIT command, 287–290

SETEX command, in Redis,
    273

sets, meaning of, 268

*Seven Languages in Seven
    Weeks* (Tate), xi

sharding, in MongoDB, 169–
    171

shell protocol, HBase, 122

simple dictionary, 40

SINTER command, in Redis,
    269

small_vclock, 84

snapshotting, in Redis, 280

sort, as URL parameter for
    Riak searches, 88

SQL, *see also* primary key
    aggregate functions, 21–
        23
    definition of, 21
    executed to PostgreSQL,
        31–32
    foreign key constraints,
        13, 15
    joins, 15–18
    PostgreSQL and, 4
    standard string matches,
        37–38

SQL clauses
    GROUP BY, 23
    HAVING, 23
    WHERE, 13

SQL commands
    CREATE INDEX, 19
    CREATE TABLE, 11, 18
    DELETE FROM, 13
    EXPLAIN, 42–43
    finding in PostgreSQL, 11
    INSERT INTO, 13–14
    ROLLBACK, 25
    SELECT...FROM, 13
    UPDATE, 15, 29

SQL identifier, primary key
    as, 11

SQL keywords
    DISTINCT, 23
    ON, 15
    REFERENCES, 13–14
    SERIAL, 16
    UNIQUE, 19

SQL statements, RETURN-
    ING, 16

Stand-alone mode, HBase, 95

star (*)
    in regular expression
        searches, 37
    in Riak searches, 88

static programming lan-
    guages, *vs.* dynamic pro-
    gramming languages, 149

stop words, 40

stored functions, in Riak, 67–
    68

stored procedures, 26–28

string matches, combining in
    searches, 44

strings, in PostgreSQL, 14

system design, consistency
    and durability in, 72

T

table logs, 28–29
tables
    altering in HBase, 100–102
    building by scanning, 115–116
    creating HBase, 96–98
    creating SQL, 11
    definition of, 21
    full table scans of, 18
    joins, 15–18
    timestamps in, 17
    unions, 18
Tate, Bruce A., xi
Tcl, 28
telnet, streaming commands via, 276
templates, in Postgres, 41
text datatype, 14
Thrift protocol, HBase
    about, 122
    building client application, 123–125
    generating models, 123
    installing, 122–123
timeout option, in Riak, 71
timestamps
    in HBase, 99–100
    in Riak, 80
    table, 17
top command, MongoDB, 158
transactions
    in PostgreSQL, 25–26
    unavoidable, 26
transform steps, in Gremlin, 231
triggers, 28
trigram searches, 38–39
TSQuery searches, 39–41
tsvector lexemes, generating in Postgres, 41
TSVector searches, 39–41
Tuple relational calculus, SQL and, 13
tuples, in PostgreSQL (ROWs), 11
two dimensional indexes, in MongoDB, 152
TYPE command, in Redis, 274

U

underscores (_), as wildcard in Riak Link, 58
unions
    in Redis, 271–272
    table, 18
UNIQUE constraints, setting, 35
UNIQUE keyword, SQL, 19
Unix build tools, 52
UPDATE command, SQL, 15, 29
URL parameters, for Riak searches, 88
URL shortener
    adding activities to, 267
    building backend for a, 263–264

V

-v (verbose) attribute, in cURL, 55
varchar() strings, 14
vector clocks (vclocks)
    about, 80
    in practice, 82–84
    Riak pruning, 84
    in theory, 81–82
vendor lock, 27
venue_id
    counting events at, 22
    setting, 22
venues, creating tables with, 16
versioning, in HBase, 99
vertex
    vs. pipeline, 228
    vs. relationship, 223
views
    accessing documents through views in CouchDB, 186–188
    creating in , 30–31
    creating views with CouchDB reducers, 200–202
    developing in CouchDB application specific, 191–192
    path for querying, 193
    saving as design document in CouchDB, 191–192
    writing views in CouchDB, 188–190

V (cont.)

virtual nodes (vnodes)
    consistency by quorum in Riak, 77
    consistency by reads in Riak, 76
    consistency by writes in Riak, 76
    durable writes in Riak, 78–79
    eventual consistency in Riak, 76
    Riak, 72–78
Voldemort database, 4, 125
voting and arbiters in, in MongoDB, 169
vtags, 83

W

WAL (Write-Ahead Log) files, 112–113
web, Riak and, 51–52
web administration page dashboard, 222
WHERE clause, SQL, 13
$where clause, running custom code in MongoDB using, 150
Whirr
    about, 125
    configuring cluster for, 127–128
    destroying cluster command, 129
    preparing, 126
    setting up cloud service, 126
whiteboard friendly, meaning of, 219
WikiMedia Foundation, publishing data dumps, 106
Wikipedia, streaming, 107–109
wildcards
    in ILIKE searches, 37
    in LIKE searches, 22, 37
    in regular expressions, 37
    in Riak, 88
    in Riak Link, 58
Window functions, using in PostgreSQL, 24–25
Write Ahead Logging, 94
Write-Ahead Log (WAL) files, 112–113
wt, as URL parameter for Riak searches, 88

X

-X PUT parameter, 55

X-Riak- Meta- header prefix, 58

XML, streaming, 107

Y

young_vclock, 84

Z

Zookeeper, 125, 132, 252, 254

ZRANGE command, in Redis, 270–271

Learn a New Language This Year

Want to be a better programmer? Each new programming language you learn teaches you something new about computing. Come see what you're missing.

You should learn a programming language every year, as recommended by *The Pragmatic Programmer*. But if one per year is good, how about *Seven Languages in Seven Weeks*? In this book you'll get a hands-on tour of Clojure, Haskell, Io, Prolog, Scala, Erlang, and Ruby. Whether or not your favorite language is on that list, you'll broaden your perspective of programming by examining these languages side-by-side. You'll learn something new from each, and best of all, you'll learn how to learn a language quickly.

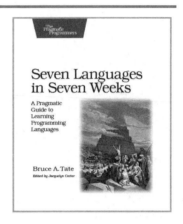

Bruce A. Tate
(328 pages) ISBN: 9781934356593. $34.95
http://pragprog.com/titles/btlang

Bill Karwin has helped thousands of people write better SQL and build stronger relational databases. Now he's sharing his collection of antipatterns—the most common errors he's identified out of those thousands of requests for help.

Most developers aren't SQL experts, and most of the SQL that gets used is inefficient, hard to maintain, and sometimes just plain wrong. This book shows you all the common mistakes, and then leads you through the best fixes. What's more, it shows you what's *behind* these fixes, so you'll learn a lot about relational databases along the way.

Bill Karwin
(352 pages) ISBN: 9781934356555. $34.95
http://pragprog.com/titles/bksqla

Long live the command line!

Use tmux for incredible mouse-free productivity, and learn how to create profession command-line apps.

Your mouse is slowing you down. The time you spend context switching between your editor and your consoles eats away at your productivity. Take control of your environment with tmux, a terminal multiplexer that you can tailor to your workflow. Learn how to customize, script, and leverage tmux's unique abilities and keep your fingers on your keyboard's home row.

Brian P. Hogan
(88 pages) ISBN: 9781934356968. $11.00
http://pragprog.com/titles/bhtmux

Speak directly to your system. With its simple commands, flags, and parameters, a well-formed command-line application is the quickest way to automate a backup, a build, or a deployment and simplify your life.

David Bryant Copeland
(200 pages) ISBN: 9781934356913. $33
http://pragprog.com/titles/dccar

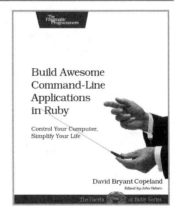

Welcome to the New Web

You need a better JavaScript and more expressive CSS and HTML today. Start here.

CoffeeScript is JavaScript done right. It provides all of JavaScript's functionality wrapped in a cleaner, more succinct syntax. In the first book on this exciting new language, CoffeeScript guru Trevor Burnham shows you how to hold onto all the power and flexibility of JavaScript while writing clearer, cleaner, and safer code.

Trevor Burnham
(160 pages) ISBN: 9781934356784. $29
http://pragprog.com/titles/tbcoffee

CSS is fundamental to the web, but it's a basic language and lacks many features. Sass is just like CSS, but with a whole lot of extra power so you can get more done, more quickly. Build better web pages today with *Pragmatic Guide to Sass*. These concise, easy-to-digest tips and techniques are the shortcuts experienced CSS developers need to start developing in Sass today.

Hampton Catlin and Michael Lintorn Catlin
(128 pages) ISBN: 9781934356845. $25
http://pragprog.com/titles/pg_sass

Be Agile

Don't just "do" agile; you want to *be* agile. We'll show you how.

The best agile book isn't a book: *Agile in a Flash* is a unique deck of index cards that fit neatly in your pocket. You can tape them to the wall. Spread them out on your project table. Get stains on them over lunch. These cards are meant to be used, not just read.

Jeff Langr and Tim Ottinger
(110 pages) ISBN: 9781934356715. $15
http://pragprog.com/titles/olag

Here are three simple truths about software development:

1. You can't gather all the requirements up front. 2. The requirements you do gather will change. 3. There is always more to do than time and money will allow.

Those are the facts of life. But you can deal with those facts (and more) by becoming a fierce software-delivery professional, capable of dispatching the most dire of software projects and the toughest delivery schedules with ease and grace.

Jonathan Rasmusson
(280 pages) ISBN: 9781934356586. $34.95
http://pragprog.com/titles/jtrap

The Pragmatic Bookshelf

The Pragmatic Bookshelf features books written by developers for developers. The titles continue the well-known Pragmatic Programmer style and continue to garner awards and rave reviews. As development gets more and more difficult, the Pragmatic Programmers will be there with more titles and products to help you stay on top of your game.

Visit Us Online

This Book's Home Page
http://pragprog.com/titles/rwdata
Source code from this book, errata, and other resources. Come give us feedback, too!

Register for Updates
http://pragprog.com/updates
Be notified when updates and new books become available.

Join the Community
http://pragprog.com/community
Read our weblogs, join our online discussions, participate in our mailing list, interact with our wiki, and benefit from the experience of other Pragmatic Programmers.

New and Noteworthy
http://pragprog.com/news
Check out the latest pragmatic developments, new titles and other offerings.

Save on the eBook

Save on the eBook versions of this title. Owning the paper version of this book entitles you to purchase the electronic versions at a terrific discount.

PDFs are great for carrying around on your laptop—they are hyperlinked, have color, and are fully searchable. Most titles are also available for the iPhone and iPod touch, Amazon Kindle, and other popular e-book readers.

Buy now at *http://pragprog.com/coupon*

Contact Us

Online Orders:	*http://pragprog.com/catalog*
Customer Service:	*support@pragprog.com*
International Rights:	*translations@pragprog.com*
Academic Use:	*academic@pragprog.com*
Write for Us:	*http://pragprog.com/write-for-us*
Or Call:	+1 800-699-7764